AWAKENING
IN TIME

Jamie

BOOKS BY JACQUELYN SMALL

Becoming Naturally Therapeutic
Transformers

and CHARLES L. WHITFIELD, M.D.

Codependence—Healing the Human Condition
A Gift to Myself
Healing the Child Within
Spirituality in Recovery

AWAKENING

IN TIME

The Journey from Codependence to Co-Creation

JACQUELYN SMALL

Foreword by Charles L. Whitfield, M.D.

BANTAM BOOKS
NEW YORK · TORONTO · LONDON · SYDNEY · AUCKLAND

AWAKENING IN TIME

A Bantam Book / September 1991

All rights reserved.
Copyright © 1991 by Jacquelyn Small.
Cover art copyright © Gabriel Molano.
BOOK DESIGN BY KATHRYN PARISE.
ILLUSTRATIONS BY STATE OF THE ART COMPUTER GRAPHICS

Library of Congress Cataloging-in-Publication Data

Small, Jacquelyn.
    Awakening in time : the journey from codependence to co-creation / Jacquelyn Small.
        p. cm.
    Includes bibliographical references and index.
    ISBN 0-553-34955-4
    1. Codependents—Rehabilitation. 2. Transpersonal psychology.
    I. Title.
    RC569.5.C63S62 1991
    616.86'0651—dc20   91-6523
                                                              CIP

Published simultaneously in the United States and Canada

Bantam Books are published by Bantam Books, a division of Bantam Doubleday Dell Publishing Group, Inc. Its trademark, consisting of the words "Bantam Books" and the portrayal of a rooster, is Registered in U.S. Patent and Trademark Office and in other countries. Marca Registrada. Bantam Books, 666 Fifth Avenue, New York, New York 10103.

PRINTED IN THE UNITED STATES OF AMERICA
CWO   0 9 8 7

A DEDICATION . . .

To my extended family—

Greg, Mark, Yala, George, Sharon, Mauri, Martha Lynn, Tom, Jennifer, Christopher, Mary Cecile, Tommy, Bob, Brett, and Brenda.

I am forever grateful for the times we've shared and for the part you've each played in my training as a wife, stepparent, and mother.

IN APPRECIATION . . .

To Linda Loewenthal, my editor and "co-pilot":

. . . for the crystal clarity, structure, precision, and integrity she contributed to this book. Sharing in its creation from beginning to end, not only mind to mind, but heart to heart. I am grateful for our relationship and its high calling.

To Greg Zelonka, my partner in our life's work:

. . . for orchestrating our demanding lifestyle with great skill and perseverance during the conception and birth of *Awakening in Time*. His love and unfaltering support often held me steady through the stormy process of creative book-making.

To John Brockman and Katinka Matson, my literary agents:

. . . for their guidance, support, and belief in me. I am grateful that they are in my life.

And to my students, friends, and colleagues—my beloved traveling companions:

. . . for their willingness to journey to the depths and share so openly with me their life-changing adventures of the Heart. They are continually my inspiration and my teachers.

I love you all.

Contents

Foreword by Charles L. Whitfield, M.D.   xi

I • **Healing Codependence: A Psycho-Spiritual Approach**

Introduction: "Awakening in Time"   3

Recovering Our Lost Selves   15

From Fragmentation to Wholeness:
The Gift of Psycho-Spirituality   24

II • **Codependence: The Shadow Side of Our Love Nature**

Needy Love Is How the Shadow Dances   41

How Codependence Patterns Are Created   66

III • **The Shift: From Unconscious to Conscious Living**

Entering the Heart Through an Open Mind   109

The Transforming Mind   114

IV • **Heartwork**

The Heart Is Where We Heal   149

The Heart's Accelerated Path   171

Relationships That Come from the Heart: An Interlude 188

V • The Return of Our Soul Powers

The Higher Chakras: How We Become
Soul-Infused Personalities   199

Relationships with High Callings   210

VI • Co-Creation: A Shared Human Destiny

Service Is "Doing Your Being"   227

Transformational Groupwork: Communing
at the Edge with Co-Creative Families   249

Epilogue: Home!   255

Appendices

Appendix One: Glossary of Transformational Resources
and Methods   259

Appendix Two: Suggested Readings for Bridging Old
and New Paradigm Thought   265

Index   275

J acquelyn Small is a pioneer in the recovery field and a new paradigm thinker and teacher. In the late 1970s I read her book *Becoming Naturally Therapeutic* and was glad to find someone who advocated such qualities of humanness in therapy because they *worked* in assisting people in their recoveries. A short time later I met Jacquie, shared some of my new material on spirituality in recovery, and we began to collaborate in workshops and conferences. Still later I read her second book, *Transformers,* and had seldom seen spiritual psychology expressed so practically and clearly.

In *Transformers* she described the chakras, or psycho-spiritual energy centers and levels of consciousness, and their importance in the healing process. In *Awakening in Time* she expands this approach into a novel and useful way of describing some of the manifestations and dynamics of codependence. While there are a few ideas in this book that I disagree with (such as the notion that the chakra system is common knowledge in Western medicine), I support and endorse the general principles that she so beautifully espouses.

Before recovery most people are stuck in the first three levels of their awareness—also called levels of consciousness—roughly equivalent to the first three chakras, or energy centers. In Stage One recovery we heal the addictions, compulsions, and other disorders that can manifest as blocks in these chakras. In Stage Two recovery we heal the ungrieved pain of these lower levels of consciousness as we evolve into and through level four—the level of the human Heart, which I call the hub of the True Self or the Child Within. This adult child and codependence healing is the longest, most painful and difficult part of our healing process. Not until this is completed can the spiritual work of Stage Three be undertaken. When to focus on Stages Two and Three recovery usually depends upon the person's prior healing and present condition.

We learn in our adventure of healing that the only way to realize God and Serenity is through our Heart, our True Self. We cannot get there through our ego or false or codependent self. We may have tried to fill our emptiness with people, places, things, behaviors, and experiences and found that they didn't work in a lasting way. The only way to fill our emptiness is to know and be our True Self and then to connect experientially to the God of our understanding.

While "the map is not the territory," maps can be useful. Jacquie uses several maps, in addition to the chakra system, to describe our consciousness and our journey. One of these is a modified Jungian map of the psyche. The map of the psyche that I find most useful is simple, and it correlates with the one that Jacquie presents: In each of us there is only one True Self (Real Self, Child Within, Existential Self, Heart, Soul) that is in relationship with *other people*, with its *Higher Self* (Self, Guardian Angel, Divine Self, Divine Nature, Atman, Buddha Nature, Mystery Monitor, Thought Adjuster), and with its *Higher Power* (God/ Goddess/ All-That-Is). By contrast, the *ego* is the True Self's *assistant* and may be *positive* ego or *negative* ego, depending on how we relate to and use it. Earthly adventure remains a Divine Mystery, while outside of our awareness our unfinished business is stored in our unconscious mind (unconscious, shadow). Even though Jacquie's map of the psyche varies somewhat from mine, I am comfortable with and support her treatment of most of its dynamics.

In keeping with Jungian principles, Jacquie describes the double-edged nature of most things we encounter in life. This is the conflict we face almost daily, working through the opposites as they tug upon and sometimes even wrench our Heart, our Child Within. As we work through these dualities and heal, we may notice that most of our ego, or false self's, shadow stuff is darkness, in contrast to our Higher Nature and God, which is mostly Light.

But there is a catch—a potential trap here. If we try to go around or bypass the darkness to get to the Light, i.e., if we try to ignore the lower to get to the higher levels of our consciousness, something (usually our shadow) will pull us back until we work through our particular unfinished business. Trying to avoid this work of Stages One and Two recovery can be called "premature transcendence," "spiritual bypass," or "high-level denial." As Barbara Harris and I have pointed out, this is seen in any number of situations, from being prematurely "born again" to having a spiritual awakening and focusing only on the Light, to becoming attached to a guru or "way." Its consequences are often active codependence: denial of the richness of our inner life; trying to control oneself or others; all-or-none thinking and behaving; feelings of fear, shame, and confusion; high tolerance for inappropriate behavior; frustration, addiction, compulsion, relapse, and unnecessary pain and suffering.

The way out of this trap is to work through the pain of wherever we may be (or just enjoy the joyous feelings). Those who are actively addicted or disordered can work through a Stage One full recovery program. Those who are adult children of troubled or dysfunctional families can work through Stage Two recovery. Throughout this book Jacquie is mindful of these necessities. For we cannot let go of something if we do not know experientially what it is we are letting go of. We cannot transcend the unhealed. And we can connect experientially to the God of our understanding only when we know our True Self, our Heart.

Jacquie breaks new ground, expanding our beliefs so we can bring our Higher Nature into our everyday life. Her writing is heartfelt, and she easily shares her own experiences. She never keeps herself separate from the reader. This kind of humility allows the reader to experience a healing unity with her as she offers her wise guidance. Having the ability to explain difficult psycho-spiritual concepts clearly and easily, she repeatedly invites us to stretch beyond the limits of who we thought we were.

I recommend this book for codependents and adult children of dysfunctional families who are in an advanced state of recovery and who want to go deeper into their spirituality. This is not light reading for the religiously or psychologically conservative. But if you want a clear introduction to an expanded spiritual psychology, then this book is educational and inspirational reading.

Charles L. Whitfield, M.D.
Baltimore, MD

I

Healing Codependence: A Psycho-Spiritual Approach

Without the transcendent and the transpersonal, we get sick . . . or else hopeless and apathetic. We need something bigger than we are to be awed by and to commit ourselves to.

—Abraham Maslow

"Awakening in Time"

Thank God our time is now when wrong
  comes up to meet us everywhere,
  Never to leave us till we take
The longest stride of soul men ever took.
  Affairs are now soul-sized.
The enterprise is exploration into God.
  Where are you making for?
It takes so many thousand years to wake.
  But will you wake for pity's sake?

—Christopher Fry

odependence is a crisis of the spirit. It is the way we give our power away as human souls—to intimates, to strangers, to projects or careers that don't come from our hearts, to societal standards, and even to a God we may not experience as connected to us at all.

And, like many of my colleagues in the recovery field, I am convinced that codependence, commonly known as the "relationship addiction," is at the root of all addictions. For in codependence, we sit back feeling impotent, believing somebody or something out there will take care of it (and us). We focus in the wrong direction, avidly fixated on the "other," instead of on the unfolding of our own truth. And this basic pattern is true whether our addiction is a relationship, alcohol, shopping, or sex.

3

However, I do not believe codependence is a "disease," as it has been recently defined. And I do not believe it is a label anyone should use to describe one's self. (For codependence is not who you are; it is something that you do.) Unfortunately, these faulty premises have permeated much of the codependency movement.

And perhaps as a result of this, the concept of codependence is currently under attack by many in the field of addiction, psychology, medicine, and the general public. This criticism is also directed at the many different definitions of codependence, so many that it has become a vague and confusing list of characteristics that describes virtually everyone who struggles in relationships. However, this does not concern me, as I feel codependence *is* in essence a facet of the human condition; that, in fact, it is a process many of us must go through as we learn how to love.

But what does disturb me—and many others in and out of recovery—is the way in which some people have used the term to label themselves as sick or weak or powerless; and how others come to feel that any sort of intense involvement—the excitement of new love, taking care of someone in pain, or being a force in your children's lives—is codependent and wrong. The distinction between codependent behaviors and true caring is often lost, creating unnecessary doubt and confusion.

Unlike many of its critics, I do not feel the answer is to reject the concept of codependence. I do feel strongly, however, that while we need to claim and understand our relationship addictions, we also must be very careful not to mislabel our natural human urges or become stuck in our addictive identities, wearing them as if they were our skin.

Some of you may have read books about codependence that enumerate its wide-ranging symptoms: lack of boundaries in relationships, caretaking or the need to be indispensable to others, low self-esteem, feelings of victimhood or powerlessness, being out of touch with one's feelings, self-neglect, and other ways of abusing oneself for the sake of someone or something one perceives as more significant than oneself.

However, despite the success and plethora of these books and the growth of the codependency movement, I know of many now labeling themselves "codependent" who are feeling stuck or restless. They feel ready to move forward in their lives and are seeking a path that will match their spiritual longings and beliefs. They are searching for a self beyond their dysfunction.

But in their search, they continue to find overly simplified approaches solely devoted to identifying them with a disease, syndrome, or disorder (mostly focusing on what they're doing wrong). Some literature and treatment programs simply stop at describing the symptoms of the dysfunction, offering superficial advice and little direction for the seeker as to how healing really occurs. Many people are recognizing that something is wrong with all the disease and addiction labels we've been using on ourselves.

For this reason, codependence must be looked at in a spiritual context, as a place in our evolution we must move beyond. Only then can we take the necessary step of embracing our imperfections, our faulty ways of loving, rather than harshly labeling or rejecting them. As the Twelve Step movement of Alcoholics Anonymous and other Anonymous groups teach, acceptance is one of the first steps toward letting go. Once we take this step, we are well on our way toward developing a larger and more fulfilling identity.

I believe *codependence is unconscious living*. It affects those of us who have not yet awakened to our innate spiritual power, who do not yet see that a destiny much larger than our painful addictive ways is awaiting us. This destiny sits quietly and patiently within our consciousness. But until we wake up and actively begin participating in our own creation story, we will continue to fall victim to the destructive patterns of codependent living.

Awakening in Time is about finding that creation story, your own individual truth and expression. It is about taking the journey inward to discover your essence. *This is not another book about codependence: it's about moving beyond it, beyond the condition and beyond the label, which for some of us has actually limited our growth.* And it has been written for those of you who want more than what is customarily offered in addiction treatment today.

Please know that I am not dismissing the entirety of mainstream addiction philosophy; there's a lot of valuable material being published. Nor am I at all debunking the tremendous healing power of the Twelve Step program, which I follow myself. Moreover, there is much value in realizing codependence exists in one's life. There are millions of people just becoming aware of the concept of codependence, and they—understandably—feel relieved that their painful condition has a name. Identifying a problem is the first step toward healing. But we must always remember that it is only a first step.

My hope is that this book will help you take that first step, if you haven't already done so, and then introduce you to an even deeper understanding of codependence as it manifests in your life. Because codependence is essentially a spiritual condition, I will be using a *psycho-spiritual* approach that synthesizes concepts from mainstream psychology, Jungian thought, and the new and growing field of transpersonal psychology, metaphysics, Eastern and Western mysticism, and Twelve Step philosophy. For until codependence is approached wholistically (both psychologically and spiritually), it will slip out from underneath our grasp and attack us in some new area of our lives.

I hope to show how codependence patterns manifest in our earliest stages of development, sometimes even in the womb. And I will explore—through the ancient chakra system—how codependence results from imbalances in our physical, emotional, and mental natures that distort our basic human urges: the urge to control, the urge to excite (or be stimulated), and the urge to merge. I will illustrate how by opening our hearts and accessing our spiritual nature, we can transform these urges into positive forces that can heal our relationships and our lives. My purpose is to help you unfold your own destiny as an empowered, spiritual person who can live without the pain of misunderstood addiction.

Because this book has been written not only for thirsty minds but for hungry hearts as well, it is not merely a collection of concepts. It is a process book that teaches you through your own direct perceptions and reactions as you read along. In many places, you'll find hints for your intuition—guided imageries as well as simple diagrams and symbols—rather than concrete ideas that engage your mind intellectually. If you participate fully, from the heart, your insights will become living principles within you: no longer *a* truth, but *your* truth. If you choose to make this reading a transformational journey, you will find yourself undergoing some of the mental, emotional, and spiritual shifts explicated herein. This, of course, is completely up to you.

In any case, I invite you forward and support you on a journey toward a whole new way of being—toward realizing you are a self that is larger than your "disease." *I encourage you to <u>awaken in time</u> to realize the timeless, multifaceted, spiritual being that you are. For I believe with all my heart that this awakening is the only way we can truly become conscious and heal our wounded selves.*

This approach to addiction emerged from my own personal history of codependence, which has been a keynote for my life. As someone who has had an unconscious pattern of "serial monogamy" and multiple marriages, I've suffered vast amounts of pain from relationship dysfunction. Yet simultaneously, these broken dreams have been a source of growth, for I've always felt a need to return to my self after each disillusionment. Along with my pain have come new seeds of truth bearing fresh insights and furthering my spiritual journey. Now, years later, I'm learning to speak about my experiences, and to heal them.

In 1975 I underwent a spiritual crisis so severe I thought I'd died. I learned some things about my marriage that ended the relationship right there on the spot. The illusion bubble had burst wide open, and there I was: bereft, with no identity at all. For I'd invested my whole self in this relationship, and now it was gone. I was no longer the person I had known myself to be and that others called "Jacquelyn." I walked around for days not knowing who I was, spending most of my time in my best friend's driveway just sitting in my car; she was away on vacation, but this was the only place I felt safe. My boss was very understanding; he met me in a coffee shop one day and simply told me to take care of myself and come back to work when I felt better. Later, I found out that in the Twelve Step program this is called "hitting bottom." I'm sure many of you reading this book have also died to someone you were at an earlier time. I know of many recovering from codependence and addiction who've experienced something similar to this. And I know others who've undergone actual near-death experiences and who also describe these feelings.

As a result of this traumatic period, I underwent deep and lasting changes in my life. Gradually, after much griefwork and processing, I realized that I had been mistakenly seeing myself as nothing more than a mirrored reflection of the conditions in my life. And I had been despondently trying to correct those conditions without tapping into—or even realizing the power of—my spiritual self, my true core. I knew I needed to continue to explore the unhealthy aspects of myself that had gotten me into this relationship and caused me to feel so needy I couldn't let go when it became dysfunctional. But I also felt I had to find the greater person I knew myself to be, beyond the unhealthy parts. For even in my pain, I sensed that all of me wasn't as torn up and sick as that one who'd died. If I was going to live at all, I realized, I had to start over as someone new, someone who I had to learn how to be.

I pulled away from mainstream addiction work and dropped my identity as an addiction therapist. I needed fresh air and a broader perspective. I couldn't find validation for some of my experiences through the disease lense of addiction: I was in need of a philosophy large enough to explain the newly expanding me. And I found this broader context and support in the field of transpersonal psychology, a field that incorporates both Western and Eastern thought and spiritual traditions from throughout the world. I brought with me my knowledge of addiction, and when I eventually returned to the field of addiction, I brought back the concepts and perspective I had gained while studying—and living!—transpersonal psychology.

This new-paradigm psychology focuses on the inner life and the psycho-spiritual realities that reside deep within us: the mystical life. The transpersonal definition of the self includes both the ego and the soul or spirit. It sees as legitimate both the ancient spiritual healing traditions and more contemporary psychological methods.

The scientists of this new psychology, also known as "human

consciousness researchers," work with nonordinary states such as meditation, dreamwork, and the active imagination of Jungian psychology, as well as with myths, archetypes, and the psychic realms of human consciousness. They make use of guided imagery, psychosynthesis processes, and deep cathartic methods such as rebirthing, breathwork, and integrative body work (which I will describe later and in the glossary at the end of the book). Some also incorporate Christian contemplative prayer, shamanic work, and Yoga into their practices. They are learning to communicate with our potent and all-inclusive unconscious mind, carrying forward the insightful work of Freud, Jung, behaviorism, and humanistic psychology.

This kind of inner work is the focus of my own healing/training institute, Eupsychia, which has been in existence since 1983. The word *eupsychia* was coined by the great humanistic psychologist and pioneer, Abraham Maslow, and it translates from Greek as "good psyche" or "well-being." My coworkers and I try to live up to Maslow's term by providing a safe, loving environment that honors all dimensions of the human psyche: its ability to work through painful experiences as well as to transcend its conditions. And we feel strongly that the healing of emotional wounds— which are at the root of codependence and many other addictions—happens when people can strengthen their inner connection with a Higher Self and a Higher Power. All of our programs are based on the premise that *we are not human beings learning to be spiritual; we are spiritual beings learning to be human.*

In fact, we've found that when people are out of touch with the inner life, they are far more prone to addictions of all kinds. They only look outside themselves for gratification and validation: they may think they have a self, but they don't realize it experientially. They are ruled by doubt, fear, and unmet needs for safety and love. Because they are too passionately involved in their relationships— embroiled in the outer thrills of romance, sex, compulsively rescuing others, and the constant melodramatic highs and lows these conditions create—they cannot act out of love or true caring. And even worse, they may completely merge into another and lose their identities entirely. When relationships become this painful and unfulfilling, people are more likely to drink, overeat, gamble, shop—anything to forget their suffering.

Charles Whitfield, a doctor and writer in the field of addiction, enlarged the concept of codependence to include not only our personal relationships but our communities, institutions, and culture. And author Anne Wilson Schaef addresses this issue as the theme of one of her most important books, *When Society Becomes an Addict*. Indeed, codependence affects all areas of our lives: personal, professional, social, cultural—and cosmic. It is that huge and foreboding. Our addictive focus keeps us from realizing our own talents, dreams, and visions. As a result, our society is suffering from an enormous loss of creativity.

For our purposes in this book, I want to note that all definitions of codependence have the same underlying theme: There is a loss of self, given away for the sake of some other—a relationship, outside authority, escape, or reward—and this "other" is the *not-self*. Therefore, our mission as recovering people must be to return to the self, our spiritual essence, by discovering our true identity within. For it is necessary to *be* a self before we can offer ourselves to others in loving relationships.

Until we develop this sense of identity, we will mistake who we are and think we are our outer conditions. Like Narcissus, we will fall in love with the reflections of life and believe they are the truth about us, as I did after my marriage broke up. We will identify with our predicaments, taking them on so completely we wind up believing those problems in living are our essence.

In fact, the very act of labeling ourselves can be codependent. Instead of saying we experienced a divorce, we say "I *am* a divorcee." We don't say we have codependence patterns in our lives; we say "I *am* a flaming codependent." We define ourselves as our conditions, which often doesn't give us room to grow beyond them. From now on, notice how you use language: you may be very subtly disowning your power as a soul—as creative and able to change. If we are to truly heal our addictions, Rule Number 1 is:

The Self Is Larger Than Its Conditions

As co-creators (for we always create along with a Higher Power), we need to work through our pasts: the wounds from both childhood and adulthood must be fully processed in order for us to heal. And then we must begin to make our lives our own responsibility and stop blaming others for our misery. We must learn to preoccupy ourselves with our own authentic expression. I call this "standing in the light of your own being." And I believe it is the eventual healer of codependence.

This return to the abandoned self may sound a bit cosmic; but I promise you it is very practical work. Right here in the midst of our daily routines, we gradually learn to respond to our inner spirit and stop reacting to outer conditions. The exercises and imageries herein will hopefully give you some tools to carry with you on this journey.

As a society, I believe we are crying out for this higher way of living. Many voices can now be heard crying, "Whoa! Enough of these unconscious ways!" Our planet is dying—and we are dying right along with it. We see families, neighborhoods, even whole cities and cultures steeped in the agony of addiction, gang wars, religious wars, illness, pollution, and hopelessness. It's time to awaken to our rightful stance as co-creators. We can't wait for someone outside ourselves to come along and save us. We must become our own sought-for rescue mission.

Are You an Adapter or a Transformer?

There are two modes of functioning on this planet at any given time, producing two very different types of people: those who are busy adapting to their conditions as they are, *adapters*; and those who are transforming and moving into whole new ways of being, *transformers*. Some are interested in keeping life unchanging and familiar, focusing on the improvement of their present situations within known boundaries; others are preoccupied with bursting the boundaries of their current conditions, shedding their old ways and going beyond. And we are all absolutely both, depending on which path we're following at a particular time in our lives.

This book is written for those in a transformational state of mind (and heart). It's a book for transformers, who are finally ready to leave their codependence and addiction behind. The following descriptions will help you better understand these two states, although the simple fact that you've picked up this book indicates that you are probably ready to transform or are already in a transformational cycle.

Adapters

People who are in an adaptive mode are living within a fairly definitive set of attitudes and beliefs, bound in by what they consider to be "real." They are concerned with the contents of their outer lives, and they aren't interested in venturing outside beliefs and philosophies long held by society or family tradition. Anything that falls outside these acceptable belief systems seems unimportant, irrelevant, or—depending upon how threatening—downright evil. For instance, someone in an adaptive cycle may be having continuous trouble with something her preacher does or says, but she will not be looking for a new church or a new religion. In fact, she might even view all other religions as "off-the-mark" or "devil worship." If she seeks out therapy, she'll seek advice from people she deems "experts" on how to fix her broken parts, based on psychological theories and techniques or religious beliefs meant to help her adapt to things as they are. And if an adapter is struggling with issues of codependence or addiction, he may seek out a treatment center that will label him sick but never go beyond this very first insufficient step. He is not looking for new beliefs, nor is he interested in transformational therapies that seem abstract or might change his consciousness, such as working with imagery or dream symbols, or really following the Twelve Steps. To him, these inner realms seem to be mere fantasy, unreal, even dangerous. Adapters want answers for specific, concrete issues. They are focused on the outer world, believing the outer life is the only life.

People in adaptive cycles function as conformists and together they are known as "mass consciousness." They will manipulate and experiment with the contents *within* their boundaries, but adapters will not go beyond what, to them, is "normal" change. These people serve an important function for society as a whole: They hold together the "goods" of the past; and they become a backdrop against which the transformer can bounce.

Transformers

However, people who are experiencing a transformational cycle cannot hold onto the status quo; it has already blown apart for them. They are changing identities, moving into a new universe. Something has happened in their personal experience that has shown them that they are more than they thought they were, and life is more than they thought it was. This event can be anything from a relationship ending painfully to a serious illness, the trauma of childbirth, hitting bottom with an addiction, or a deep and abiding mystical happening such as a near-death experience. It can also take the form of a dramatic exposure of a codependence pattern through some occurrence or series of occurrences that point out that the old way will simply no longer work. Or sometimes, less dramatically, a person may meet someone who is a transformer or become exposed to and fascinated by new kinds of information—books, movies, or artistic expressions that speak of the mystical or hidden realms. And something (someone) inside of them recognizes these new ideas as true. No longer interested in the same kinds of relationships, they are seeking new ways to grow and new friends and partners to grow with. However they got there, these people have burst the boundaries of their previous belief systems and have become seekers of a new way.

Those of us with this mindset are becoming *transpersonal,*

moving beyond an exclusive focus on the personal life into an identification with the world around us. Transformers see themselves as part of a bigger picture. Seeking advice and strategies that "fix" them is no longer gratifying. Many have died several times, some to alcohol and drugs, some to marriages or other significant primary relationships, some to careers, roles, or social groups. But they are beginning to see these "deaths" as necessary for their growth.

Those of you currently undergoing a transformation cycle are likely feeling an urgency to let go of any codependence patterns that are limiting your true expression and that of the people you love. Many of you are ready to see yourselves in a whole new way—as *bigger* than your problems and as worthy of more than continuously getting lost in outside events and other people. If this is your truth, I sincerely hope this book provides sustenance and loving support for your seeking soul.

Recovering Our
Lost Selves

Humankind has long felt a void, that there was
something missing in its life. . . . That which
is missing has been with us all along, although we
are only now turning to it in a serious way. It is
our Spirit, our Self.

—Charles L. Whitfield, M.D.

Many people with codependence and addiction issues have
been caught up in their suffering for so long, they've never
gotten around to "doing their being." Often as a result of
dysfunctional upbringings, many of us sacrificed our true vision
and talents early on in life, turning instead to the outer allure of
codependent entanglements and melodramas. That budding ac-
tress in you, the poet, or great adventurer—or those leadership
qualities you had during elementary school, those little awards you
won—these were signs of your creativity emerging from the source
of your being. Many of you were never encouraged to continue
developing these gifts, or were even discouraged. As a result, you
let them go, or put them aside, perhaps hoping that someday you'd
pick up where you left off.

But that day never came. You've been taking care of your
alcoholic husband; you've been obsessed with your role as parent

15

and caretaker; your career took a bad turn and you've been recovering workaholically ever since. Or you've been drowning your pain in a substance, or working jobs you can't stand in order to maintain a lifestyle that no longer thrills you. Or perhaps life became particularly difficult due to illnesses or unforeseen events, maybe even tragedies. For whatever reason, your spirit got put on hold while your ego took care of your outside life and became so outer-directed you forgot where you originally wanted to go. Now perhaps you've said "Enough!" And you feel a compelling urge to retreat and go inward to find the whole person you were meant to be. This is the beginning of the co-creative path.

But in addition to uncovering our sublime natures and native creativity, we also must recover our abandoned shadow selves, those negative selves we'd rather deny. Because so many of us were taught that painful feelings, or even natural human urges, were not to be felt, we repressed them and still may not be able to claim them as our own. They've become our shadow, following behind us wherever we go. We may hide our emotional truth much of the time, only letting one side of ourselves show while another side seethes within us, unable to be heard. Or perhaps we are completely out of touch with our emotions, unconsciously collecting unfelt hurts or rage. Until we legitimize our feelings and learn to express them, they will keep us locked in extreme highs and lows, the emotional turmoil we all know as codependence. When we do reclaim our disowned parts, both positive and negative, we will then quite naturally settle into a larger self, the self that we've always been but didn't know we had a right to be.

For just as caterpillars turn into butterflies and ducklings into swans, we, when we're all "grown-up," become a *self*. This self is that place in consciousness all humans seek, where we feel complete and fulfilled. And it resides down underneath our codependence patterns, *at the very roots of our being*. Like the princess who's been kidnapped and raised as a pauper but one day is told she has a kingdom to inherit, we, too, are realizing we have a destiny far greater than preoccupation with dysfunctional involvements. It's time now to deepen—to seek our inner source once again, so we can fulfill our true potential, which is waiting just around the corner from our dysfunctional past.

Now I'd like to actually introduce you to the many selves you'll meet along your journey from codependence to co-creation. As you become aware of them, you'll see that they already know how to transform your life; each has a sacred function in your process of awakening. And each one is worthy of your recognition and gratitude, for without any one of them, even your negative selves, you can never be complete.

The definitions that follow can be used for reference as you read along in this book. Keep in mind that they are not scholarly; they are *living* definitions that will enable you to formulate a mental picture of the characters who live on your underneath side. Recognizing these selves and their source is the first step toward integrating them.

Higher Power. This is the impersonal and formless Energy Source, the Creator. Although It originates beyond this realm, It fuels and compels our entire living process. Some people call It "God." Some call It "cosmic consciousness." In the movie *Star Wars*, the Higher Power was "The Force." Those of you in Twelve Step programs have likely already come up with a definition you're comfortable with. Others of you may want to spend some time contemplating this crucial power.

When we honor the Higher Power's principles of love—of truth, goodness, and beauty—we are using our energy as a creative positive force, and we feel serene. When we violate Its laws of love and wisdom which are in fact our nature, we feel isolated, heavy, uninspired, and out of sorts. Our creative powers grow dim, and we are likely to misuse our energies in codependent pursuits. When we are aligned with our Higher Power, we are not only creative; we are inspired and illumined. The Higher Power is an electromagnetic circuit we plug into. It is available to all who recognize this energy and choose to bring It into their lives by aligning their personal lives with Its principles and qualities and then expressing them. In order to connect with our Higher Power, we simply need to be still and listen. Our intuition already knows the sound of Its voice.

The Higher Self (or the Self). This Self is *an organizing principle only*, which draws Its energies from the Higher Power. It is our core nature, or root-consciousness from whence we've sprung. It is the Ideal of each completed human being. C. G. Jung defined the Higher Self, or Self, as he called It, as a central unifying archetype around which all other archetypes are grouped and ordered. An archetype is the ideal image of anything we wish to create or become; according to Jung, archetypes reside within the collective human mind. The archetype of the Higher Self is the blueprint for all of humanity, its masterpiece. And It is the blueprint for each individual as well.

Many believe Jesus, the Buddha, and a few other great beings who've manifested on this planet perfectly exemplified this divine blueprint. For this reason, most of us should not expect to completely become this Self at our current stage of evolution. But we *can* be aware that the Higher Self represents our wholeness (or holiness). And It can therefore function as a guywire to guide us toward completion as human beings.

The Higher Self is synonymous with what most people call "the soul." We experience It as an attitude of calm lightheartedness—a deep sense of well-being. The energy of the Higher Self can take form and live *as* us anytime we manifest our wholeness, even for a moment. And since Its nature is to unify, It will clothe Itself around whatever identity we put on: the things we say "I am" to, we become. This is why it's so important to be careful how we use those magical words, "I am." This is how we can unconsciously become identified with a condition or a limited trait.

The Higher Self is both our *source* and our *goal*. And it's important to remember this while reading this book. Sometimes I'll refer to It as our abstract source, which I will call the Higher Self. At other times I'll speak of It as our wholeness, which we attain when we unify our fragmented parts; in this case I'll call It the Self. Both terms will always be capitalized, to honor their archetypal nature (as will all other archetypes throughout the book). This Higher Self is the Co-creator par excellence! For it is *by, through, and as* the Self or Higher Self that we continually evolve into more expanded and integrated people.

The Ego. This self is the ruler of our conscious life, the executor of our identity. It is our personality and individuality. And it is responsible for meeting our basic needs for security, pleasure, belongingness, self-esteem, and love. If it fails to do so, we will become needy, and very likely try to meet these needs through codependent behavior patterns. The ego is also limitation; it decides which boundaries we live within and call "reality." It throws everything else out, labeling it dangerous or irrelevant. (Adapters often have very strong egos.) It makes sure we don't become too overwhelmed by the contents of the unconscious mind.

The ego can split into two selves: sometimes it is the approved-of *persona*, the facade we like to show others, a positive, integrated self. However, this persona breaks down when we become too needy, and the ego then reverts to the *shadow*, our disowned fragments or impure selves that otherwise remain hidden. In addition, the ego serves as a buffer zone for the soul, or Higher Self, which is entering into time through us from a higher (deeper) dimension. The soul is too light, innocent, and insubstantial to withstand the harsh conditions of the outer life.

When our ego is gratified, it is in alignment with the soul: it has presence, or potency, and wisdom here in the ordinary world. Eventually, it becomes merged into the soul as a *soul-infused personality*, which I'll discuss at length later in the book. When the ego is not gratified, it focuses backward, re-active to the conditions of our past. Until the ego purifies and integrates its shadowy fragments and learns how to meet our basic human needs, we will have no foundation upon which to build a whole and balanced Self. Though it can be contrary and sometimes try to rule us, the ego is our friend.

The Shadow (the deficient or negative ego). The shadow represents all our disowned, despised, and repressed traits. It lives buried in the closets of our subconscious minds safe from our judgments. The shadow is our "dark side." It acts out for us all those denied emotions and urges we wish we didn't have. For instance, if we're prudish about our sexuality, it acts out our "vamp" side behind our backs. If we insist on always being kind and loving for all the world to see, it will express our other side by sometimes taking over and harshly misbehaving. It is an emotion-based self, slippery and hard to catch. And it is grounded in fear, drama, and competitiveness; it can destroy our relationships if not tamed. Its sacred purpose in our transformation is to remind us of our emotional unfinished business, of what we're trying to skip over or leave behind. Jung called it "our sparring partner," the opponent who exposes our flaws and sharpens our skills.

Whenever you repress an emotion, or deny an issue in your life—such as pretending an insult doesn't hurt, or insisting you're not having trouble with alcohol when it's obvious you're alcoholic—these repressed emotions or unresolved issues will go underground into the subconscious mind. Because it takes so much energy to repress disowned feelings, the shadow will eventually pop out and make a fool of itself (you!), or in some other way bring the issue to the surface. The shadow is our awakener; it will eventually bring out of denial all our unconscious ways.

As you study this book you'll see that our codependence patterns come from the shadow's fears and illusions about how to love and be loved, and until we make them conscious (recognize and own them), we are likely to act out, manipulate, or otherwise behave codependently through this negative, non-purified ego. (Because of its importance in the unfolding of codependence, I've devoted an entire chapter to the shadow.)

The shadow dissipates or lightens when we accept it. We may still swing from negative to positive states, but our lives will become manageable because the extremes will disappear. When our shadow does manifest, we'll know it is time to listen to its message rather than act on its impulses. We need to see that the shadow, too, can be our friend.

The Positive Self (positive, purified ego). The positive self is the healthy ego, which has integrated the shadow, become conscious, and is therefore open to the Higher Self's messages. It is the evolving individual personality, our learned self who is always correcting our mistakes. It is our straight-A self, our purified or forward-moving ego, which is busy integrating the shadow as well as the Higher Self, or soul.

This positive self keeps us moving toward our next right identity. It is centered and enables us, as egos, to live from the heart. But it is a part of our ego—its highest expression—and completely of this world. The Higher Self utilizes our positive self for the purpose of incarnation: For the positive self can actually merge into the Higher Self for periods of time. During these high times, we feel truly inspired; we become co-creators.

The Observer Self. To make anything conscious, we must separate the knower from the known. For only when we have perspective on our conditions can we see and understand them. Observer self is the knower, the activator of consciousness. This self is an agent of our Higher Power's mind and its function is to notice and re-mind. But this is not an intellectual function; it is a *felt awareness*—an inner knowing. The observer self reminds us *in vivo* of anything that is standing in the way of our truth.

I think of my observer self as sitting on my shoulder, gently poking me into consciousness anytime I go to sleep. It will occasionally whisper in my ear, "Just notice what you are saying now. You are repeating yourself over and over again." Or, "You just walked to the phone booth again to call that man for the sixth time." This self brings us into the present moment, making us fully conscious of what we are doing. Then, we have a choice as to whether or not to continue our current activity. We may choose to anyway, but at least we'll be doing it consciously. Often, to help us let go of a pattern, observer walks us through our dysfunctional behavior while we're wide awake, acutely aware of what it is we are really doing. This can be very uncomfortable but is often necessary to our healing. Without this dispassionate self we'd never be able to recognize the truth beyond our wounded ego's definition of it; we would never evolve. In certain practices of Buddhism, observer self is called "the fair witness."

All of the above are characters in our game of life. And as you can see, each one of them, mighty and small, is vital to our awakening into wholeness. But most of us have been unaware of these selves and therefore have not been fully tapping our inner power. We may also have been unconsciously, or codependently, misusing these selves: judging instead of observing; acting out our shadow rather than embracing it; using our vision of a bigger self to beat ourselves up for not being perfect; or searching for the Higher Self in one another. As spiritual beings with a nature that is creative, we're always busy either creating or mis-creating something; we have no other option. Unfortunately, much of our creative energy has been wasted simply repeating over and over the patterns from our families of origin, like robots. These patterns will cease once we utilize these selves in their true form.

As we explore the issue of codependence in these pages, we will begin weaving together the various selves you've just met. They will emerge as an integral part of this reading, just as they emerge in you. And you will recognize them as they appear. As one who is traveling this journey with you, I've found the writing of this book provided much healing for me. And it is an honor to be sharing this experiential knowledge with all of you. For I don't consider myself an expert. No one outside us can be an authority on our unfolding Self. There can be guides—people who are more experienced on the path or skilled in areas of specific knowledge—but never experts.

From my work with thousands of people for over two decades, whether in my workshops or in my daily interactions, I now understand that at some point, we must each do the psycho-spiritual work required to recover these lost selves and literally re-member our wholeness. Otherwise, we never make it Home. For I believe that we are not one self, but many—until like blossoms we fully open and express our whole nature. Until then, many of our selves will remain buried in the nethermost depths of our psyches, feeling lost or abandoned and unable to evolve.

So where is the whole truth of our Self to be found? Well, certainly not in the varying schools of mainstream psychology (though each has made an important contribution to this quest for the Self). The divergent disciplines of psychology don't even agree on what human nature is or how positive change really occurs. And obviously, all of our truth cannot be found in any one of the warring religions; they disagree even more vehemently with one another than the psychological schools! And they often do more to separate people from their innate spirituality than anything else. When we put all of psychology and the roots of religion together, we're getting closer to the truth.

This next chapter is devoted to exploring the perspective of transpersonal psychology, which, as I pointed out in the introduction, integrates the spiritual teachings of the various world religions with the schools of psychology that have developed in the past century. I call it a psychology of wholeness, because it offers a context in which we can integrate our many selves and finally realize the Self we always were but never had the tools to discover or the perspective to see.

From Fragmentation
to Wholeness: The Gift of
Psycho-Spirituality

In the core of our being we are singular and
unified; at the surface of our interactions with the
world, we are multiple and dispersed. In transformation we seek to recover that original unity.

—Ralph Metzner

The addictions field has done an excellent job of helping us
name our addictive conditions. We have been forced to wake
up and take a look at how we are giving our very lives away.
Addiction and codependency treatment is replete with knowledge
about each and every addiction and dysfunctional behavior we are
capable of.

However, something has been missing, not only from some
recovery books, but from most of our treatment of addiction and
codependence, and I believe this "something" is our whole Self. I
know of no place where reductionism and psychological myopia
are more rampant in today's world than in the existing field of
mainstream addiction treatment. This is a strong statement. And
there are, of course, exceptions.

It is a fact that most hospitals' and treatment centers' programs report high degrees of recidivism (some as high as eighty percent), and many such programs are folding, having failed to meet their goals. Yet many still in existence continue to focus almost entirely on the negative, sick, or fragmented aspects of people. For they view clients—as well as their families—exclusively through the lense of disease and dysfunction. There seems to be very little interest in or understanding of the concepts of wholeness, the repressed sublime, creativity, core goodness, or the inner healer. Clients' inner strengths that have developed over years of struggle with addictions are often unacknowledged, and clients and their families are given little hope for becoming wiser or greater selves, or for understanding the positive aspects of their crises or the transformative nature of humankind. I am often reminded of the comment made by India's great social reformer and sage, Sri Aurobindo:

> I find it difficult to take these Western psychiatrists at all seriously . . . yet perhaps one ought to, for half-knowledge is a powerful thing and can be a great obstacle to the Truth. . . . They look from down up and explain the higher lights by the lower obscurities; but the foundation of these things is above and not below. (Satprem, *Sri Aurobindo or the Adventure of Consciousness*)

Many treatment programs recommend or include the Twelve Step programs of Alcoholics Anonymous, Narcotics Anonymous, Overeaters Anonymous, or Codependents Anonymous. Yet if you review these treatment programs' philosophies, you can see instantly that they are merely giving lip service to the principle of Higher Power, the real healer of the Twelve Step approach. They themselves have become the experts. And they look to their clients for verification. But "fixing clients" is a myth. Anytime we believe someone else is our savior, another addiction has set in. Giving our power away to others, at whatever level, is codependence, leading to more entrapment in lieu of the hoped-for freedom of recovery. The only power we should surrender to is our Higher Power, and this always happens within the Self. The focus of treatment—if it is to be really life-giving and lasting—must be on clients finding their *own* strength and inner healer. And, they should leave treatment believing in *themselves*, not in some expert or program.

I know a woman who checked herself into treatment for codependence while in deep grief over a relationship breakup. Before her relationship blew up, she had made huge strides in her self-esteem while working with therapists and in groups with a transpersonal and Gestalt therapy orientation, as well as faithfully attending Alcoholics Anonymous meetings. Her ego was settling into an expression of her creativity once more. She had reentered school to study her new-found love, social work. And she was working part-time as a counselor at a halfway house for women. Although her relationship had broken up, it was the healthiest one she had ever experienced. She'd been happy much of the time and was learning a great deal about herself before the heat got too high. The suggestion of marriage was acceptable to her, but he wanted children and she did not. In response to their fear of losing each other, they had begun acting out codependence patterns that one day caused her to panic and prematurely end it all.

While in treatment, she wrote me often. I could feel her self-esteem begin to wane. She was accused daily of being incompetent and codependent, and she was cajoled into believing she could only be with graduates of that particular program from then on, even when she returned to her small home town, where she was close to many people who'd never even heard of this out-of-state program. Over and over she was reminded that she was an abused child, but she was never given any opportunity to release these early childhood issues.

I maintained my contact with her in spite of the mandate that she spend time only with the people from that program, because I began fearing for her sanity. Even with the help and encouragement of many of us who had known her before, she was incapacitated with fear and self-doubt for months after this experience. In my opinion, allowing a group of people to take her over was her biggest codependent problem—more damaging than the relationship with the prospective mate.

As I've pointed out, *naming* and *claiming* our codependence and addiction issues, our fragmented and wounded selves, is a vital first step in the process of healing into wholeness. But there is a further step that must also be taken and rendered legitimate if we are to fully heal: We must focus with purposeful intention in the direction of the transformation that we seek. And this requires an inward orientation, for it is our outer focus on the multiplicity of our conditions that has made us act codependently in the first place. In order to learn who we truly are, we must turn within where we can see beyond our codependent behaviors, beyond our exclusive focus on others and the ego's dysfunctional ways.

Our deep questions and inner longings cannot be satisfied by focusing solely on our ego issues. In the last chapter we saw how many selves are involved in our awakening! When we make use of only disease-oriented theories of addiction, or Freudian and behavioristic psychologies, we study the eggshell and leave the insides of the egg unnoticed. We cannot comprehend our essential nature by focusing so narrowly on our mistaken identities as only addicts and egos. We are not just our shadows and we are not just our shells.

Today we in the addictions field suspect that *all* significant relationships have their ways of being dysfunctional. When our problems in living become this universal, mainstream addiction treatment and psychology—which utilize mostly medical and socio-behavioral systems for recovery—are too limited in scope to address the entire problem. What is required is a healing of the human soul. And for such an all-embracing task, we need to employ a model of reality that offers us all that we know of the Self: the current findings of both science and religion, including the literature and experiences of the mystics and sages throughout history. We need an expanded view.

As I said earlier, the fragments of our original Self split into little subpersonalities as we pass through the trials of living. And these various "little selves" are usually in conflict with each other. For instance, there may be a self who loves sex, yet another one who is ashamed of having sexual feelings. Or there may be one self who enjoys being irresponsible, loving to just play around or "veg," while another self fusses at us for not always being grown-up and responsible. Sometimes our heads tell us one thing, while our hearts (or experience) tell us the opposite. Roberto Assagioli, the developer of Psychosynthesis, was the first in the field of psychotherapy to utilize this principle of "subpersonalities" in therapeutic work. Once in a Psychosynthesis training session I heard the statement that these subpersonalities, or fragmented selves, act just like a committee. And you know how committees are; their members seldom agree!

We need to re-collect these lost selves, now living outside the Self (or our awareness), denied and disowned. For it is only through the process of integrating our fragmented selves and gradually gaining a sense of oneness or wholeness that we come to know our true potential. The words *wholeness* and *health* are actually derived from the same Old English word, *hal*, meaning "sound," "complete." We know intuitively just by the way we use language that we don't like feeling split. When we feel heartbroken, disappointed, or hurt we say things like, "I've got to pull myself together," "I'm coming apart at the seams," or my relationship is "splitting up." We speak of breakdowns and cracking up. When we are feeling good about ourselves and our lives are running smoothly, we say, "I feel complete," "My life is coming together," or "Finally, I'm of one mind about the issue."

And this theme of "from fragmentation to wholeness" (a phrase explicated by transpersonal psychologist, Ralph Metzner) is ancient, unfolding steadily throughout the pages of human history. As Erich Neumann reminds us in *The Origins and History of Consciousness*, Osiris is the god or archetype in Egyptian mythology who represents this completed journey back to wholeness: "I have knit myself together. . . . I have renewed my youth. . . . I am Osiris, Lord of Eternity." And in the ancient Sumerian myth of Inanna (also known as Ishtar), this lovely goddess of the higher worlds has to sacrifice her wholeness and enter into the evil, fragmented, hellish world of her dark sister Ereshkigal, going all the way back into the archaic levels of unleashed passion and rage to merge with the deep feminine instincts. Only through reclaiming her denied other half could Inanna then truly possess the powers of wholeness. Her story is beautifully told by Jungian Sylvia

Brinton Perera in *Descent to the Goddess.* I believe this ancient theme is coming to full fruition today in the emergent field of transpersonal or psycho-spiritual psychology. Here we can focus on our bigger Self, the person we want to become: the path of inner transformation becomes visible.

A Psychology of Wholeness

The teacher or therapist with a psycho-spiritual orientation is sometimes accused of embracing ideas that are too abstract or esoteric to be relevant to everyday life. As a pioneer in the integration of transpersonal psychology into the field of recovery, I've often heard the question, "What has all this got to do with addiction?" I remember such an incident back in the early 1970s when I tried to conduct a training workshop for our field representatives of the Texas Commission on Alcoholism. I entitled this workshop "Meeting Your Higher Self." And I received from my coworkers a rush of memorandums whose thrust was, "Look, Jacquie, we can't even get our budgets to balance. We certainly don't have time to learn about our Higher Self!" And again, that question: "What's this got to do with alcoholism anyway?" I'm sure some of you who are reading this book can relate.

Transpersonal psychology is the new kid on the block. Nevertheless, more and more therapists, doctors, and counselors are making use of transpersonal methods. It is at the cutting edge of psychological systems that began with Freudian analysis and have included the schools of behaviorism and humanistic psychology. It goes beyond these other schools because it involves an inquiry into the whole Self, including the soul: it includes our spiritual life. For this reason, I can think of no other psychology that comes closer to the basic tenets of Alcoholics Anonymous, Codependents Anonymous, and the other Twelve Step programs. The goals are identical: a passion for knowledge about how to move from an unconscious sleep state into that of a conscious being, from being drunk and in a stupor to awakening fully to one's responsibilities as a co-creator. Carl Jung participated in the beginnings of Alcoholics Anonymous by advising its founders to seek deep healing for the terrible plight of addiction. His famous phrase "*spiritus contra spiritum*" meant that he saw the alcoholic's craving as a spiritual one that only a spiritual experience could counteract or heal.

Psyche is the root of the word "psychology," and it means soul, or spirit, something many psychologists seem to forget. The psyche is huge, our total Self. She knows herself both inwardly, as the unconscious mind, and outwardly, as one who experiences events in time. To the psyche there is no difference: her outer world is merely a manifestation of her rich inner life. Psyche knows exactly who she is. On the other hand, as I've said, the ego mind—a much smaller little character—divides the psyche up into pieces and tries through fragmented knowledge to define her.

Like the ego mind, mainstream psychology has cut us up into so many little pieces that we've almost forgotten how to conceptualize wholeness. Psychology has historically taken the personality, or ego, as its unit of study, neglecting the deeper aspects of our nature. Consequently, most of our psychological methods have not reached deeply enough into the psyche to disturb her slumber and divulge her secrets. She hears no calling to awake. For without the influence of our Higher Self—including the vast collective unconscious mind where we meditate, dream, imagine, intuit, and envision—we are cut off from the spirituality that is our essence.

Transpersonal psychology is attempting to bring back a respect for the wholeness of the Self. Its goal is to move forward along the trajectory of our unfolding lives, to help us manifest the theme "from fragmentation to wholeness" so that we can actualize our full potential. It is the first psychology (because it includes the work of Carl Jung) that explains the client's process as being a hero's or heroine's journey, an inner awakening or pilgrimage back to our spiritual source. This journey has been known throughout history by many names: the Tao, the Way of the Christ, enlightenment, the shamanic journey, kundalini awakening, the middle path, the Royal Road, the path of Initiation, the hero's journey, or simply "going Home," to name only a few.

Yet, this expanded psychology also utilizes and honors knowledge from other psychological schools that have preceded it. It is a synthesis of what has come before but is evolutionary because it contains all that we now know from studies of mystical states and nonordinary states of consciousness. It honors both ego integration, which was the focus of these earlier psychologies, and ego transcendence, the ways beyond ego that enable us to rise above our conditions and transform our being.

Therapists of this new psychology know that ego integration must precede ego transcendence. In other words, we cannot transcend an ego we've never developed. People with weak or unhealthy egos wind up in back wards of state hospitals, unable to cope with the outer world. I've seen examples of what the late Buddhist master Chogyam Trungpa called "spiritual by-pass," where people use spiritual practices to try to step over unassimilated childhood experiences and other painful biographical events. This can be the worst kind of denial. Again, the ego is our friend, and it plays a vital and purposive role in our functioning. We cannot pass it by.

Transpersonal psychology says the ego and Higher Self must form a congenial pact and choose to work in harmony; otherwise, we cannot evolve. For our healing is a *two-way process*: First, we must go *back* and look at how our ego became fragmented and our growth became blocked. The development of our ego actually happens in the body—in its first three energy centers, or chakras. As children, when our needs are not met on any of these three levels—physical, emotional, or mental—we become stuck and our adult lives will be unbalanced. When we clear these chakras through much inner work (which we'll explore later in this book), we then have the ability to move in a *forward* direction (which we'll also look at in this book). The very word "transpersonal" has two meanings: to go through and to go beyond.

This new-paradigm psychology helps us transcend our limits and become greater and more evolved. It guides us toward a Self much larger than our conditions. This Self bursts the boundaries of the ego mind. We experience this when we tap into our numinous higher nature during moments of meditation, prayer or invocation (which I'll explain later), trance, or other ways of going into the inner worlds. These spiritual experiences can create profound and lasting change in people's lives, showing them in a flash the potent beings they are and revealing to them their deep connection to the universe.

Without the context of a spiritual psychology, when people have experiences beyond what mainstream psychology deems "real" (such as a mystical experience during one of the processes described above, a dramatic incident of hitting bottom, a near-death or rebirthing experience), they have no place to go to be validated for these awakenings and therefore may become convinced they are mentally ill or merely New Age flakes. And when there is such a lack of validation, these experiences can become what are now being called "spiritual emergencies," a term explicated in the work of medical researcher Stanislav Grof and his wife, Christina Grof. People who undergo such emergencies often feel compelled to go underground, becoming isolated and secretive concerning issues that relate directly to the very ground of their being! This splitting off from the deepest aspects of the Self can, of course, lead to severe feelings of alienation, confusion, and various types of addiction. Those who've had these experiences need the support of others who've had similar histories or who understand these processes. To this purpose, my training institute, Eupsychia, has created a network of individuals throughout the United States and Canada who are equipped to handle calls from people having such difficulties. (See the appendix for more information).

Psychotherapy with a transpersonal approach can provide similar support and affirmation for people in search of wholeness. For example, in a therapy session where my client has curled up in a fetal position expressing tremendous fear as well as force, I will observe that she may be re-living aspects of her biological birth (an experience which psychology is increasingly acknowledging can be remembered by the unconscious mind). I would encourage this symptom, inviting her on through the fearsome re-living of her birth or whatever she is re-collecting, rather than attempting to stop the process and calm her down. Or another client might be re-living a "past life" by describing these events to me. I may not even believe in reincarnation myself, yet I honor the fact that my client is actually having this experience. I would encourage him to enter into the imagery and follow it through, never discounting his experience or trying to bring him into my own "reality." Sometimes work in nonordinary states requires the exact opposite approach from that of a traditional therapist. Transpersonal therapists know that it is not out, but *through* that heals us, so they believe in increasing the very symptoms others might choose to medicate and make disappear. Transformational or new paradigm groupwork also provides such a context, and I will explore these groups at the end of the book.

All this may sound strange to some of you who have never had to endure an explosive visit by your giant unconscious mind. And as a result you may feel transpersonal psychology is not for you. Let me assure you that the transpersonal approach has much to offer us all. For it is one of the only schools of psychology that fully legitimizes a Higher Power, which we all must connect with in order to truly heal. I believe it is crucial for people with codependence issues to begin to recognize the realms of consciousness beyond their personal biographies, which many of us have become overly attached to.

Moreover, modern research into human consciousness, perinatal psychology, quantum medicine, and the effects of imagery and prayer on healing are validating the psyche's deep wisdom and breadth. Soon the nonordinary will become ordinary as research and methodology fully catch up with us, and we see that human beings really grow and transform through deep inner experiences. Our society is about to realize that the psyche is both outside us (as ego) and within us (as spirit).

Some people are currently learning how to function in these two modes of consciousness simultaneously, the inner subjective world of the psyche and the outer objective world of the ego. These "walkers between two worlds" are becoming a new breed of conscious explorers who identify with the greater, more cosmic pattern of our wholeness, yet remain grounded and relevant in the outside world of regular activities.

How Psychology Is Expanding

Below is the spectrum of psychological approaches that exist thus far, along with existential and transpersonal approaches, so that you can see new paradigm psychology in the context of the other schools:

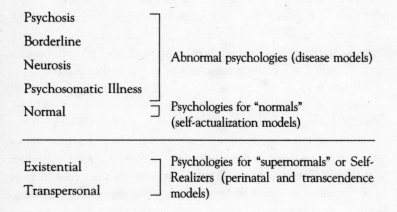

Psychosis
Borderline
Neurosis — Abnormal psychologies (disease models)
Psychosomatic Illness
Normal — Psychologies for "normals"
(self-actualization models)

Existential — Psychologies for "supernormals" or Self-Realizers (perinatal and transcendence models)
Transpersonal

The psychology for "normals" was prevalent in the 1960s and 1970s during the humanistic era of Fritz Perls, Carl Rogers, Gordon Allport, Virginia Satir, and others who felt that the earlier mechanistic or behavioristic disease models were excluding our pro-active aspects, our healthy needs to move beyond just being average. People like Ram Dass, Marilyn Ferguson, Victor Frankl, Stanislav Grof, Jean Houston, Abraham Maslow, Francis Vaughan, and Ken Wilber have served as bridges into the now emerging existential and transpersonal psychologies.

These two deeper realms take us closer to the source of our wholeness, where our existential issues concerning life and death reside. As a young college graduate declared to my son recently, "I know why I go to work; I need money and a career. But what I *don't* understand is why am I spinning around on this mud-ball called "earth"! And more deeply, these psychologies affirm that we all are able to access the collective unconscious mind (as Jung described it) that contains the totality of human experience back to the beginning of time. Here, we can directly experience processes many of us know as "religious experiences," peak experiences, or spiritual awakenings. We meet our Self: the spiritual co-creator and expresser of the mysteries.

Ordinary therapies honor and promote gradual sequences of incremental growth, with very few surprises. Nonordinary therapies honor and promote powerful death/rebirth sequences that include both disintegrative and integrative stages. Death experiences can be dramatic and painful, caused by the loss of a loved one, a career suddenly falling apart, or a traumatic divorce. But they are the catalysts behind our growth. And they enable us to be reborn as expanded beings. The concept of death/rebirth is crucial to our transformation and will be further explored in a later chapter, "Transforming the Mind."

The symbolic and abstract worlds are also part of the transpersonal consciousness. When we learn to decipher them, symbols can become powerful teachers, as in the following example from my life, which I recounted in one of my newsletter articles: "I was re-living in my mind the death of my stillborn baby. As I was feeling the darkness of death enfolding me, everything turned black, and once again I was enveloped in the finality of death. In the midst of this experience there was a flittering of light within my mind. The light was playing around in the darkness until suddenly something merged and a giant triangle overshadowed me, with death on one side and birth on the other. And at the top sat in perfect repose the Divine Child. I felt I had been reborn." I had temporarily merged with or accessed the archetype of Rebirth. Death and birth as I had previously understood them—as opposites—had come together, beyond the illusory dichotomy. And they offered me an experience of their true nature, which is one continual rebirth. And I got it: We are always aborning. So why feel so attacked by the death part?

As we go deeper into the psyche, we begin to make sense of our codependence patterns of relating—all the ways we try to hold on. We begin to see that our fears, our needs to manipulate and control, our self-doubt, our ways of going unconscious—all these patterns cannot be broken by merely recounting our childhoods.

We need to access our Higher Self, the soul. Psychology is having to address these deeper aspects of the psyche because we are asking deeper questions. The whole field of psychology is expanding because we are. We are going for it! Many people are telling me they are consciously choosing to clear out their psyches completely—even though they know at least part of this process will be painful.

This book is for them, for all of us who are searching for our wholeness. These pages explore the relationship between the spiritual quest and addiction, tested in outer reality by this author's twenty years' experience in the fields of addiction and mental health. I know now, after practicing a transpersonal approach with thousands of you who have addiction problems, that people heal more rapidly and more completely when following this approach. The reason for this is that they are being given a context within which to explore themselves more profoundly. As Twelve Step programs have proven, contact with our true spiritual Self is how we heal our addicted selves. I've come to realize that without touching the sacred and the beautiful in life, we begin to die.

We Are Spiritual Beings

People who call themselves "addicts" and "codependents" are perfect candidates for the transpersonal or psycho-spiritual path. For addicts are flyers! They love explorations into uncharted territory. They are the mystics, poets, artists, and muses of the soul.

Most people with codependence or other addiction issues tell me they've been mystical since childhood. The spiritual dimensions of reality have always been predominant in their lives, even though during adulthood these dimensions may have been hidden under layers of drama and addiction. They were often once criticized for being dreamy-eyed kids who lacked discipline or the ability to concentrate on the *real* world. For them, the *other*worldly has always felt more familiar. But they took this early criticism to heart and went about letting go of their spontaneous, childlike curiosity, perhaps becoming obsessive people-pleasers—a seedbed for the breeding of codependence—learning at an early age to give their power away to others more "wise" and "knowing" than themselves. But that dreamy-eyed kid who lacked full interest in the "real" world was their true and rightful Self, their soul.

Many who suffer the pitfalls of addictive lifestyles have fallen into dysfunctional patterns while seeking a higher, more creative and meaningful way to relate here in this mundane world. They often tell me that they were born feeling like strangers in a strange land, and have lived with a deep sense of isolation. People close to their mystical memories are homesick. Many have become out of touch with their true natures, never having fully committed to being here in this world at all. "Beam me up, Scottie, there's no intelligent life on this planet!" is the cry of the person caught up in codependence who has not yet re-connected with his or her spiritual essence. Surely there is a better place than this, they feel! And this combination of feeling like a misfit in life while simultaneously possessing a highly developed and close-to-the-surface mystical consciousness can be dangerous. These people are more interested in seeking a way out or back to that "other place" where they truly feel at home than bothering to try to make it here in this world. And they may choose addictive relationships, sex, chemical highs, overeating, causes, or gurus to fill the empty spaces within their hearts, the gaps of unfulfillment. They will give their power away to almost anyone or anything, so desperate are they to find that something or someone to guide them home.

But another possibility, which many never realize, is to go within and discover the inner Self, our wholeness, which is just waiting to express. Because the Self is greater than our conditions, It is at home in any location; It can be *in* this world and yet not *of* it. The Self accepts with gratitude whatever life brings.

Mythologist Joseph Campbell said that we seek not so much the meaning of life as we do the experience of life—the rapture of being alive. And everything we need to experience life fully is already within our blueprint, the Higher Self, only to be awakened and accessed for this rapture to be felt. In our workshops we use the maxim I've included in the preface: "We are not human beings learning to be spiritual; we are spiritual beings learning to be human." Dominican priest Matthew Fox, an interpreter of the teachings of the Christian mystic, Meister Eckhart, and the author of the concept "creation spirituality," pleads with us to remember our mystical heritage. Not only would each of us be better off, but so would the world, says Fox:

> Mystics must come out of the closets, must gather to share their stories that we might set fire again to our tired and cold civilization. These stories can inspire us to acts of prophecy which can awaken our hearts, renew our cultures, and hasten the resurrection of Mother Earth. (*The Coming of the Cosmic Christ*)

Today, I believe many are ready to take the next step—to cease this outer seeking and go inward to do the psycho-spiritual work required for true healing. The journey of the astronaut continues to teach us much about outer space; now it's time to make the journey of the "intronaut" and explore our inner space—the God within.

The thirteenth-century alchemists spoke of humankind as a "wingless bird" stuck in its alluring conditions for so long it has become too heavy to fly. At some point the wingless bird's soaring spiritual counterpart arrives on the scene, a "winged bird" with the advantage of a loftier vista. It attaches itself to the disempowered one, merging with its nature so it can lift it up and lead it back to freedom. Maybe we all are truly waking up. And perhaps . . . just perhaps, we are going to learn how to fly!

❧ II ❧

Codependence:
The Shadow Side of
Our Love Nature

What is the way of the world, and how does it move?
What is the way of the heart, and how does it heal?
What is the path of the Soul, and where does it lead?
To home, Dear Friend, to home.

—Gary Zukav

Needy Love Is
How the Shadow Dances

I stood upon a high place
and saw, below, many devils
Running, leaping,
And carousing in sin.
One looked up, grinning,
And said, "Comrade! Brother!"
—Stephen Crane

According to Carl Jung, at the very core of our humanness exists a dualism—the shadow and the light. Before we can manifest our light and become that winged bird, we must first come to know and accept our shadow.

Most of us know that every person (and all situations) have both their positive and negative sides. Yet many of us ignore our dark side, pretending we don't have negative feelings and denying them expression. As a result, our hidden side undoubtedly rebels, forcing us to act out our disowned feelings, usually whenever we are under stress. This is our shadow at work. For, as mentioned earlier, the shadow is the container of the aspects of ourselves we perceive as intolerable, of all our repressed emotions.

The shadow is our holy grit: its sacred purpose is to bring all our unconscious, denied feelings into conscious awareness. It makes such a fool of us with its antics that it forces us to get real and deal with the parts of ourselves we're trying to skip over. The shadow is our anti-self or negative ego, and it serves as the polar opposite of our positive ego as we learn to discriminate between our truth and untruth. Jung said it is an "apprentice" as opposed to the "Master-piece," which is the Self.

In this chapter, I want to introduce you more fully to your shadow. An understanding of this anti-self is essential to our study of codependence. For codependence, seen in its entirety, is *the shadow side of our love nature.* It is our shadow self that "does codependence."

The shadow is a product of all those old repressed hurts left over from our earlier years, which are now lodged in our subconscious minds and create our current self-destructive patterns and feelings of insecurity. In our refusal to allow these denied feelings expression—either because we've been ashamed of them or didn't recognize their existence—we have not allowed our shadow to be faced, understood, accepted, and released. Unless we stop denying this split-off and unwanted self, our healing will be on hold. And our lives will be fraught with the imbalanced emotions of codependence.

Before we further examine how the shadow and codependence have developed and how we might clear the psyche of our childhood and adulthood hurts, we need to look more closely at the way the shadow actually manifests in our lives. The first step out of denial and into healing is always *recognition.* And for this reason, recognition (re-cognition) is a key process in this book. For it is a way of re-membering who we are in wholeness, our essence; literally, how we collect our members.

Again, we all know intuitively that we have a negative side; we carry this ill-formed or uncivilized self around with us, hoping to keep it under control, intent upon hiding it from others. Carl Jung, who is most often credited with developing the concept of the shadow, called it "the skeleton in our cupboard." But as most of us know from experience, the shadow won't stay inside. Trying to keep our shadow hidden is like trying to hold a ball under water. If we let go for an instant, it will bounce out into the open for all to see. And the harder we push, the more extreme our shadow's reaction will be. Often, when we are repressing some unwanted truth in our lives, up comes the shadow to embarrass us with some kind of outburst. It takes over and acts out the part we are denying.

You can tell when your shadow is dominating you, because you will feel guilt or shame or a deep sense of humiliation about your behavior. For instance, I might be pretending I really like someone I actually can't stand, and out of the blue I'll grimace or say something negative about the person. Or I could be pretending I'm not bothered by something, yet I become intense and behave defensively. Or I'll be going along quite cooperatively with some planned activity (something I really don't want to do at all), and at the last minute, I'll act out or quit. Often it is our body language that betrays our shadow's secret feelings; we hunch over, we won't look someone in the eye, we stand too close or too far away, or we grit our teeth. Other times we utter words we don't recall having said. Because the unconscious mind seeks wholeness, the shadow will automatically manifest the feeling we are trying to ignore.

You might remember the radio show back in the 1950s called *The Shadow,* with its ominous lyrical prelude: "Who knows what evil lurks within the hearts of men? Only The Shadow knows." And this is absolutely correct: The shadow knows. It senses the whole picture with an uncanny psychism. We might be able to fool others and even ourselves for awhile, but the shadow—no way! We can never slip past this primed and overly sensitive emotional character; it will not be denied no matter how hard we try to pretend it doesn't exist.

Until we become fully realized beings, a goal very few have reached on planet earth, we will always have a shadow to a lesser or greater extent. It acts out in all sorts of unconscious ways; usually it is those closest to us who know our shadow best—we control, possess, obsess, and project. But if we can *recognize* and *accept* the shadow, it will lose its power over us. It will de-activate, for it will no longer have a purpose, except to join in and help us celebrate life.

For as I said in an earlier chapter, the impure shadow is not only our disowned, unacceptable, and despised parts; it is our pre-conscious and unclaimed transpersonal wholeness as well (which, by the way, we also unconsciously fear, mistakenly feeling these powerful spiritual forces will overwhelm us). It is a mixture of both the *darkness* of our repressed feelings and the *lightness* of all our unacknowledged and unformulated qualities of holiness. Once its moodiness and over-reactions settle down and its energies become less intense, it then releases its gifts to us, which are truly amazing: It gives us substance, enriching us with psychic intuition, vi-brance, and a luscious passion for life, which comes from all our struggles with emotional pain. In fact, without inclusion of the shadow in our conscious awareness, we are split off from our very life-force, afraid to fully involve and express our whole truth. Without it, we can never be complete. It's time we took our shadow's hand, joining with it instead of pushing it away.

Here's a visual description to help you envision your shadow: Think of your ego as a "body ego" which has taken form in order to absorb all the dense harshness of the earth, serving as a buffer zone for the soul, which is only light. As the soul enters the ego's world, its loving and carefree nature will begin to lighten up the ego—literally! When the soul merges with the ego, a whole new kind of self takes form—*a soul-infused personality*. But until the ego becomes totally transparent with the light of the soul, what's trailing behind the ego? Its shadow! The ego's judgments are in the way, blocking the rays of the soul and creating a shadow self. It is only our judgments that hold our shadow away from its transmu-tation into light.

According to Jungian John Conger, the "character armor" that Wilhelm Reich (one of the fathers of Western psychology) spoke of is a correlate of the shadow. Character armor is made up of body rigidities and defenses that hold us away from our real feelings. One of the clearest examples is how people cross their arms over their hearts, fidget in their seats, or almost fold into a pretzel when being spoken to directly or intimately. Newcomers to group therapy or Twelve Step programs often defend themselves in this manner. When we armor our bodies and our hearts, what are we defending? Character armor is a defense against being known; we believe if we are known, we won't be acceptable or loved. The shadow, according to Conger, is the *emotional* body's character armor.

It is our own unwillingness to honor our negative self that keeps the shadow activated in our lives and its armor in place. We must come to terms with the fact that we are *both/and,* rather than either/or, the shadow and the light. We *can* learn to love and accept our disowned half. And when we do, the shadow will become an irrelevant concept: we'll have no need to judge ourselves as "good" or "bad"; we'll *just be here,* doing our being, involving fully and passionately in life.

The Shadow's World
of Projections and Storylines

According to Joseph Campbell, we'd better have a very big story, or no story at all; it's those "little stories" in the middle that get us into trouble, limiting our potential and keeping our shadow hidden and active:

> Anything from the past—such as an idea of what man of this, that, or another culture might be, or should be—is now archaic. And so we have to leave our little provincial stories behind. They may guide us as far as structuring our lives for the moment, but we must always be ready to drop them and to grab the new experience as it comes along, and to interpret it through new eyes. (*An Open Life*)

A big story would be: "I'm a daughter of God here on this earth with a divine purpose to unfold my spiritual destiny." Or, "All that I ever need to be is already contained within me." Or, more scientifically, "I'm both the particle and the wave; I'm all of it, just like my cells show me that I am!" And to have no story at all would be to live in a constant state of meditation, where we drop all ideas about who we are and live fully in the here and now, allowing the Higher Power to define us.

But until we become fully enlightened and can relax completely into the wisdom of our inner lives, we create an outer game of life we call "reality." We create "storylines" and "projections" and then become trapped in them. We think, falsely, that our outer conditions and other people are causing our feelings and creating our situations. When we were children, others *were* in large part responsible for the situations we found ourselves in. In adulthood, however, as if viewing a movie, we often see all our own inner needs and processes unfolding as events coming at us from the outer world. Marie-Louise von Franz, quoting Jung, said that a projection is

> an unconscious, unperceived and unintentional transfer of subjective psychic elements onto an outer object. One sees in this object something that is not there, or is there only to a certain degree. This creates a "hook" on which one hangs a projection as a coat on a coat hook. (*Projection and Re-collection in Jungian Psychology*)

These storylines and projections, as part of the shadow, come from deep within our unconscious minds. They are outgrowths of unintegrated events or feelings from our past. And they will remain our story only so long as our past hurts remain unhealed. For once the emotions heal, the energy goes out of the story; it no longer holds our interest. For instance, if you are an adult child of an alcoholic, you may still be suffering from years of abuse in the form of physical or emotional battering or neglect and the pain of witnessing parents who acted out from their addicted selves. (As many of us know, codependence is rampant among ACOAs.) Or you may be suffering from the legacy of a different but equally harmful childhood. You may also have experienced a trauma in adult life that you haven't yet been able to examine, work through, and integrate. Until you can look back, draw forth, and embrace your injured selves, you will likely continue to act from those battered places. Your shadow will rule your present relationships. I do not mean to imply that working through the pain is a simple process; there is a lot of anger, hurt, and sorrow for most of us to process. However, it is important to realize that eventually, if we commit to our healing, we can be free of our suffering and the trappings of our past. But first we must recognize how projections and storylines actually affect our lives, so that we can begin to break through the limitations our shadow has created.

Jung felt that people who pretend they have no shadow can become the bane of society's existence. For instead of acknowledging it, they cast their shadow out onto the world, expunging these "evils" from themselves and seeing them only in others. Then, the rest of us have to live with the heavy effects of these unconscious projections—for they can manifest as hate and war. When people try to walk off and leave behind these unloved aspects of themselves, they become powder kegs waiting to explode.

The following is an example of projection: A woman named Anne had trouble accepting her sexuality, because she was raised in a puritanical environment where sexuality was denied and treated as "bad." If she had sexual feelings and evidenced them in the slightest, she was labeled "indecent" or "a vamp." As an adult, one night at a party she met a woman who was obviously quite at home in her feminine sexual self. This woman behaved in an innocent, spontaneous, and friendly manner toward the men in the room, fully present and glowing. Anne's response was to say to herself: "Yuk! She's one of those loose women!" And she walked out of the room with her storyline, in a state of panicked emotions. She was feeling upset and afraid to associate with this other woman. Why this over-reaction? Because the other woman's behavior was stirring up something inside Anne that was crying out to be expressed. Anne was re-acting from the negative side of the pole—her shadow—denying a part of her true self. She'd cut herself off from an aspect of herself that was real, natural, and holy—her own sexuality. This is the shadow at work.

A more extreme example of this is the modern-day Evangelist who preaches hellfire and damnation to the rest of us for sinning and then is caught with a "lady of the night." Or a great political leader who is caught embezzling money from the people's social security funds, while telling the people to save their money and pay more taxes to their government.

I know other people who have devoted their lives to working on causes for a better world. And they do an excellent job. Yet, they've tried to deny their own inner war. They work all day in the office for peace. Then, they arrive at home tired and all bent out of shape and yell at their spouse and children, shaming them for not honoring the "true" planetary cause with zeal. This is also the shadow.

The shadow can also act out in more subtle ways: Let's say I'm driving along in the car with you and you are gossiping about someone you are obviously jealous of. Instead of feeling empathy for the person you are putting down, I become weepy for you: "Oh, isn't it terrible?" I say. Suddenly I'm over-reacting. I've become embroiled in your feelings about this person I don't even know. What is that? The shadow. When I am ashamed of my own negative feelings, such as jealousy or rage, I will become over-identified with others who are expressing these feelings more directly. I will latch on and piggyback on these situations. This is one of the passive, oblique ways the shadow can operate.

The shadow can also manifest collectively. We as a society constantly project, calling other countries "evil" for the very crimes we ourselves commit. An example would be the United States—as it invaded third world countries and built up nuclear weapons—calling the Soviet Union the "evil empire." We also may view a whole race or religion as wrong or evil. When we cannot own our "evil," we will automatically project it onto others.

Some people become caught in a tape loop. Perhaps they are obsessed with a victimhood theme, for instance. Victimhood becomes their storyline. When we hear someone spinning around in victimhood, we tire of him very quickly; for I believe on some deep level we all know we are meant to release our past. When a person identifies himself as "victim," he is latching onto only one side of a polarity. His complement, "savior" or "perpetrator," will remain inside, disowned and repressed. Therefore, he undoubtedly will project these inner, denied ones onto others, continually searching for someone "out there" to save and/or perpetrate him. These storylines beneath our projections easily can become addictions; and they serve as mental barriers to our healing. We walk through life with a self-image that does not reflect who we truly are, founded upon a wounded or partial self. My physicist friend, Fred Alan Wolf, provided me with an insight into this matter I'd like to share with you:

> The new physics indicates that we humans play a far more significant role in the whole universe than was previously understood by any earlier model of reality. In essence what it says is that every action we take produces multiple possibilities, and nothing is firmly fixed or determined. Actions in the present can have repercussions in the future, as many already suspect, but also repercussions for the past—which many do not suspect! In other words, the past is mutable—not fixed, either. This may be surprising, but it is perfectly consistent with the world view of the new physics.
>
> In the area of addiction and healing, this has profound implications. The blaming of one's past actions for one's present state, from the new physics point of view would be a rationalization. The present state of the person's consciousness is actually producing the past.

It's not pleasant to see how we might be using our past to keep ourselves away from unfolding our potential, yet we must each admit that this is a distinct possibility. In fact, I believe it's not our past we fear as much as it is our future. We've survived our past! But many of us use it to keep us from what is to come next.

On the other hand, denial of our past never works either. Our personal history provides important clues to our patterns of dysfunction, as well as our true talents and skills. *If we are to heal, we must make our past conscious and stop acting from it and blaming it—the past must be recognized, owned, accepted, forgiven—and dropped!*

"Do you wish to know the name of your prison?" I once heard a wise man ask. "Your prison," he said, "is *your past.*"

Recognizing Your Shadow

Again, in order to free ourselves from our past, we must first make conscious our shadow's ways of acting out its storylines and projections. Below are some of the concrete "symptoms" I will experience when my needy shadow is running the show. I hope they further enable you to recognize your shadow.

1) I will perceive certain types of people in my life as "enemies" or "dangerous" and feel that I am being "victimized" by them. I may even obsess about my troubles. My sense of trust is at stake.

2) I will perceive some people as better than me—saviors, teachers, or paragons of truth or authority, putting them on pedestals and falling devotedly to my knees. I believe other human beings hold the key to my salvation. When I'm honest with myself, I feel demeaned by this: I am giving away my own intrinsic wisdom.

3) On the other hand, I may see myself as the strong or better one, in charge of another person, and then I will set about "doing" his life for him (or at least trying to improve it). I give away my time and energy to this person and barely have any time left over to express my own talents, desires, and dreams. I'm filled with resentment and frustration with him, but if I'm honest, deep down inside it's myself I blame.

4) I will fall madly in love with someone who is not available or appropriate for me (a married man, a priest, a well-known womanizer). My deep ability to relate and care is wasted on irrelevant "romantic" pursuits that keep me excited and preoccupied with the thrill of drama and newness. I am therefore spared from having to make myself truly vulnerable in relationships that are ongoing and real. My passionate nature is being misdirected.

5) I will perceive others as "experts" on my health and well-being and will give my own creative power of rational and intuitive thought over to another "smarter person," believing this other can label me accurately, diagnose me completely, and eventually cure me of my ills. (This is similar to Number 2, above.) My own

intelligence is sacrificed. I stop thinking for myself. After awhile, a slow fury begins to build.

6) I will sacrifice my physical body, emotions, and mental energy to a "cause" that I believe is more important than my own life. I'll work without money, buying into others' perceptions that I must dedicate myself to a selfless project—do something for "service to God"—and give away my talents and hard-earned skills. Then later, when I feel truly used and abused, I will see that the "cause" I was working for was someone else's idea of service, and not necessarily mine—or God's—at all! My compassion, or what I thought was compassion, begins to turn into either apathy or rage.

7) In general, when I get any kind of "clutched" feeling in my gut that makes me want to act out—scream, run, control, lie, hide—this type of behavior usually means my shadow is activating. Remember, the shadow is part of our emotional body. When we are being dominated by its energies, we feel super-sensitive and reactive.

Other Ways the Shadow Manifests

The shadow, because it is emotional in nature, usually requires intense emotional-release work in order to heal (which we'll learn how to do later in the book). Again, the shadow is the container of all your *emotionalisms* (stuffed and loaded emotions). It is the one who is always in touch with what you are feeling and simultaneously denying that you feel at all. This is why it is so hard to pin down. *All* emotions, by their very nature, are vaporous; they are indistinct and oblique formations, like smoke or fog. They move from positive to negative in illogical ways. The minute you notice them, they change into something else or disappear. I'll be feeling possessive, then angry, then self-pitying, then I'm no longer enraged, I'm in tears. Then I feel a surge of emotional love for the one I'm condemning, then sentimental over our lost friendship, then I feel hurt. I collapse into a heap of helplessness and become a little girl; then suddenly, I act strong and vicious. Then I feel shame. Will the real Jacquelyn please stand up! This is how emotionalism feels. It is made up of *pent-up* emotions that burst forth because our valid anger, hurt, fear, or sorrow was repressed. These real emotions do not come from the shadow. They are healthy and natural, part of the positive ego. But they *do* fog up our intellect's ability to think clearly. And our intense emotional over-reactions are especially shadowy and disconcerting.

The shadow is also very psychic. It can pick up what's happening in a whole group of people in less than a second, but we might refuse to acknowledge its insights. Then it will sit in the basement of our psyche until a great amount of repressed energy builds. Suddenly, the shadow will feel disgusted: It'll say, "My God! When is she going to get the picture?" Then, "Grrrrrr." She breaks out and bawls someone out in a giant over-reaction. Or she stomps out of the room, saying something she'll later regret. Introverts may not do this shadow dance as explosively as extroverts do. But the outcome is often the same. Being passive-aggressive or sneaking away can be a loaded *non*-reaction. So is whispering into someone else's ear or scheming behind people's backs, inciting others to act out our shadow for us. And most often, these behaviors backfire. Remember, the shadow is a trickster; it *will* get our attention if we try to deny its feelings.

And the shadow manifests when we get caught in dualisms, that is, the need to see ourselves and others as all good or all bad. Have you noticed how just after you've experienced a "high" time, you often will act out negatively afterward? Often when we get a strong spiritual "hit," we feel we've spoken with God, or had a healing— and we may have. But immediately afterwards we try to prove to ourselves that we're omnipotent or omniscient or something else unrealistic. This is our failure to realize what "perfection" means; we try to live only on the positive pole. So, of course, we then unconsciously make sure we fall. "Being good" or "high" or "spiritual" is *not* perfection; this is just the ego's false notion. Our error is in trying to hold onto the positive side addictively: From a fifteen-minute meditation, we will begin meditating an hour;

then three hours; then a day; then, fasting and meditation; then, deep breathing, fasting, and meditation. Do you see? "If a little bit's good, more will be better": the addict's theme song blasts away. And soon we'll have a crisis and have to stop. And then we'll (hopefully) gain another lesson.

The Shadow's Gifts

It is crucial to remember that our goal is not to relinquish the passions of the shadow. Imagine a couple walking around all day, every day, with plastic smiles on their faces, quoting positive affirmations to themselves and others all the time. Imagine a lyric soprano singing an Italian aria with no passion, with no ability to bring tears to people's eyes. These scenarios have no substance; there is no allurement, no risks, no mystery, no awe, no surprises, no yearning, no differences. Most of us would rather be dead! And, in fact, this type of Self-denial *is* a form of death.

I want the right to be mad at you sometimes and the opportunity to stand up for my differences. I want to be able to be in a bad mood. I want to express to you my fears or secret desires—even when they don't sound very "holy." Sometimes I'd like to surprise you, to be full of life! Jung said our shadow is what keeps us alive. I am convinced that it is truly a sacred self, and that we must learn to honor the positive role it plays in our lives. According to Conger, the shadow's holy purpose becomes known to us by our experience of it:

> The purpose of the shadow is to provide the human soul with the opposition and tension to develop tough inner resolve and determination to clarify through the challenge of the opposites. (*The Body as Shadow*)

As I said earlier, if we are conscious of our shadow, we can watch it and learn a lot about who we are and how we respond to the world. Anytime I get into denial around an issue in my home or work life, my shadow will act out royally—and expose the lie. Usually, she'll make everybody angry by becoming overly emotional and exploding over an issue no one else sees as significant. And even though I can't stand her at the time, I'm later thankful. Looking back on the situation, I can see the lesson it held. Then, usually much, much later, I really see the gift.

And sometimes the shadow will literally get to the truth of a situation. For example, once in a temper I ordered a person out of my house (and my life!) for being so loud and uncouth in front of my small children. Later, I found out this person was capable of extreme brutality; my intuitive shadow had picked up on this fact, even though I'd had no real evidence of it before. Another time I attempted to be in a therapeutic relationship with an acquaintance who was unwilling to do anything about his feeling of total rejection by all the women in his life. I finally terminated the relationship, telling him that I, too, felt like rejecting him. I told him he smelled bad and wore awful clothes, his hair was a mess, and his constant moaning was getting on my nerves. Later, he called to thank me for the best therapy he'd ever had: he'd cleaned up his act, gotten a good job, and found a new girlfriend!

But again, we must become conscious of our shadow's ways and be able to tame them; otherwise, we will be at their mercy. The process of coming to terms with our shadow is very much like managing and helping a hyperactive child. We express our feelings, see them in operation, and love them, over and over, until these energies subside. We observe our process as it is occurring, making our lives conscious as we go. And we do so by making use of our observer self, which I described earlier. The observer self is "a moment in time" that stops us right in between the action and the re-action (or the stimulus and the response). It offers us a choice: We now can choose whether or not to act on an emotion. The observer self is the tamer of the shadow. When we utilize it, we will stop swinging from extreme to extreme, for we'll see rather quickly how this behavior affects us and those we love.

When you feel yourself moving toward some over-reaction, bring out the observer self and watch yourself go for it—consciously! You'll probably have to act out your shadow pattern for your observer self at least one time in order to make it conscious—and this will be the most uncomfortable time of all. Without one bit of you in denial, you'll see your shadow in all its glory. Once we bring the observer self into our lives, it will have an ongoing dialogue with our shadow's many voices and all the taunting images that challenge us when we're trying to get past a debilitating habit. By clarifying these images and our energies—and getting to know them—we eventually will integrate our shadow self. Our positive ego will take dominion over our shadow fairly easily, if we are willing and courageous enough to look ourselves squarely in the eye.

So, welcome, dear shadow. We recognize you. And I, personally, am feeling grateful for you right now—even though some of your antics have nearly killed me in the past. You relentlessly demand the very best from me, not allowing me to bypass anything I need to look at. I thank you for that, and I invite you now to come along with us on this journey to wholeness. I'm choosing to bring you along—because frankly, dear comrade, I admire your spunk!

Codependence Is the Shadow Side of Our Love Nature

When we can recognize and own our codependence patterns, the shadow no longer will have hold of our love nature. But until then, this unintegrated shadow will periodically explode into our outer lives, doing its dance for all to see. When in codependence, we play at loving and being loved by trotting out aspects of our shadow's nature and flinging them at one another in "needy love." *Needy love is how the shadow dances.*

Codependence is the "dis-ease" of unequal relationships. It's a classic case of psychological projection, and, as I've explained earlier, of giving our power away. We become so enmeshed with another person that we lose our boundaries and become one dysfunctional entity playing out opposing polarities: I'm weak, so he is strong. I'm "spiritual" and always kind, so my partner gets to be the bastard. He never feels anything, so I'll act out his feelings for him. She's the alcoholic and neglects all family responsibilities,

so I have to take care of her—and everyone and everything else!
I can't make money, so she's the financial wizard I have to beg from
for pocket change or a new pair of pants. He's the "good father"
type, so I get to neglect the children. My business partner has
never made it in life on her own as I have, so I lend her my earned
prestige, my reputation, my power, and my money. Then hopefully, I've made her feel equal. Right? Wrong. Nothing like this
ever works; it all becomes self-defeating.

Codependence is our unmanifested potential in relationship. In
codependence, we are not bad or sick, just uninformed. Unfinished. To get beyond it, we must focus beyond it. Instead of saying
I *am* a codependent (which stops the process and freezes it in
time—it's a small story!), we say "I *have* these codependent
conditions that manifest when I go unconscious in my relationships. These are the ways I keep from being myself."

There is a cardinal rule about loving: Until we love ourselves
and honor our positive ego for needing what it needs, we can never
expect to really love another, or even have empathy for what
others might feel or need. We must become responsible for
meeting our own needs directly in ways that do not harm us or
anyone else. No one—not even an intimate life partner—can do
this balancing act for us. *With* us, yes. But *for* us, no. For we are
self-evolving organisms! To fully *be* requires that we do this sacred
work on our own. In *The Prophet*, Kahlil Gibran offers the
following profound teaching for lovers:

> Sing and dance together, and be joyous,
> but let each one of you be alone,
> Even as the strings of the lute are alone
> though they quiver with the same music. . . .
>
> For the pillars of the temple stand apart,
> And the oak tree and the cypress grow
> not in each other's shadow.

In order to avoid each other's shadow and not *act* from codependent urges, here are some suggestions for conflict resolution that
will help keep us within our own power:

1) We do not project onto others our predicaments or states of mind.
2) The resolution of external conflicts with others necessitates the *prior* resolution of our own inner conflicts.

In other words, when we are perceiving someone else as "our problem," we may need to sit with our emotions for awhile and contemplate how we might have helped to bring the situation on ourselves. Then, searching deeply within our own hearts, we may see how we've been denying our part. Perhaps we were too naive to believe this person could do such a thing. Or perhaps we have a similar habit but can only see it in that "other." In the end we may come to the conclusion that the other person *was* negligent in some way, but we'll be better able to resolve the issue if we can articulate the part for which we are responsible. (I do not mean to imply that anyone necessarily invites tragedy or abuse; some things are out of our conscious control. But often we *do* try to hide our role in the guise of victimhood.)

Anytime a charged issue comes up and we feel the urge to act out, the following steps will clear the projection:

1) Claiming the issue as our own.
2) Discharging the irritated energies or pent-up emotions around the given conflict appropriately (with a therapist, close friend, or by ourselves privately through physical and/or emotional expression: crying, screaming out, moaning, or raging into a pillow).
3) Then transforming the energy into some other type of expression—our own work, our own creativity—an expression that will take care of us and what we need, appropriately and truthfully.
4) When we are better able to step back from the situation, we can approach the other person(s) involved to discuss the issue. Because we have achieved our own clarity, others can—and usually will—see their part without becoming defensive.

We can see now that there are two modes of living for each of us. The inner way is the way of self-responsibility, wherein we always say first, "What's the lesson in this for me?" We then dive in and learn about *our part* in the conflict, how we may have set it up either blatantly or passively by just allowing it to happen. The outer way—the way of projection—is where we put our own inner processes out onto others and then watch as these "uncooked seeds" are thrown back at us. This outer way keeps us locked in addiction and storylines. It blocks us from seeing our own patterns and from the healing that self-responsibility eventually brings.

When the shift is made from outer projection to inner responsibility, everything relational begins to fall into place. *This is the shift from unconscious to conscious living.* Instead of carrying our old storylines around in our heads like precious belongings, we possess the free attention necessary to focus inwardly on our unfolding future, the urges that emanate within. We learn one of the greatest lessons in the healing of codependence: that we are not responsible for others' feelings or misplaced hopes and dreams. Nor are they responsible for ours. We begin to see that we each create our own personal reality as a stage upon which we either celebrate our life's experiences together or create a melodrama wherein a painful lesson in loving plays out.

The Power of Guided Imagery

Now, I'd like to pause for awhile to do some inner work. But before doing so, I want to say a few things about the power of using symbolic imagery.

Guided imagery is a way to use our powers of creative imagination, which can be much more immediate and effective than analytical thinking. The guided imagery exercises interspersed throughout the book are designed to offer you a direct experience of the concepts you'll encounter as we go along, converting them into dynamic activators of your minds and hearts. Like everything newly created, a truth must begin in the mind. Hence, the purpose of guided imageries is to show your intellect a *living truth*, which can then eventually move into our hearts. A living truth is an idea that has become clothed in form by your imagination—an idea that can be felt in your heart and will create change in your life.

Before you begin the imagery that follows, it's important to remember that everyone does not see pictures when doing this work; *inner seeing* can seem more like thoughts, symbols, or spontaneously arising feeling-states. *All* of your senses, not just your inner eyes, are used for inner work. You may get a whole mental flash all at once concerning the meaning of a pattern or issue; a shiver may run up your spine; or your heart may fill with the feelings of sorrow, joy, or forgiveness. Some people can even smell aromas or hear voices not existing in this reality. Just let come whatever wants to come, with no judgment and no invest-ment in the outcome. This process can profoundly affect your psyche.

Many people think they are imaging fairly superficially at first, only to realize later that these images, symbols, and thoughts were inspired, though sometimes subtle. In practicing the imagery work throughout this book, you'll discover that your inner Self has a way of giving you the kinds of images and insights you will be able to recognize. The meanings you attribute to these inner experiences are yours and only yours. Universal meanings learned from books or other people's interpretations are often beside the point (and can even get in your way). Learn to trust your own interpretations. And if some outside source aids your own findings, that's good. If it doesn't, just ignore it. When you are willing to experiment with imageries, these "gifts of the spirit" will teach you without much effort on your part and greatly enhance your healing process.

Now, let's image our shadow for awhile. This exercise will invite your shadow to expose itself to you, which is a crucial step in your healing process. Take some time now to consciously enter into a quiet space within your heart: the healing of your shadow self is a very sacred moment in time.

A friend can read these instructions to you, pausing wherever there are some dots. Or you can read this imagery onto a tape and guide yourself through it. Or you can study this imagery until you know it by heart. Allow yourself enough time between suggestions to envision them. Keep the voice-tone (even if it's inside your own head) *calm* and *even* throughout. And when undergoing the imagery, do so in a quiet place where you can sit or lie without being disturbed for awhile.

Meeting Your Shadow
A Guided Imagery Experience

Close your eyes, and begin to tune out the outside world. . . . Allow your body to settle down . . . and release the tensions of the day. You can use your breath to gently enter into your body, letting go of any tightness, or discomfort you may be feeling. . . . Softening the body . . . Letting go . . . Remember, you have a body but you are not your body only. Feel yourself surrendering to your inner Self and allow your consciousness to just float around through the inner experience that follows.

Take some time now to check out your emotions. See if any are rocking around in your body anywhere. If so, just breathe your breath into these emotions until they begin to quiet. . . . Becoming still like a lake with no ripples . . . Allow your emotions to settle down. . . . A lake with no ripples can perfectly reflect the sky, just as quietened emotions can perfectly reflect your truth. . . . Take a few balanced breaths and feel your emotions beginning to release you, becoming open and receptive to whatever spirit wants to bring forth during this experience. . . . And remember, you have emotions, but you are not your emotions. . . . Your emotions come and go. . . .

Now, take a little time to clear your mind. . . . See if you have any ideas or expectations floating around in your brain. . . . If so, feel them beginning to release, leaving your mind free and clear as a beautiful blue and cloudless sky. . . . Feel yourself leaving this concrete reality for awhile, as though you are drifting into space. . . . Just relax . . . and feel yourself deepening . . . a little more . . . and a little more . . . (longer pause).

Now, from a deep place within your mind, envision yourself dressed as you are today sitting by yourself on a sofa in an empty room. You are quietly reflecting back over your life . . . all those experiences, some of them painful, that you've been through. . . . Just allow some of these events to surface as you sit here alone on the sofa. . . .

The times you were terrified . . . lost . . . or alone. . . . Or times when you've lost someone dear through separation, or death. . . . Just let yourself be with these memories . . . (longer pause).

Now, reflect on that part of you who just couldn't handle some of these situations—who had to go underground and be private about how you felt. . . . Take some time to reflect on the whole quality of your childhood . . . (longer pause).

As you sit in deep reflection, you look across the room and notice a trapdoor in the floor that you'd not seen before. It is closed. Note what the door looks like. . . . As you look at it, you begin to hear something stirring underneath the door. . . . And you get up and walk toward the door. . . . Notice what you are feeling. . . . As you go forward, you decide to put on a violet cloak that is hanging on a hook, and to light a candle to take with you. . . . These are gifts from your Higher Self. . . . Take some time now to put on the cloak, and to light the candle. . . . Stay very close to your feelings as you do this . . . (longer pause).

Now, open the trap door and peer in. . . . Notice what happens . . . and allow the imagery to unfold . . . (longer pause).

[Note: As the door is opening, you might put on, or have someone else put on, some music without words that swells with a heartfelt melody. This enhances the experience, but is not essential.]

Now, see your shadow as plainly as you can . . . (longer pause). And remember, you are in charge of this experience: you can bring your shadow up into the room, or you can go down into the cellar where it lives. . . . If you are willing, encourage your shadow to reveal itself more fully . . . (longer pause). See how it's shaped . . . or dressed . . . its stance . . . or attitude . . . (longer pause). Now, call it by name!

Have your shadow speak to you if it will, and tell you what it needs. . . . Attend now to what it says or shows you . . . (longer pause). See if a dialogue begins between you and it; just allow this to unfold spontaneously. Perhaps you need to say something to your shadow. . . . Allow the two of you to relate . . . and stay very close to your feelings as the images appear. . . . (Take plenty of time here.)

Gradually, now, the images begin to fade in a mellow whitish-grey light. . . . Allow the scene to fade . . . and as the shadow is dissipating, love it as much as you can! *Feel this love in your heart—as much as you can muster . . . (longer pause) . . . and thank your shadow graciously for whatever it did or didn't do with you just now . . . for just being who it is. . . . Tell your shadow goodbye . . . (longer pause).*

Take some time now to appreciate your shadow self . . . as much as you possibly can . . . as you begin removing the violet cloak, taking some time to put the cloak away and blow out the candle, putting it back where you found it . . . (longer pause). Now, you are back on the sofa in the empty room, dressed as your current self, alone once more. . . . Just remain in quiet reflection for awhile . . . (Longer pause).

Now, slowly allow your mind to settle back into this reality, and once again become aware of your surroundings. . . . Take your time coming back here. . . . Now feel yourself fully back in your body. [Here, the guide's voice becomes stronger, more directive.] *Feel your body touching your seat. Still retaining all that happened on the inner plane, feel yourself being back here fully. Make this feeling real. . . .*

You might want to move around just a little, so you will be in touch with your body as it awakens from this experience.

Processing Your Imagery

Take some time now to ponder all this before you begin any other activity. You may want to continue with your inner work for awhile, if you and your shadow brought up something important. Or, if the imagery has subsided, you may want to jot down some notes on what transpired—a poem, a picture, a symbol, or a few thoughts. If you don't want to write, you might engage in some spontaneous ritual or movement. You may want to pick out an object or some concrete symbol that you can keep as a reminder of this shadow self, so you'll be easily reminded of more insights as time goes by. (In ancient Egypt these objects were called *amulets*, and Native Americans call them *fetishes*.) Imagery work is like dreamwork, and it can all disappear rapidly if you don't concretize it somehow. Profound insights may pour in as you do so. Just let yourself be with this inner experience for awhile—and trust whatever comes.

It's important not to move into an analyzing mode too quickly after an inner experience such as this. Let your intuitive, more right-brained self remain in charge for awhile. But afterwards, you will want to process the imagery more fully, with intellectual insight and integration. So later, when you are more fully back into ordinary reality, here are some things you might ask yourself: What is your shadow's name? And what did it look like? How did you feel upon meeting it? Could you ascertain how it felt exposing itself to you? How long has this self been with you? Did it feel familiar? Or were there surprises? Where are some of the places that it's been? What are its characteristics? Its needs? What is the quality of your relationship to this shadowy experiencer self—the one who's undergone much of the suffering and confusion in your life? How did it feel about *you*? Take note of your insights, for this exercise will aid you later as you more fully accept this disowned self.

Now, if by chance some of you feel you had no experience at all or that you were just intellectually making it all up, please just let all this be for now. Any kind of "making up" is still coming from within your own mind, so it has a meaning and a purpose for you, no matter how much you may want to dismiss it. Anything that occurred is part of your process, even if you're feeling that you did not do it right. There is no such thing as failure in psycho-spiritual inner work. It is all "grist for the mill." Please do not try to manipulate the experience in any way; just be with it as it was. Whether you realize it or not, you are exactly where you need to be in your process of awakening. (This general "processing" pattern can be followed for the other imageries in the book.)

In the next chapter, I want to take you back through your developmental years and show you the ways many of us have gotten blocked or off-track and the gift each of these limitations and distortions can bring us. We will see how our ego has become overwhelmed from time to time, succumbing to the shadow's over-reactions and fashioning storylines that contaminate our current relationships.

While reading the next chapter, you may activate feelings you haven't experienced since your early childhood years. These feelings may be painful, but please keep in mind that this pain is part of the healing process. You are making conscious, emotionally and mentally, any "uncooked seeds" you still may have from those old wounding experiences.

As you read along, keep your observer self intact to re-mind you that you are more than your shadow and the conditions it's created. Visualize your Higher Self from time to time, and even dialogue with It if you need to. In fact, before going on I'd like to help you visualize this Higher Self with a short guided imagery. It is crucial—as you journey back through your past to see how your codependent ways developed—that you know on a deep level that your past is not ultimately who you are. You have a greater Self awaiting your recognition once you face your outworn fears and illusions.

Again, if you cannot visualize or feel your Higher Self in this imagery, do not be concerned. The intellectual knowledge of this Self will help you remember its presence as you read through these pages.

Visualizing Your Higher Self
A Guided Imagery Experience

Take some time to relax your body and focus on the breath, allowing your breathing to settle you down while you go inward and focus.

Now close your eyes, and gently breathe into your heart. Feel it expand as though it's being bathed in fresh air and particles of warm light. . . . As you feel your heartspace becoming emptied, feel your deeper and Higher Self begin to emerge from a tiny mustard seed within your heart, gradually becoming larger inside of you . . . slowly filling you up from the inside out . . . until It has merged with you completely. . . . You are It, and It is you. Stay with this feeling until it becomes real. . . .

Now, slowly open your eyes. . . . And for as long as you can keep this consciousness, realize that you are looking at your world through the eyes of your Higher Self.

How Codependence
Patterns
Are Created

The ego is a marvelous fiction . . . a false
mirror . . . a novel written by ourselves about
ourselves, and the very first step on the Quest is to
disentangle ourselves from its seductions. . . .

—Yatri, *Unknown Man*

We were born about twelve years too soon," Joseph Campbell
humorously declares in his book *Myths to Live By*. If we
could have stayed safely in the womb until we were big enough to
take care of ourselves, we wouldn't have been at the mercy of the
significant grown-ups in our lives. As Campbell points out,
members of many other species know how to fend for themselves
instinctively from the moment they hit the earth. However,
human children are born in a totally dependent state. And because
so many of us had unenlightened parents, we may have been
consistently mistreated through unconscious, or possibly conscious, cruelty, neglect, unfair expectations, or inconsistent attention to our needs.

As we study the first three levels of human development or
unfoldment in this chapter, we'll see clearly how our dysfunctional

codependence patterns were bred in those early years as a defense against the treatment many of us were subjected to. But first I want to point out that the onset of our codependence and addictive patterns—indeed our entire learning process—didn't begin when we landed on the delivery table after birth; our ego's first schoolroom was the womb. Research in the new field of perinatal psychology evidences this fact. While still unborn and preverbal, our organ of information-gathering was not the intellect, but our whole selves—instincts, physical sensations, feelings, and intuition. We learned through *experiential data*. And, unfortunately, because this wholistic learning happened throughout our being, in our very cells, it is the hardest to later correct.

To complicate things even further, unborn babies are still undifferentiated from their mothers' emotions and physical ingestions. By the time many of us were born, we'd already encoded the message that drugs are good: our mother may have drunk or taken drugs when we were growing inside her; or doctors may have inundated her with drugs during her pregnancy and our delivery. And this kind of drug-intervention may even have saved some infants' or mothers' lives. Therefore, many of us learned before we were born: When something hurts, medicate it; make the pain magically go away. I—and many others—believe drug addiction may originate partially in the womb. In addition, we may have experienced our mothers' emotional instability, her moods and feelings, while still *in utero;* as a result, many of us were born with emotional imbalances, still enmeshed in our mothers' emotional life. This, of course, can be the onset of codependence and needy love—indeed, even a borrowed life!

Once we are born, the problems begin to multiply. Parents who need their children emotionally for a sense of worthiness or ego strength demand unrealistic behavior from their tiny offspring; they may expect them to be perfect, always to shine, exemplifying to others the supposed values and worth of the family. As a child abuse caseworker, I saw children younger than eighteen months old who had learned to eat every bite of their food without spilling a drop; otherwise they knew they'd be knocked across the room. I also saw cases where children lived amid so much emotional drama, they learned from their grown-up family members that fighting and half-killing one another can lead to romance or to passionate lovemaking. Children in alcoholic families learned from the addict how to self-medicate and escape through substances; from the co-alcoholic they learned how to control and manipulate. Others may have grown up with parents who had troubled marriages, and one parent may have turned to the child for nurturance and support, creating a syndrome Dr. Patricia Love has called "emotional incest." And many were sexually abused by one parent—or even both—leaving them with deep emotional scars and seriously distorted messages about their sexuality. These are the kinds of terribly damaging stories many of us grew up with, everything from "you're here for my pleasure" to "drink till it goes away."

In homes where certain values and storylines proudly upheld the family code of honor, the offspring may have been coerced into living up to these prearranged standards; and if they failed, they were labeled inferior, immoral, or sick. When traditional values do not happen to fit with a child's individual nature and destiny in life, a terrible rift can occur between the child's inner and outer self.

Societal values can do equal harm. We've heard often that "children are to be seen and not heard," for instance. Then what is a child to do with his or her natural childlike spontaneity and joy? These natural feelings are repressed, to later emerge as a pleasure-seeking shadow self, or a person who is so frightened of feelings that he or she becomes cold and unfeeling. The following is an example from my own life:

My son Tom is the son of a West Pointer, and his grandfather had served in two wars with General Patton. He learned early on that strong men are brave and do not show fear or much emotion. They stay in control. His young ego was being trained to be a courageous soldier. When Tom was a very precocious four, we went to see the movie version of *Charlotte's Web*. The story is about a spider who dies in the end after everyone has fallen madly in love with her. When she died, I noticed little Tommy was rubbing away his tears, shyly looking around to make sure no one was watching him. I leaned over and whispered, "It's okay to cry. This is very sad. See, nearly everyone is crying." With this permission, he fell into my lap and let the tears come. Later, during our drive home, Tommy blurted out, "I don't think most men know that!" "Know what?" I asked. And he said, profoundly, "I don't think most men know that it's okay to cry." He had been pondering this proposition for about twenty minutes.

Many of our early childhoods were replete with these kinds of half-truths. Based on what? People's false notions and unexamined beliefs unconsciously passed on from generation to generation. We take these values for granted, thinking they are true "because *they* said so." And robotism sets in. It's up to each of us later on in life to make these beliefs conscious and change them when they no longer fit. Otherwise, our shadow will begin to magnify in strength, deeply repressed underneath the weight of these automatic responses to life.

The Human Chakra System: Bridge Between Body and Soul

Before we can truly change, or become a larger Self, we must make fully conscious our unwanted patterns. In the last chapter, we saw how the shadow can manifest in our lives. Now we must take the next step and look back through our early years to see how the shadow, in the form of codependent behaviors, came to be. We must be like an operator in an assembly line who realizes each product is coming out damaged; she doesn't try to fix each separate article, but stops the machine to take a look at the source of its miscreations.

The first three stages of development I will explore in this chapter involve the formation of our ego's physical, emotional, and cognitive natures. In order to be human each of us is required to build and inhabit a sensual body, emotional feelings, and an intellect. At first, when we are infants, the body is all ego. In fact, we could safely call it a "body-ego," because there is no distinction between our physical structure and the emotional feelings it carries: one affects the other directly. Later we develop separate— yet still interconnected—emotional and mental natures. You'll learn that these first three levels of development are part of a universal pattern, the human chakra system; every chakra is representative of a totally different level of consciousness, containing certain qualities and specific trials we all must undergo in order to develop adequately at each stage, and then move on. But the shadow's ways can become predominant and manifest codependence patterns galore if our ego is weakened or imbalanced during our crucial early years, and these levels of consciousness may become distorted as a result. In our country where, as Anne Wilson Schaef says, "society itself has become an addict," there is little chance many of us will make it through these stages of physical, emotional, and mental development without some degree of dysfunction woven into our ego's patterns.

When we are continuously wounded, our ego carefully weaves itself around these wounds by building up defensive blocks, just as a physical wound will create a scab. These psychological defenses are absolutely necessary when we are children; otherwise, we could not survive our dysfunctional families. However, these defenses become unnecessary limitations when we grow up and are able to fend for ourselves.

The following are examples of how childhood issues can linger: At the first level of consciousness, while establishing your basic sense of security and safety in the world, you may have become over-controlling of yourself and others in order to feel safe. Or during the second stage, while your emotional life was developing, you might have built an ego that chose to withhold feelings, or that distracted you when you were threatened by intimacy or emotional needs that were never expressed honestly in your family. Or because you never felt loved as a child, you might have developed an ego that seeks others to make it feel lovable, and you feel your very *life* depends on them loving you.

And if these first two stages aren't demanding enough on their own, our ego's architecture is *hierarchical* in nature. This means that if a distortion occurs at level one, it will be carried forward to level two, taking on more distortion and emotional force, and bringing all this dysfunction to level three, our mental nature—where our ego blooms in all its radiance as a whole personality. Then we've got an intellect ruled by ideas, attitudes, or values that are unhealthy, unrealistic, or too protective to allow us to grow into our full potential. This kind of impaired mind will build into it all the urges of codependence—*the urge to control, the urge to excite, and the urge to merge.* When recognized, faced, and turned around, these very urges—which we'll explore in depth—become our avenue to bliss and love. But first, we may need to do a lot of inner work. For in order for our old wounds to heal, they must be at least partially reopened, the old scabs removed.

The human mind needs a picture or scaffold to hang ideas on in order for us to truly understand their essence; hence the need for icons in a church, symbols and mantras in every kind of religion, or even diagrams in a science manual. Similarly, in order to grasp the full meaning of our personal histories, we need a structure around which to organize our experiences. The chakra system provides such a structure.

The Seven Chakras

Physical Location	Human Issue	Gland Affected	Color
1st chakra—*base of spine*	Security/safety or survival needs; issues of being grounded or having a firm foundation.	Adrenal	Red
2nd chakra—*sexual or sacral center*	Passion and belongingness needs; issues pertaining to sexuality, childbirth, and the creative urge.	Sex Glands	Orange

The Seven Chakras (cont.)

Physical Location	Human Issue	Gland Affected	Color
3rd chakra—*solar plexus*	Issues concerning self-esteem or self-identity.	Pancreas	Yellow
4th chakra—*heart*	Issues concerning love; giving love, receiving love, and loss of love.	Thymus	Green
5th chakra—*throat*	Issues relating to one's individuated, creative expression in the world and comprehension of the whole of which we are a part.	Thyroid	Blue
6th chakra—*third eye* (between the eyebrows)	Issues pertaining to compassion for the world and aspiration to serve the whole.	Pituitary	Indigo
7th chakra—*crown* (top of the head)	Concerns the power to manifest truth unambiguously; being one's Self, beginning anew, or God-realization.	Pineal	Violet

The various forms of Yoga practiced in Eastern cultures teach that we are seven-layered, and these layers include the workings of both the ego (the lower self, chakras one through three), and the soul (the Higher Self, chakras four through seven). And it is precisely because the chakra system includes both our higher and lower selves that it offers an ideal way to focus on our wholeness in a concrete way. This system is the basis for Chinese medicine and many Eastern religious paths. For in Eastern philosophy, which is much older than our Western psychological schools, there has always been an honoring of both ego and soul.

As Arthur Young points out in *The Reflexive Universe*, all biological systems and many philosophical systems contain these seven levels of consciousness in some form or other: the seven notes of a Western musical scale, the seven major colors, the seven major planets, the seven primary glands in the human organism (see the chakra diagram above). And in the Bible, Jacob's ladder had seven rungs we ascend toward heaven. Nature has shown us over and over again that we develop according to a divine and orderly scheme.

In many spiritual philosophies, the chakras are viewed as a ladder of subtle energies we climb to build a Self. They are vortexes of spinning energy, or vibratory centers, that mold themselves into seven differing forms of human expression. These levels of consciousness are not seen but *felt*. For emotion is e-motion; it is our movement of energy, or spirit. And we all know that our emotions and feelings differ from time to time, depending on our state of consciousness. Our energies can be low or high, from passive, heavy, dense, and rocky to light, refined, and smooth, depending upon which chakra level we are functioning on at a given time.

For those of you new to spiritual science, do not think of these chakras as existing literally. Remember, the Self is an organizing principle only; it has no form, so the chakra system is a metaphor for how we grow energetically. You can think of the chakras as the Self's architecture. They are not found within the physical body; they are circulating along the body's main axis, up and down the spine, in the energetic or etheric body. These subtle-moving energies are how the urges and feelings of our soul communicate with its physical instrument.

Although ideas about the chakra system vary somewhat in different cultures, the fact that it exists will soon be common knowledge in both Eastern and Western medical settings. Many within the healing professions concur that these seven major energy centers hold an important key to human health and evolution. In fact, medical doctors find that when a chakra's energies are inactive or overly active, physical disease and emotional imbalance can occur right at that chakra's station, thereby affecting our body's organs, glands, and nervous system. The chakras are the gateways through which the soul enters our physical bodies and our lives.

Once again, the first three chakras represent the development of our ego, the learner self, our experiencer. If we had all been brought up in perfectly balanced families, where honesty, creative expression, and individual potency were truly valued, our lower chakras would be clear, allowing our soul to shine through. We would have learned how to do our being. The chakra system would then function like a flute; the soul or Higher Self would blow right through, creating a pure and harmonious melody, each tone absolutely pure. And that song would be our lives. Without any work at all, we would express our authenticity even before we could talk.

However, because none of us had the good fortune to be brought up in a household of saints, our chakra energies have likely become to varying degrees blocked, imbalanced, or distorted (all these words describe the same phenomenon). One, two, or all three of our lower chakras may be damaged. And if we were abused, our chakras will be that much more imbalanced. As a result, instead of being open, these first three chakras may have become constricted with shame, anger, fear, or other negative emotions. Or they may only be half-opened, or too opened sometimes but completely shut down at other times. We may even be arrested at a given level of functioning—devoid of that chakra's particular quality, whether a sense of security, sexual energy, or personal power. In any case, our lower chakra levels need to be reexamined and healed so that the soul can more fully enter our lives and the upper chakras of the Higher Self can express.

As any good social worker knows, we must first understand the system we're presently involved in and trying to impact before we set about to make changes. We must take on and understand the ways of "earthlife" before we can disidentify from our conditions and co-create improvements here. Hence this chapter is devoted to getting to know and understand the functioning of the first three chakras. But before I continue, I want to remind you again that as important as these first three levels of development are, they are not all of who we are; the remaining four chakras are expressive of the Higher Self. Beyond level three of our development, we'll see there is another world, one in which the ego undergoes an initiation of fire and is purified, learning to forgive its past and accept its conditions. This begins happening at the fourth level of consciousness, the Heart, which I'll explore in the next chapter.

In this section, we will look at each level of ego development; then we will focus on what relationships in our life look like when we are carrying forward distortions on any of these levels; thirdly, we will look at how to heal the imbalanced chakra; and finally, we will discover the gift each chakra or level of consciousness offers us. As you study these stages of growth, allow your whole Self to involve in memory and reflection; try to experience your sensations, feelings, and even emotionalisms, as well as honoring your thoughts and intuitive wisdom. You may find that you have more than one imbalanced chakra; in fact, most of us are at least somewhat imbalanced on each of the three levels. Please be gentle with yourself and be careful not to judge or categorize yourself in any way. Keep reminding yourself that this is a journey of discovery and healing; it is not designed to give you easy answers or simple diagnoses.

Level-One Consciousness: Our Physical/Instinctual Nature

As little babies, we are only physically and sensually aware. We yell when we're hungry, cold, tired, wet, or need to feel safe. At first, we barely care who gives us these pleasures and conveniences (as any brand-new and disappointed mother or father will tell you). When these needs are met, we coo contentedly in our cribs. Soon, we begin to prefer our mother, or primary caretaker, and then Dad or other significant others are gradually acknowledged.

The first chakra is our grounding rod, referred to as "the root chakra" whose energies gather and settle at the base of our spine. It is the "reds" of the earth. It rules the adrenal glands and controls our physical/sensual life. At this basic chakra level, we are preoccupied with *handling our primary needs for safety and survival.* No other needs are recognized. *We believe we are only our bodies.* This is the fundamental survival level of consciousness where we develop a strong *will to live.*

Some parents are so neglectful and abusive that their children, even as adults, never make it through this stage completely. They have a shaky will to live, and may be plagued with a constant urge to "take themselves out"—through drugs, alcohol, sex, and in some cases, suicide. At its extreme, being stuck at this level can lead to paranoid schizophrenia, where the person has no sense of reality beyond meeting his or her basic survival needs. The shadow has taken over. Feelings of terror, fury, isolation, and despair dominate this level when it is imbalanced or never completed. A person may feel he or she is never safe or secure.

When stuck at this chakra level we are ruled by separatism: a bumpy, dense consciousness where we feel it is "me against the world." Here, we will be completely identified as *a physical being only,* in a stage of complete soul-forgetting. This base level of functioning is one most of us do by instinct. If the first chakra is intact, adults don't have to focus much at this level, unless their very lives become threatened. When this happens, they can behave in a subhuman and uncivilized fashion full of rage and aggression in order to defend against physical harm. They literally "see red." I call this my "cave woman consciousness." This chakra is the center of our dynamism, our very life-force. When imbalanced, this powerful force can run rampant and get us into serious trouble.

When we are stuck at this lowest level of consciousness, our sexuality can become domineering or even bestial. The sexual urge is geared toward physical release and partners are sought out purely for one's immediate gratification. A first-chakra couple may go "on automatic" and become downright animalistic in their drives to dominate or aggress. There is often no inkling of love; only need. Survival is the keynote. The shadow, if denied expression of its natural sexual urges, might contain overwhelming aggressive/sexual obsessions that burst out compulsively in harmful ways.

And although we may no longer function at this basic survival level, many of us do have imbalanced first chakras to varying degrees. Therefore, certain security or survival issues, if not recognized, can crop up in our current relationships and act out through our shadow. Here are some of the comments I've heard from my friends and clients who have first-chakra issues: "Every time something threatens the loss of my money or my home, I go into such panic, I can't even think." "I need a strong mother figure in my life; I just never feel safe enough." "I can never stand to be alone, so I'll befriend almost anybody."

As mentioned earlier, when we grow up with people who abuse us, we create psychological defenses against these unsafe and uncomfortable relationships. We develop personality quirks, fragilities, or neurotic disorders. Later in life, we may seek out partners to live out these early patterns of victimization and abuse: until made conscious, they will act out through us. Imbalanced first chakras are an especially rich haven for codependence patterns concerning the need for excessive control of self and others.

The Urge to Control

This basic urge is set up by our ego to stabilize, hold steady, or remain strong, grounded, and fully present in our relationships and in our lives. This urge, in itself, serves a positive function. When we are damaged at this level of development, however, we have an excessive need to be always on top of things. And often accompanying this is a strong need for others to see us as being always right or good. There is little tolerance for criticism, even the constructive kind. Underneath this need to control is the fear of surprise, spontaneity, or change. There is an overwhelming need to ward off shattering instability. For many from severely dysfunctional families, any kind of surprise is associated with crisis—the melodrama of quarrels and fighting, and the inability to predict whether or not one will be safe from one moment to the next.

I once knew a man whose shadow functioned so rigidly that even in his forties it would not allow him to leave his mother—or even their house—without his experiencing paralyzing feelings of anxiety. His father had been a Protestant minister who wanted all his family members to be "moral." This father was obviously afraid of his own human urges and had unconsciously passed his fears on to his children. It had created in his son (my client) a shadow so strong that it forced him to live a severely limited lifestyle in order to keep that shadow at bay. He was afraid of being known. For if he were, he felt others might discover that he was "evil" or "bad." Intense psychotherapy over several years finally made it possible for my friend to become a member of a small men's social group that played shuffleboard on Friday evenings in his neighborhood. This was the beginning of his frightened shadow's integration.

This chakra is a seedbed for codependence. People with first-chakra imbalances need others to take care of them, to sustain them financially and/or emotionally; or conversely, they may need to take care of others to feel good about themselves. Often, those with first-chakra issues attempt to fill all the needs of other people—as they wish their parents had done for them. Giving parentlike support to mates and friends, or getting it from them, is a form of wrong relationship: It places the persons in dependency roles vis-à-vis one another, when in reality, they are of equal status.

Too many unmet survival needs in childhood can create such unequal relationships later on in life. These relationships demand unrealistic guarantees and unending amounts of dependency. And they force the people involved into belittling codependent roles. We've heard of the "baby doll" syndrome, where a grown woman acts like a child in order to get others to meet her emotional needs. Or the "Peter Pan" (or Jung's *puer aeternis*) who refuses to grow up, requiring a more mature adult to take care of him. Or the "mother hen" syndrome, where a man or woman cannot stop caretaking, often to the great annoyance of those in their lives. Either role—the dependent or the caretaker—is a codependent stance.

Relationships with a First-Chakra Imbalance

John was emotionally neglected by his mother until she died when he was six, at which point he lived with his physically abusive father. By the time he was in his teens, he'd left home, finding refuge in a shelter for runaway boys. With the aid of a social worker, John entered a trade school when he was seventeen. There he met Mary, who was five years his senior. This was the first relationship that ever made him feel secure. He and Mary fell in love and dated all through their trade school days, then married. John seemed to take great pride in being Mary's husband and loved to show her off to people as "his." Mary admitted that she enjoyed this feeling of being so special from the beginning of their relationship.

One day, however, everything changed. Mary went back to school, and her circle of friends began to expand beyond her home life. John was threatened by her other relationships from the start—those with men and women. One day when Mary was speaking favorably of one of her professors, John became convinced that she was in love with him, and he hit Mary during a violent argument. This had never happened before. Then, over the next several weeks he began to obsess about the professor; he started playing shadow games. He acted out, inventing wild stories about his own whereabouts, trying to convince Mary that he had a lover. And he had sporadic rage attacks. Eventually he became too dangerous for Mary to be around. She entered into therapy with me and used a battered women's shelter several times for protection until she finally got the courage to leave John and begin a new life. John came to a few therapy sessions but never seemed willing to change. Although he intellectually understood his issues, he would still fly into uncontrolled rage whenever his security was remotely threatened.

The minute he felt himself to be in danger, John's first-chakra issues became activated. His undeveloped emotional body sounded an alarm, and irrational feelings of mistrust and abandonment cropped up that did not befit the current situation. John was anxious anytime his mate was not around. Feelings of jealousy, paranoia, and possessiveness ran rampant. In such a scenario, even when the partner adores the person and never leaves his side, feelings of extreme neediness still dominate the psyche. I feel that people such as John should leave intimate relationships alone until they can build a stronger ego. I heard a few years later that John had lost two other relationships.

Healing Our Wounded First Chakra

We each have our ways of feeling fragile, insecure, or doubtful. But instead of allowing ourselves to feel these feelings in the heart (meaning we claim them honestly and directly), we often hide behind our relationships with significant others. We "buy" this false protection, afraid that we can't stand what we'll find if we look within and feel our pain. In this way we lose touch with our ability to be alone and take care of ourselves; we fall into one codependent relationship after another. Until we learn that we ourselves are capable of meeting our basic security needs, we will be brought back to this early level of consciousness and remain fixated on our fear—or, if deeply wounded as John was, paranoia.

If you have first-chakra issues—whether they take the form of overcontrolling those around you, losing control and acting out, or protecting yourself from life so you don't lose control—you need to invoke the quality of true *discipline*. "Invocation" is an active way to pray, and one that lacks passive religious connotations. It is a way of aggressively calling out to our spirit, being willing to do our part. I'll more fully explain invocation in the next section. For now, simply ask the Higher Power within to help you realize discipline. And remember, "discipline" comes from the same root word as "disciple." It is the act of bringing oneself face to face with the truth in every situation. Most of our untruths are imbalances—too much of this, not enough of that. Discipline arights these incongruities. It helps us follow through with authenticity rather than going unconscious and behaving codependently.

Because so many power-hungry authority figures have misused this quality so horribly, discipline has unfortunately become an ugly word. These "control mongers" apply *their* rules to other people even when these standards don't befit them. When we were young, we didn't have a choice; we had to allow ourselves to be "disciplined." Now that we're grown, we should never discipline ourselves to act in ways that go against our gut, just because someone else thinks we should. This kind of yielding is classic codependence! Only when we discipline ourselves in the areas of life that *we* choose do we become true disciples.

People with first-chakra issues need to apply discipline to their current relationships over and over again until healing begins to occur. This discipline should take the form of reality testing with partners and calling forth the observer self to begin noticing control needs when they appear. These behaviors take the place of acting out (as John did). Ask yourself, "Why am I feeling jealous right now?" Then communicate with your partner: "Sara, I felt like you were flirting with him. Are you attracted to him or is it my imagination?" Or "Jim, I'm feeling like you don't want to be with me right now. Am I making this up?" These kinds of questions must be asked repeatedly, until the qualities of trust and openness create a new landscape for our relationships.

First-chakra work requires a lot of understanding, support, and patience from ourselves and others. If you feel you've got a lot of repressed material from your early childhood traumas, you may want to seek experiential therapies that take you into your feelings, so you can release these painful emotions and find relief. Such experiential therapies bring you back to your past, so you can see the roots of your first-chakra imbalance by actually re-experiencing the original pain. Such therapies include Gestalt "Open Seat" or Progoff's Journaling methods, movement therapy, expressive artwork or sandplay therapy, music therapy, role-playing and psychodrama, and experiential family therapy. They also include regressive therapies such as breathwork, re-parenting, process hypnosis, rebirthing, or cathartic bodywork. (See Appendix One for further explanation of these therapies.) Repressed emotional issues can be so deeply buried within the psyche that talk therapies may not reach them.

Twelve Step programs such as Emotions Anonymous or Codependents Anonymous also can be safe outlets for expressing feelings and working through them. Sometimes extensive psychotherapy is required for those who are severely damaged. These first-chakra issues are the hardest of all to heal—for they are experienced as issues of life and death. Learning to remain open and honest about one's feelings and one's plight is crucial if one is to heal from first-chakra imbalances—or, for that matter, from any woundedness.

My own experience with basic survival needs baffled me for the longest time. I never understood my "fragility pattern" until I began therapies that took me deeply enough into my psyche to access reliving my birth. I was a complete puzzle to myself: I was a fortunate child and had functioning, loving parents who loved me. However, I was born weighing a little over four pounds, two months premature. I bonded with a male doctor who saved my life and nurtured me for the first few weeks of my life. Many of my security issues are wrapped up in this fragile beginning. I tend to place strong, dominant males on pedestals, believing they will "save" me. Sometimes I forget that I'm grown-up now and know how to take care of myself, because this fragile feeling state is part of my reality. When I act from this wounded place, wanting someone "bigger" to take care of me, I am coming from my shadow.

The First Chakra's Gift

Each chakra, or level of consciousness, also has its spiritual side, a high quality that becomes a skill (skills the rest of this book will help you discover). When our first chakra is balanced, and our ego learns to feel safe and protected, we will then open to the first chakra's spiritual essence. When this chakra is grounded, it offers us the spiritual quality of *Truth*, or *Authentic Being*.

People who have the ability to be practical and take care of their own basic survival needs have made it through the trials and tests of the first chakra. They've passed through one of the "gates of initiation" and have become able to fend for themselves in this world (unless they're in crisis, when they may need to depend on others). When our first-chakra issues are resolved, no one else will have to take care of us. Nor we, them, although, of course, we still have healthy needs for community, love relationships, and friendship. And knowing we are self-sufficient, we begin to act as our truth and authenticity. For without this ability to live in the world, we have seen how we are at the mercy of life's conditions and dependent on other people to make our lives work for us. Then, we have no free attention to put toward our spiritual goals.

We say of people who reflect a pure first-chakra quality, "He has presence." "Her feet are firmly planted on the ground." "She has a lot of integrity." Or "He seems at home with himself."

Level-Two Consciousness: Our Emotional/Relational Nature

Many believe that codependence is largely a second-chakra issue. For it is here that we develop a feeling nature and the creative power or force that drives us to express. When the second chakra is imbalanced, *we believe we are our feelings and our intense urges:* we feel driven by them. And as we know, addiction to imbalanced emotional states and relational needs is the bedrock of codependence patterns.

At this level, we develop the *will to feel*. And this manifests in the physical body as urges to act out of passion or emotion. If second-chakra issues are unresolved, our feelings can make us appear frantic, too needy, or overly sensitive. The second-chakra drive emanates from the sexual center of our organism, which is situated in the physical body about three centimeters below the navel. This consciousness level also rules issues of childbirth, and even the eliminative functions: it is the source of all urges to release built-up energy or constriction, and it is most often experienced as a need to push, usually with some accompanying emotional expression. It is the "oranges" of the worldly passions.

The second chakra is the developmental stage where the ego learns *to make life passionate and relational.* When activated and flowing smoothly, there is an abundance of life-force and an increase in physical stamina that is accompanied by a sense of well-being or quiet joy. However, when this chakra is half-opened or imbalanced, there can be a sense of blocked energy or extreme, almost uncontrollable sexual urges accompanied by negative emotions such as jealousy or rage (which, as you've seen, can also originate in a damaged first chakra).

If as children our feelings were constantly ignored and/or disapproved of by significant grown-ups in our lives, we most likely developed emotional imbalances; we probably stuffed most of our feelings into the subconscious mind and became disassociated from them entirely. As adults, we continue to act in response to these feelings. Again, robotism sets in. And the shadow resides in the dark as a huge powerhouse of repressed emotion. I believe that this is the origin of both sex and love addiction. People who obsess about sex and eroticism are attempting to get a lot more than sexual pleasure from their sexual encounters. They are attempting to fill a host of unmet intimacy needs from somewhere back in their development. As a result, they are playing at intimacy but are scared to death of the real thing. They seek out an array of sexual partners who will "give them their life," or nurture them out of a constant state of depression, or as one friend used to say, fill the "bottomless black hole."

Sex can also release deep emotion in a nonaddictive way, sometimes during sexual orgasm. People may at times frighten their mates when making love because they connect with deep feelings of hurt, rage, terror, or other emotions often related to physical abuse, childbirth (which is often experienced as physical abuse), or other repressed issues. Sometimes people will cry out, and their voice will not even sound like it is theirs; it is deeper, ancient, emanating from cellular memory. Have you ever had an experience such as this? If so, you will understand the magnitude of the powerful force that drives the second chakra.

We all know that in sexuality we procreate. But we may not have realized that artists and inventors are doing the very same thing: they, too, merge with something other than themselves (a musical instrument, a piece of clay) and create an offspring—a masterpiece. To our unconscious instinctive mind, the process is the same. When the urge to give birth to something new hits our imbalanced second chakra, we turn toward pleasure-seeking; our longing for a "turn-on" ignites like a flame. And we mistakenly reach outside ourselves toward the world's titillations and glamours, desiring to merge with these sensual allurements in intense involvement. But because we don't know who we are, these outside attractions become our objects of gratification, and we give our power away to them. We may do this by always needing a love partner, no matter how he or she treats us, or by attaching to a lover in a clinging, overintense way (always focused on him or her at the expense of ourselves), and/or seeing our partner as the cause of our conditions, as responsible for our happiness, depression, or anger.

And if this is not enough to make us crazed and unfulfilled, many of us have been raised to believe there is scarcity in the world—not enough of life's treats to go around—so with *first-*chakra possessive fervor, we grab onto these outside fascinations, hoping to keep them entirely for ourselves. Again, chakra development is hierarchical: what we learned from the stage before will carry forward into the next level of consciousness. When our first-chakra poverty consciousness combines with our emotionally addicted second chakra, we have a fertile ground for the emotions of jealousy and possessiveness—sometimes even hatred. We become addicted to the need to feel special and turned on, and when we don't get our fix, we think we are dying and we lash out.

On the other hand, our passion center is the place within our consciousness where we learn to merge with life and others with enthusiasm and a desire for intensity. It's the seat of our creativity.

The urge to be turned on and delighted—to "feel high"—is our natural feeling state! Devoid of these energies, we would not be attracted to anything: we would have no interests. Allurement draws us to our destiny by pulling us toward the projects and people we require for our true expression.

The Urge to Excite

When our second chakra is imbalanced, we have an overwhelming *urge to excite*, creating too much passion and drama in our lives. We stir things up. "Fire by friction" is how we throw ourselves into tailspins of activity that thrill us. The more dramatic and agonizing, the better, say those of us addicted to melodrama and passion. Living on the edge, we feel alive! We thrive on the intensity of conflict. We even start battles when none need to be fought. Then we have to use our highest skills to resolve what we ourselves created. This is the negative side of our feeling nature, and it can ignite in any of life's situations—at our job, as parents, in friendships, and in romantic relationships. We love excessively, or we don't love at all. When something feels good, we love too much; when something frustrates or scares us, we withhold and cannot show our love. We erroneously think that extremes are ways of feeling vital and alive.

In romantic relationships, we often will create roles for ourselves that keep us caught up in drama and away from our true emotions: Don Juan, the seductive manipulator, the tease, the *femme fatale*, the hysteric. These subpersonalities become the shadow's pleasure-seekers: "I'm just a stranger passing through the night; I won't be around in the morning" is one such desperado myth. Or "I'm just 'a good-time gal' who knows all the tricks and doesn't need anything back. Use me, abuse me, but let the good times roll." And these pursuits often lead to the sob stories we give in to out of self-pity: "I've got tears in my ears from lying on my back in my bed crying over you." "If the phone don't ring, you know it's me, 'cause I'm gone from you forever."

Struggling through life "looking for love in all the wrong places" is often the loneliest game in town. There is constant rejection, lack of intimacy, competitiveness, and the need to be eternally youthful, sexy, and sensational—a breeding ground for chemical addiction along with codependence. There is very little security or love that can emerge until these second-chakra illusions are put to rest, or at least made conscious. We cannot use others as our "tools" for personal excavations through troublesome deficiency needs, although, because we're so other-directed, we may think we can. To heal, we must slow down and look at ourselves.

Unless we become conscious of how we are misusing these powers of allurement and attraction—which are actually the magnetic and binding forces of Love—we will search out other codependent people as "objects" to turn us on. What we are really seeking is not them, but the feeling of being revved up. This is the addiction! We forget that our "turn-on" is *our* responsibility. We confuse outer stimuli for the inner calling to be fascinated, creative, expressive, and forever new. We've become out of touch with our real Self, or inner Beloved. And so we fall in love with "drama kings and queens," the shadow's playmates.

Second-chakra imbalances arise in early childhood, usually in family systems that evidence emotional/sexual dysfunction. Children may not have been protected from adults' frustrations, outrages, hysterical reactions, or sexual/romantic melodramas. These children were caught up in emotional enmeshment—not knowing which feelings were theirs and which belonged to the grown-ups. Or sometimes their parents' feelings were so explosive and dangerous there was physical abuse, and the children were not allowed to feel at all. They simply had to shut down in order to survive and they then became completely out of touch with their feelings. Some children were forced to take sides with one parent, or asked to become the emotional support for a dysfunctional and unhappy parent; again, a form of emotional incest. They may have felt responsible early in life for their parents' feelings; in other words, it was all their fault. This creates an adult shadow who feels it is the cause every time a loaded emotional issue erupts. Unclear and erratic emotions, feelings of over-responsibility, and poor respect for their own and others' emotional boundaries can be the result.

Often people with second-chakra issues were given random attention in response to their early expressions of need. As a result, their adult shadows may act out dramatically in order to be noticed, through hysterics or rageful temper outbursts. Morever, during childhood, their sexual feelings may have been inappropriately stirred or repressed, creating confusion about what love and sexual feelings really are and about the difference between pleasure and pain. In our work, we've found correlations between eating disorders and emotional or sensual/erotic confusions, as food is a symbol for "giving and getting" or controlling emotional/sensual gratification. Many anorexics and bingers have been incest victims or erotically mishandled or abused when very young. Their attitude toward sexuality and sensuality is founded in ambivalence and shame, for they very often confuse parental and sexual love.

As you are reading this, some feelings may be coming up for you; you may be becoming aware of some important aspects of your own early childhood; or you may be seeing some of the ways you've been confused about your sexual and/or feeling nature. Please know that if this is happening, it's the beginning of your healing—a recognition! Now you are free to go on and release the old hurts and misunderstandings that may still be living in your body. You may want to seek out a good friend or safe therapist to help you express these emerging issues. This is old stuff that needs to be released in the good company of someone loving who will understand. And remember, you are larger than your conditions!

Relationships with a Second-Chakra Imbalance

Uneven and unfulfilling relationships are the keynote for second-chakra imbalances. We become caught up in emotionalism, even explosiveness, often neglecting and otherwise thwarting the very intimacy we seek. Here's a true story, though it may seem like a soap opera, that perfectly exemplifies second-chakra imbalance:

Lea loved her husband Tom very much. They had married two years ago, even though Lea knew Tom might not have the ability to be a faithful husband. He had told her that he had been addicted to sex and to being flattered by young, attractive women. And so the two of them had agreed to seek therapy together, to work this problem out. In their two years of marriage, there had been no incidences of infidelity and an element of trust seemed to be budding, although there was still much work to be done.

One evening Tom called home to tell Lea he had to work late. A group was in town for a national board meeting he needed to attend. After Lea hung up the phone, a paranoid voice boomed in her brain saying that he was lying; that he was really going to meet Joy, an old girlfriend. Lea began quietly to obsess on this thought. She tried to go to sleep, but couldn't. She was consumed with the idea that Tom was with Joy.

Finally, in a fit of emotion, she flew out of the house in her bathrobe, determined to find him. She drove to the hotel where the board meeting was to be held, and in a psychic furor, parked right beside her husband's car. Next to his car on the other side was a red convertible with a bumper sticker that read "I Live for Joy." This "proof" made Lea livid! She charged into the hotel lobby and demanded to know the room number of the purported board meeting. There was no such room reserved. She started out the door in a fearful rage and fell into the arms of an oncoming guest, who turned out to be one of her husband's employees. "What are *you* doing here?" Lea demanded, to which he replied, "I've come to use the phone. There was no phone in the meeting room." And he led her to a separate building on the hotel grounds where the board meeting was indeed taking place (sans anyone named Joy in attendance).

The mind—and indeed, the universe!—will provide us with all the clues we need to support a paranoid notion. We will "see" what it was we came to see. A frightened ego cannot hear the voice of truth underneath all the fear, illusion, and drama. Lea learned that evening about the depths of her unresolved distrust of Tom, even though he had shown evidence of becoming a devoted and faithful husband. She realized painfully that it might take several years of living with him before she felt the beginnings of safety. And she saw her own addiction to drama, which she had inherited from the women in her family she had modeled after—all of them beautiful women who were actresses or beauty queens and had used emotional outbursts and passionate romance as a way to get much of what they thought they wanted in life.

Soon after this incident, she realized in a therapy session along with Tom that part of why she had been attracted to him in the first place was the thrill associated with winning him from other women. People like Lea often require drama in order to feel turned on and in love. She had confused the thrills of true love and tragic romantic drama since childhood.

Like Lea, when we begin working on ourselves and are willing to see our patterns, they may become exaggerated and obvious—as though they wish to cooperate. Both Lea's and Tom's codependent compulsions needed to be exposed and understood in order for them to do the extensive emotional work necessary to heal the addictions involved—his, to sex and flattery; hers, to drama and *him*! Until this point, their therapy had focused almost exclusively on Tom, his needs and emotional healing. Now, clearly Lea's work would really need to begin.

Healing Our Wounded Second Chakra

Those of us with second-chakra issues must be careful not to act on our feelings of attraction or passion without first examining them. And at the same time we need to realize that allurement and desire are the very roots of love. When we can let ourselves act from this love rather than our fear of it or of not getting it, a wild love affair ensues between us and something we are to create, whether it is a relationship, a career, or a piece of art. These feelings of "in loveness" are nothing to be ashamed of—ever! And in fact, they can heal us. Like the artist, the poet, or the mystic, when we can give this energy permission to express creatively through our own gifts and talents, the compulsion to express these powers through one another in dysfunctional ways will abate.

One way to balance our second-chakra urges is to visualize or ask our Higher Power to send us the quality of *spiritual discrimination.* Again, look for this greater power within yourself—call upon your Higher Self to bring forth this quality. Invoke it. Spiritual discrimination prevents us from misusing the second chakra's powers of allurement. This quality will act as a balancer of our indiscreet expressions of passion. It will help stop us from offering these "gifts of the heart" to the wrong people and projects. We can only learn spiritual discrimination through practice, through trial and error; it doesn't simply manifest overnight. It might help to ask your observer self to remind you every time you feel yourself slipping into your special brand of codependence. Learn to recognize your signs of neediness, and sit still with them rather than acting them out.

But in order to fully realize spiritual discrimination in our lives, we must learn what truly attracts us; and to do so, we need to listen, not only to our observer self, but to our other voices within. This is called following the mystery and partaking of it consciously, listening to the sacred call. We must be quiet and ask ourselves: What *really* excites us? What *really* turns us on? Are they healthy desires, these things that thrill us? Or are they distorted desires stemming from too much "lack" in our lives? We all feel a pulling inside us. Responded to consciously, this inner call is purposeful; it will teach us what really inspires us, what we truly wish to become involved with. Love and fascination are our lifeline— literally! But until we begin to honor our own self as creative, we're likely to just give these fascinations away in irrelevant and self-defeating codependence.

An example: I might form a crush on a history professor who expresses my passion for world history through the language of inspired thought. Later, I realize that it is my own passion for history I'm in love with, not the professor (who happens to be married and unavailable). If I'd acted on falling in love with *him,* I would have likely been left unsatisfied, if not miserable—and probably addicted. Once I begin teaching history myself, however, my own creativity brings forth a joy that is truly mine.

When we act out of true attraction, we are doing what Joseph

Campbell calls "following our bliss." But until we learn to honor our inner call, we may feel alone and empty as we struggle with repeated loss and disappointment. Most second-level consciousness views the world through a lense of romantic glamour and illusion. We dream hazily of merging with someone or a group of people in an ecstatic union so intense it wipes out the doubting self that has not yet re-connected with its source.

As with first-chakra issues, emotional and feeling-level addictions are not easily released through talk therapies. Because they function dynamically, these feelings must be re-contacted and felt through, not simply talked about. We need to go back into our pasts through imageries, deep body work, music, trance, or some method that will remind us of the feelings in our cells and in our hearts we're trying to ignore. We need methods that will help bring these feelings up and out. Eugene Gendlin's focusing technique is an example of this type of therapy, as is breathwork, movement therapy, or any of the therapies mentioned earlier in the chapter and enumerated in the glossary at the back of the book. The body always knows the truth of our being, and we must employ it if we are to truly heal.

I want to offer you a brief example from my own therapeutic practice. Sue was sitting in my office telling me about a problem she was facing in her life; she said she felt a huge knot in her heart. When I asked her to tell me about it, she began describing the feeling, and soon she was discounting it by moving into her head and analyzing where this feeling might have come from. When she paused, I said quietly, "Susie, I want to play some soft music for awhile, and together, let's reflect about your past, where this feeling must have come up a lot." She agreed. She closed her eyes and began to listen. As the melodic violins and piano moved into her heart, Sue began to weep. After a time, when the feelings began to subside, I asked, "Are you getting any pictures or reflections in your mind you'd like to share?" She replied, "I'm four years old, sitting at the supper table, and my dad is yelling at me, calling me a bad girl." And she put her head in her arms and wept violently until her body was limp with relief. Afterward, we talked for quite awhile, and I could see that she was lighter. She had made a deep connection with her past, which provided great insight and helped her with her current difficulty.

Painful feelings must be emptied out, like squeezing toothpaste out of a tube. And they will not go anywhere until they receive the blessing of truthful expression in a setting where we feel safe and supported. Once released, we can see our situations in life with more clarity.

The Second Chakra's Gift

When we learn to balance our energies of passion and allurement, charm and seduction, we become vital forces for the soul's quality of *Goodness* in the world. Our feeling nature becomes harmless, our love nature grounded in wholeness and truth. Goodness is not perfection. And it is not something we achieve; it comes naturally to us when our emotional body is cleared of all over-reaction. When we develop this trait, we can no longer intentionally hurt another. Instead of being filled with intensities that compulsively express, we are quieter, more refined, yet fully involved in life. And we see the Goodness in everyone and therefore become fully responsive—instead of reactive—to others. This, of course, is the healing of addiction. And it is how heaven is created on earth.

People who make it through the second chakra's "gate of initiation" and come out the other side in one piece (for the trials are great!) are people with balanced emotions. They've withstood the tests of extremes and are now able to function in the world in the midst of uneasy conditions without losing much poise or force. Goodness is *godliness*—high love! But being in a state of Goodness does not mean we will never over-react or act out of misdirected passion, for many of us become emotionally polarized at times in our lives. We all have weak moments. Moreover, those of us with second-chakra issues have bodies that are highly sensitized to feel. And it is precisely because we often can literally feel the feelings of others that we must learn to construct boundaries so that we know which emotions are ours. When our second chakras are balanced, we make great therapists. We can be trusted to act from our hearts.

Level-Three Consciousness:
Our Mental/Intellectual Nature

If our emotional bodies were uncontaminated or unharmed by the time we reached this level, we would develop an intellect that draws reasonable conclusions, makes choices based on wisdom and integrity, and has a solid yet not fixed sense of identity. This is the level where we *seek a self-image that tracks with our ideals.* The third chakra awakens our personal morality: our values and ethics. It is on this mental level of consciousness that we develop our ideas, attitudes, and beliefs—our life stance. The third chakra is our ego's power center, the solar plexus chakra. It's here that our ego formulates the face we show the world, our identity.

The color yellow, symbolizing the bright and pristine intellect, is associated with this level of consciousness. Scientific minds, which can analyze, categorize, label, and dissect information in logical, linear ways, draw upon the energies of the third chakra. For it is the famed "left brain." When we have a well-developed third chakra, it provides order and proficiency in our lives. We feel grounded in the ways of the world. The third chakra governs our thoughts: it's where we dream of future goals and can think realistically about how to meet them. Third-level consciousness is where we develop our intellects and fill them with the attitudes, beliefs, and identities we wish to align with. It is here that we develop the *will to know truth.*

But unfortunately, by the time most of us have reached this level, we *have* been wounded, and we create unrealistic beliefs about what truth is. It is impossible to have a clarity of mind until the emotional body is balanced and serene. For instance, if I'm angry at you and have not expressed it, my "truth" will be that *you* are my problem. Later, after I've expended all the hurt (which is usually buried under anger), I may have a whole new understanding of what that anger really was. We must first release our emotions' hold on us by purging them in an appropriate manner. Then we can think clearly.

When the third chakra is imbalanced, *we think we are our thoughts.* We cannot step outside our own belief systems. Because this third level is still an ego level, most of us still believe our life is happening outside us. We do not know ourselves very well at this stage of our awakening and are likely to opt for the wrong choices, sometimes unconsciously thinking emotional entanglements and competitive struggles are our reason for being. And then, when we fail in relationships or careers, we think (and feel) that we *are* this failure, and we become depressed and disillusioned. The intellect becomes attached to stories about who we think we are supposed to be, and then we feel intense pain when our dreams don't come true. We can even become physically sick with ulcers or other stress-related illnesses as a result of our faulty identification. Materialism can easily become our god. At this stage, we attract to ourselves lessons about power, greed, success and failure, ego dominance, dogma, competition—in other words, the lessons of separatism and fragmentation.

The Urge to Merge

Because we live in the material world, it is natural that we should desire material success. But if unmet needs exist at the third level, these illusory status symbols in the outer world can become addictions. Such things as money, power, fame, lifestyles, titles, and physical appearance become our whole identity. We believe we must have them in order to feel good about ourselves. And we also may become overly attached to other people, who become our reason for living, the very heart of our identity. This is a mis-directed *urge to merge* with something or someone who gives us stature, because we lack this feeling on our own. This is codependence.

The third level can become a haven for the egomaniac, who

acts from need and will do almost anything—no matter how self-defeating in the end—in order to feel important: spending money one hasn't got; bragging about feats never accomplished; wearing outlandish or inappropriate clothes; boring people with long, drawn-out stories about one's self; using "objects of gratification," such as beautiful, sexy lovers, or famous friends, to impress others.

Often people with third-chakra issues were cruelly rejected or abused as children, and consequently they are especially needy for respect and love. Their feelings, ideas, and individuality were never acknowledged or appreciated. And, as a result, they may have trouble learning to think for themselves and often can only mirror the values of their parents, peers, or others they perceive as authorities. They even attempt to merge into others' identities— sometimes relying on them completely to make decisions, provide a social life, and to even simply get through the mundanities of each day. They are often completely outer-directed and outer-determined. Author and psychoanalyst Alice Miller believes many such adults experienced "soul murder" as children, never having been given the chance to feel good about just being themselves.

When people stuck at this level become parents, their children's lives are likely to be ruled by dogma, usually religious or patriotic in nature. As a child abuse caseworker, I was shocked to learn that the most abusive families fell into one of two groups: the religious or the military! Parents with third-chakra imbalances (who are often carrying forward "uncooked seeds" from the lower two chakras as well) may abuse their children if the children do not comply with their black-and-white standards. Then, these children will also have damaged lower chakras; they'll often either buy into the dogma or angrily react against it in some equally rigid and harmful way.

Parents with third-chakra imbalances may also train their children to become success-oriented materialists. Some of these children grow up to be adults who feel they must fake it, bragging or displaying the fruits of success they may not think they've genuinely achieved. They may feel as if they are phonies, that if people knew how unlearned or unskilled they really were, they would not be loved. They may have built up such a false image of who they are that they feel lost and completely out of touch with their inner Self any time a success begins to show signs of crumbling.

Today, we have a category of people known as "yuppies" who are doggedly pursuing material goals. By their mid-twenties or thirties, some of these people are already showing symptoms of work-aholism, love and sex addiction (or its opposite, inhibited sex drive, from living with so much physical exhaustion and stress), alcohol and drug addiction, and severe marital difficulties. In our work, we are seeing younger and younger people in need of emotional and spiritual help. Many of them realize they have been seeking their identities in a dying materialistic paradigm that has failed to gratify their real yearnings.

Another sign of third-chakra imbalance is the compelling urge to label, pigeonhole, and categorize ourselves and others.

Relationships with a Third-Chakra Imbalance

People with damaged third chakras often seem very grown-up, responsible, and intelligent while being focused on and preoccu-pied with the external world and all its status symbols. However, they lack a real sense of Self and, in the end, often fail themselves and those they love. Here is a very sad example of such third-chakra imbalance:

Merv was from a wealthy family whose members were highly respected in the business world. When I first met him, I thought he was the most successful young man I'd ever met. Handsome, friendly, and brilliant, he was well on his way to becoming a millionaire by the age of twenty-five! After graduation, Merv's financial successes came quickly as a result of a number of intelligent investments in the stock market. By age thirty, he owned his own brokerage firm on the East Coast. He'd married a lovely woman, built a beautiful home in an affluent neighborhood, and had become a proud father of two children. On the surface, it appeared that he had it all. His wife adored him, and they were very popular with their many friends. Merv was active in the community, and his daughters were growing up with grace.

Then, one day the market crashed and his investments began to plummet. As his career fell into disarray, Merv started using prescription drugs to sleep. He became a social recluse and his family and friends began to note serious changes in his personality.

One day Merv's brother got married, and Merv didn't show up at the wedding. We were all quite alarmed, having seen him the night before in a despondent mood. On his brother's wedding day, Merv had shot himself in the head, leaving a note that said he had failed his wife and family. He was in his early thirties when he took his life.

When his financial empire began to crumble, Merv had experienced an ego death. He'd compared himself to his friends and found himself wanting. Although highly intelligent, Merv could not find a bridge to another level of being. His faulty intellect got in the way of a deeper intuitive knowing that "we are more than what we look like." He had become identified with his story of early success, wealth, and power.

Healing Our Wounded Third Chakra

Paradoxically, the ego's intellect is the key to our transformation—for we *can* always change our minds. This third level of consciousness is a jumping-off place: it's where we choose our reality, and can take the first step toward transforming our lives. Our minds can recognize the fact that a change is needed and then set about making that change. Our feelings will follow our mind's direction. The mind also can learn to surrender and say "I don't know," thereby opening to new ideas, instead of always pretending to be on top of everything.

To begin to heal our third chakra, we need to ask our Higher Power, or a power within, for the gift of *spiritual direction* or *intentionality*. With this quality we become motivated in the right direction—inward—and no longer have a need for ego games.

One way to invoke spiritual direction is to ask ourselves difficult questions about our true goals and beliefs. Have you thought about your evolutionary goals lately? Where do you think you are headed? And what part do you plan to take in this endeavor? Reflecting on what the future means to you is an ideal way to start your inner quest—and it will keep you moving in the direction of your Higher Self. The school of Agni Yoga, the "Yoga of fire," reminds us that the future is a magnetic force—a spiritual call—that relentlessly urges us on toward the fulfillment of our personal destiny.

To overcome third-chakra imbalances, we need the attitude of the mystic: We focus inward on our subjective, numinous life and let go of our ego's dysfunctional, outer-directed search. (I'll go into depth about this shift to the inner life in the next section.) The voices of our injured selves will most certainly crop up and preach to us from time to time—speaking in a mode the Buddhists call "monkey chatter"—but a higher mind will be in charge.

I heard a joke recently: "God is dead; He's been replaced by 50,000 social workers!" And it's true: it often seems that our first steps on the spiritual path are psychological ones. We find groups, such as Twelve Step self-help groups or workshops using psycho-spiritual theories and methods, that begin to awaken us to our ways of living in limitation. And these groups are very important. For at this stage of our awakening, we start to see that we've been misusing our will, emotions, and love nature, as well as our minds. This realization can be overwhelming if we don't have some support and validation for our emerging and vulnerable new self. We feel as if we're bursting out of an egg, still very sensitive and fragile from having been confined so long in the constriction of our old life. Often a lot of support, as well as patience, is required as we await our next right step.

I remember feeling very alone when I began to open to new ideas back in the late 1960s. My friends, many of whom were either training to be therapists or were involved in orthodox religious denominations, gave me all sorts of labels while I searched around for people who could understand my deeper quest. Often, I found comfort from great spiritual books and meditation groups until some fellow travelers appeared in my life.

In fact, one of the greatest aids to the transforming third chakra is bookstores that carry spiritual and psychological literature. Allow yourself to roam around these stores until some area of philosophical thought or spiritual practice attracts you. Then, gradually you may begin to practice and live these ideas and methods, expanding your old world view. (I've included some suggestions for your reading in the appendix.)

The Third Chakra's Gift

The ego's task at this level is to build a mind that allows the soul to shine through, a process I'll develop in the chapter called "The Transforming Mind." At this third level of consciousness we begin to make the shift from ego-dominance to soul-dominance. Then, the soul quality, *Beauty*, can emerge through us. Emerson called Beauty "God's handwriting." Beauty is right proportion: balance and harmony. This quality is very pleasing to our senses and is an obvious cure for the extremes of codependence, for in Beauty, everything is in right relationship.

Beauty arouses our imagination, teaching us to view life poetically: we can see what was previously invisible, the wholeness behind the fragmentation. When we perceive Beauty, our lives take on a higher meaning and purpose, for we begin to see a divine order behind our little storylines and dramas; and we start making sense of our lives. Our creativity is awakened, and according to author Madeleine L'Engle, when we are creative, we can let go of our ego's control and learn "to ride the wind."

The third chakra's gift of Beauty is our passkey to a higher order. We learn to merge with whatever we are focusing on—not in the ways of codependence, where we lose touch with ourselves vis-à-vis others, but in the ways of artistry. We consciously *become* what we study: a tree, a blooming flower, a waterfall, a certain quality, a more wholesome identity. And we merge in the way we were intended to merge, no longer giving away our power to others in codependent, unconscious activity. Instead of using our imaginations wrongly, attributing a higher value to others, we become "imagineers"—utilizing our sacred power of imagination to see our own wholeness and thereby co-create a new life.

The urge to merge is actually a function of the soul, as are the urge to control and the urge to excite (which we'll see more clearly in a later chapter). But when the ego has been damaged, these urges become misdirected, as we've seen. When we let the soul shine through (which it can only do when the ego is cleared of old hurts), the urge to merge becomes a mystical craving, a desire to merge into something higher, to become a part of the oneness that is true existence. But until we surrender to a Higher Power and direct our devotion upward or inward, we throw this sacred quality out into the world and onto projects that will bring us only material or egoistic rewards, or onto other people who are struggling at the same levels of consciousness we are.

Again, to reclaim our lives we must seek gratification from within ourselves for awhile, allowing the inner richness of our right brain to catch up with our now overly developed critical, analytical left brain. Then, later, after connecting with all our powers and gifts (and problems and pain) we'll feel cleansed, refreshed, and stronger. Then we will be more fully prepared to come out again and serve the world in the love and authenticity of one who is transformed. Our Beauty stands revealed.

Now we can see more clearly how the urges of codependence were spawned during our first three stages of ego development. And hopefully we also realize that we've undergone these trials of mistaken living for a purpose: We have substance! We've become wise to the ways of the world through all this struggling to become ourselves. And as we grow wiser and stronger, we are better able to spot *Truth, Goodness,* and *Beauty* behind the most mundane—or even painful—aspects of life. This new vision opens the door to a greater reality, a reality which is unfolding right here on earth for "those who have eyes to see and ears to hear," as the teachings of Jesus declare. This is the divine power of recognition at work.

What a time we've all had learning which emotional urges to

respond to and which to neutralize or ignore. We've been so terrified
of engulfment and/or abandonment that we've learned to turn our
feelings on and off like light bulbs! We've charmed people into a state
of intimacy and then turned around and controlled the situation so
intimacy could not occur. Or we've tried to hold onto people we
didn't even want because we couldn't stand the thought of being
alone. Or we've just merged right into them and completely disap-
peared!

To evolve beyond our codependent stances we must let go. We
have to stop giving ourselves away and surrender our harmful
self-protective patterns *in spite of our fearful feelings*. These fears
will abate when we practice living right on past them. As I said
earlier and Carl Jung so aptly taught: The way to heal is not out,
but *through*. We must learn to stay conscious and observe our old
ways as they transform *in vivo*: While I'm running to the phone to
check up on that special person in my neurotic fashion, I say to
myself, "Jacquie, notice that you are rushing to the phone in this
neurotic fashion. Just watch yourself acting out this event." In this
way, I become separated from the condition I thought I was for
those uncomfortable few moments. I thought the event was going
to "get me." So I had to "get it back." But when I stop and ask
myself what it is I'm really seeking, I realize that these feelings are
coming from my past. The feelings are there all right, and they
won't just go away. But now I have a choice: I can act on them,
or I can just watch them with a little empathy for myself. I can sit
there and love myself as much as I possibly can. After all, I say,
this is my little ego's way of once again trying to protect me from
pain. My ego may be deluded, but it wants to be my friend. As I
sit there trying to get hold of my shadow's pushy ways, I may even
write down all those things I wanted to say on the telephone—
getting the energy out of me and onto the paper. Then, I'll see that
the energy has abated; it only wanted to express. As Jungian
analyst Marie Louise von Franz said in *Projection and Re-collection
in Jungian Psychology,* "The fire of an inordinate passion looks for
that which will extinguish it."

Please keep in mind that by healing the wounds from our past,
we not only heal our emotional body, we aid in healing humanity's

as well! Most of us have experienced the same kinds of sorrows, longings, disillusionments, and joys. These inner feelings are universal, for we're all one soul. When any one of us becomes a little lighter, we have more light to shine out onto our troubled world and all its peoples. We don't need to carry lanterns; *we ourselves are the light.*

Now, let's stop reading for awhile and do some inner work. By now, you may be feeling a little kinder toward your shadow and be fairly convinced that you are indeed a larger Self. If so, your mind is now better prepared to support your repressed emotions if they choose to expose themselves and seek release. The following imagery offers you an opportunity to work with your magical powers of healing. This exercise utilizes the Triangle, the wholistic symbol for Creativity; for It is the only geometric design where three straight lines—representing the thesis, the antithesis, and the synthesis, which are necessary for all creative endeavors— intersect and make a whole. And this symbol activates within us anytime we focus with intention on creating something.

See how deeply you can enter into the following experience as it spontaneously occurs within you. Again, you may want someone to read this to you, or you might tape your own voice reading it. In any case, you should find some quiet place to do this imagery, a place where you will not be disturbed.

Healing the Emotions
A Guided Imagery Experience

Gently inhale and exhale until you feel yourself calming down from your activities. Now, gradually allow an image of yourself to emerge from within your mind. See yourself sitting in the middle of a Triangle—as a point in the middle. . . . [You can put on quiet, transcendental music as you begin to image yourself.] *Feel the Triangle forming itself all around you . . . right where you are. . . . Let your senses really create this sensation. . . . Now, notice how you feel sitting in the midst of this great structure . . . how you are sitting, what you look like. Notice as much as you can . . . (long pause).*

Now, very slowly, allow this Triangle to become filled with a warm and gentle blue light . . . until you can feel yourself being enveloped in it. . . . Bring this light into your solar plexus . . . and on up into your heart . . . (long pause).

When your heart is full, imagine a point in the center of the sun . . . way out there in space where the heart of God resides. . . . Gradually now, allow yourself to merge with this heart in the center of the sun . . . (long pause). Feel your mind . . . your heart . . . your body becoming filled with the energy of the sun . . . (long pause).

Now, sit for awhile in calm reflection . . . in the center of the sun. . . . And just let this experience fill you to the very core of your being. Breathe it in with long, slow breaths . . . (long pause).

Very slowly, now, feel yourself returning here . . . and coming back into your body. Feel your feet, your arms, your face. You may want to move around a little to bring your consciousness fully back. . . . Take some time to feel yourself being totally present in your ordinary reality.

You may want to write some things down after this experience, or process it in any of the ways I described in the last chapter.

All this preoccupation with our past can seem somewhat tedious and exhausting, but this kind of in-depth exploration is necessary if our "apprentice-self," the impure shadow, is to come forward and integrate. I'd like to remind you again that healing is a two-way street: to once again be whole, we must return to our past to retrieve our lost and fragmented selves. And simultaneously we must reach forward and learn to merge into the brand-new identity that is awaiting our recognition. This newer self will be closer to our whole Self.

As we move into the next part of this book, we'll begin looking at our four higher chakras, drawing the spiritual qualities of our soul, or Higher Self, into our ego's ordinary life. Accessing these higher chakras will provide the spiritual force necessary to unleash the gifts of the three lower chakras: our Truth, Goodness, and Beauty—our essence. And this, of course, will accelerate and enhance our healing into wholeness. We'll still need to do more work on our lower selves, but now our Higher Self will help take us through whatever ragged and unprocessed "stuff" we still have to balance and integrate. When we are in touch with our Self, we'll be amazed at the power we then have to transform our codependent, addictive ways.

Now let's look beyond those old "wrinkles in time," our outworn past, and open to a future that is inviting us to move on. In the next four chapters, we'll become acquainted with both the masculine and feminine aspects of our higher nature, the transformed Mind and the open Heart, which combine to make a Self that is far bigger than our conditions, our shadow, or our positive ego. We need to expand our vision now to include our whole inner life—our soul's entire psycho-spiritual reality. Returning to the original Self is the journey of the mystic, and it is our true purpose and destiny. Pir-O-Murshid Inayat Khan, the head of the Sufi Order for the West, said it this way: "The mystic does more than quote scriptures; he not only says 'seek ye first the Kingdom of God,' his whole life is absorbed in that seeking."

Fortunately for us, from the beginning of time our Higher Power has sung a melody in the depths of our being. It has been telling us to work on our wounded ego selves while also focusing on our numinous inner life. When we do so, the ego's dysfunctional ways of thinking will gradually fade into the background of our minds. The ego will gracefully bow out of its dominant and needy stance, and enter its rightful role as a temple in which the soul can do its creative work of imagination, insight, and illumination.

As you read further now, you'll be taking in the worlds of both your ego and your Higher Self. And, from this point on, as my "inner guide" has lovingly remarked, "May the intensity of your ego become the Joy of your soul!"

III

The Shift: From Unconscious to Conscious Living

It is the worst thing when [people] do not know how to escape from the old rut. It is dreadful when they approach new conditions with their old habits. Just as it is impossible to open a present-day lock with a medieval key, likewise it is impossible for [people] with old habits to unlock the door of the future.

—Agni Yoga Teachings

Entering the Heart
Through an Open Mind

If man wants to grasp the whole of reality
he must practice until he succeeds in awakening
other faculties which have always been there,
within him, but which are still asleep.

—Omraam Mikhael Aivanhov

The Heart is the fourth chakra, the meeting place of our two natures—the lower and higher selves. When I say the word "Heart" in front of a group, nearly everyone in the room comes up with at least two or three of the following associations: feelings, softness, feminine, being there for another, acceptance, forgiveness, true caring, love, vulnerability, Christ-like, warmth, soul, spirit, innocent, childlike. All these words are associated with the Heart. For the Heart is a human Ideal, a universal principle or archetype, that holds the qualities and powers to heal our wounded experiencer selves—the ego and its shadow.

And simultaneously, this level of consciousness takes us to a higher dimension of ourselves. It opens the gateway to the three higher chakras (five, six, and seven), or our Higher Self's nature. The fourth level of consciousness shifts us into whole new ways of being, where we feel—rather than acting on—our feelings and enter into a co-creative relationship with others and the world. *It is in the Heart that we make the shift from unconscious to conscious living.* Because It is a universal symbol with so much deep meaning, I will capitalize the word "Heart" from now on, unless I'm speaking of the anatomical or nonarchetypal heart.

Most cultures have honored the Heart as a Great Feminine Principle in some form and as the Creative Principle as well. The Heart is The Mother of the World, Goddess, Mother Mary, The Great Earth, Kwan Yin, Shakti, Binah, and more. It is the Great Nurturer, for It gives us continual life by lovingly carrying us in Its womb through all the stages of our lives.

The Heart is too big to be understood through the analytical intellect; it can only be known through metaphor: as a chasm, a womb, a temple, a vessel, a chamber, the center of the lotus, the breath of God. The Heart is a *space*—not a thing. And it is our absolute Truth. It is that place in consciousness where our identities are not just ideas we *think* about who we are; our identities here are intuitively *felt*. And in this way they (we) are *known*.

The Heart chakra is the first level of consciousness beyond our ego's limited intellect. When we enter the Heart, we are in an inner sacred temple where true forgiveness and understanding become possible. This is the consciousness level where we clear out our old hurts, where we grieve, and where we heal. For example, when dying to an old identity, you feel grief about the loss in the Heart; and when you're awakening to a new identity, you are nurtured by the Heart until you gradually stop feeling raw, exposed, and inexperienced.

In addition, the Heart imbues our ego's personal emotions with the soul's expanded sense of compassion for humanity, and in this way binds together the personal and transpersonal. For instance, if I've lost a child in death, I will feel my own grief as well as compassion for all mothers in the world who have lost children. All separateness dissolves in the Heart. Here we all know the same suffering, and we transcend boundaries of race or creed, or even species.

While the ego's intellect can study isolated facts without linking them, the Heart just naturally links them, seeing the relationships among them all. What often remains a mystery to the intellect is usually not a mystery to the Heart. Where the mind's intellectual arguments divide us, the Heart unites us; almost any controversy can be solved through Heart-felt communication. This is why when the going gets rough in a relationship, we may hear ourselves say to our partners, "Please come from your heart." Or, "Does this decision you're making have heart?" Moreover, scientific research has shown that therapists who work from the Heart are more effective than analytical and emotionally reserved therapists. I've described this Heart-felt therapy of high-functioning counselors in my earlier book, *Becoming Naturally Therapeutic.*

The Heart is our life-source, not only physically (for without the heart no other organ could function), but also emotionally, mentally, and spiritually. Contrary to the teachings of this culture, It is a far more powerful part of the Self than the mind. Again, we can never fully comprehend It intellectually, only intuitively; the Heart brings along with It a divine science! Even when you are in unconscious denial, the Heart will often activate right in your chest and tell you something doesn't feel quite right. A certain stimulus may strike you and you'll react without thinking; your body will alert you with symptoms such as a pounding or heavy heart, or nervous stomach. Without the Heart, the mind cannot really function: we've all seen how when our feelings are in turmoil, when our hearts are newly in love or breaking because of loss, we cannot think straight or solve a problem accurately. In addition, when our thoughts and intuition cannot agree, we feel pulled by the opposing forces of what the intellect thinks *ought* to be and what the Heart *knows* as true. We need to learn to listen to the Heart's soft voice.

But before we can come fully into Heart-consciousness (the fourth chakra), we must first open up our ego minds (the third chakra). Because it is limited, the intellect does not easily acknowledge or make room for the healing and unitive powers of the Heart. However, the Heart has a way of slipping in sometimes and catching the intellect off guard. But it is usually a tragedy, such as a heartbreak, that brings the Heart to the forefront, transforming the mind sometimes rather suddenly, shattering our mental constraints, and even changing our lives. In our work, it is quite touching when a normally rigid, dominating, and fearful man has an experience that opens his heart. (For this seems to be more difficult for men than for women.) He softens, his face changes, and tears flow down his cheeks. Then, he begins to have revelations about his loved ones and how much he's held himself away from their lives. Before our very eyes, these men transform, gaining gentleness and wisdom. But most of the time, the mind is in control. And because the intellect has been taught to think only "objectively"—in just two shades, black and white—it is restrictive in these four primary ways: 1) It sees life dualistically—as being either good or bad; 2) It sees the outer world and its conditions as our only ruler—our only legitimate life; 3) It is goal-oriented—seeing growth only as success; 4) It misunderstands the crucial healing concept of transcendence—seeing it as a sudden irrational stepping past what is concrete, legitimate, or scientific. The ego's intellect has disempowered the subjective nature of the Heart, which just naturally sees all colors and shades of gray.

However, the mind is paradoxically a gateway to the Heart; for it also has the power to open and take in new ideas, or to step aside and let go of its hold on us. It can think, and it can quit thinking and lead us to meditation. And it can soften its rigid boundaries and embrace the principles of wholeness. In the next chapter we'll see how the four egoistic ideas above can transform through four inspired revelations. And we will study each transforming mental shift in detail. We will see how the ego's mind can merge with a higher Mind—one that thinks beyond the confines of linear, left-brain thought. While the Heart is the feminine aspect of our Higher Self, the Mind is the Heart's masculine counterpart and the Higher Self's intellect. And It is the bridge into the Heart's processes. As you'll learn in the "Heartwork" section of the book, at the fourth stage of awakening we fully enter the Heart as Mind and Heart become one, bringing us the powers of Wisdom and Love as well as those of purification, invocation, creative imagination, recognition, and vision.

When the Mind says "yes" to the Heart, we accept our feeling nature and intuition as valid, and our soul can more fully express. The Heart then becomes our agent of transformation. Like an alchemist, It takes the dross of our experiences and magically refines it into the qualities of our Higher Self. Our unconscious and stagnant ways of relating are reborn as true passion and creativity. The Heart provides vision and inspiration to the Mind; and the Mind, in return, makes the Heart's mystical ways conceptually legitimate to the ego-dominated intellect.

There is no turning back once we begin to see with the eyes of the Heart. It's as though a whole new life takes up residence in our bodies. We enter into a new universe, one that is both familiar and yet brand-new. For it is through the Heart that all our personal sorrows can rise up and meet a greater life, a deeper understanding, and a more powerful love. It is through the magical mystery of "Heartwork" that not only we, but our whole world, is transformed:

> To behold with the eyes of the Heart; to listen with the ears of the Heart to the roar of the world; to peer into the future with the comprehension of the Heart; to remember the culminations of the past through the Heart; thus must one impetuously advance upon the path of ascent. Creativeness encompasses the fiery potentiality, and is impregnated with the sacred fire of the Heart. (Agni Yoga Teachings, *Heart*)

Let's look more closely now at how our transforming minds open and make way for the Heart to enter. To learn to live "from the Heart," we need to once and for all say good-bye to the lower intellect's limited rule and its codependent ways of defining us by our conditions. We must learn to think and feel anew.

The Transforming Mind

Be not conformed to this world: but be ye
transformed by the renewing of your mind, that
ye may prove what is that good, and acceptable,
and perfect will of God.

—Romans 12:2

The mind is an incredible mechanism. It is the filter that sits
between our conscious and unconscious lives, defining what is
acceptable and real. Once the mind decides what is legitimate, it
creates a mental boundary. This boundary then circumscribes our
universe and becomes our limitation. We unconsciously say, "This
is all the 'reality' I can handle." Webster's *Third New English
Dictionary* provides a perfect opening definition:

> [The mind is] that which reasons; the doer of intellectual work. It
> organizes groups of events which it perceives, classifies, transforms
> and coordinates. . . . It is a biological organism but is not organic
> in nature. It has to be experienced as emotions, imagination or will.
> It can act as an organizing whole or split into dissociative parts.

What the dictionary doesn't say is that the mind is a magician. It
serves as both the creator and the slayer of truth. According to the
Buddha, the mind is a conjurer of both the unreal and the real; it
can create sickness, and it can create cures. It can make things

114

seem ugly, or call them beautiful. It latches onto ideas and makes them your world: it decides what your life is. If the mind were always clear and in touch with absolute Truth, it would be an impeccable spiritual guide.

Enlightened beings possess such a mind: they make a distinction between the ego's intellect and "Big Mind" or Mind, which is Jung's collective unconscious mind and which they tap into for greater wisdom. But, quite frankly, most of us are not even close to being fully enlightened and do not possess a clear thinking apparatus. As we learned during our study of the third chakra, our intellects are often contaminated with fables based on undigested half-truths or complete falsehoods about what life is and who we are. Nevertheless, we often worship these doctrines, convictions, ideas, and beliefs, giving them authority over our lives: our all-powerful intellect becomes a "false god." In order to function positively, the mind must remain a slave—never the master—of our consciousness. The human mind must learn to live in surrender to the higher Mind.

For the mind to become enlightened, it must die to its old and outworn ways. But let me warn you: *One of the hardest addictions to release (or die to) is our addiction to dogma, judgments, and opinions.* To die to what we've believed was true is a desolate experience; we can become confused and depressed. We may even feel at some points that we are going mad: But as I once heard Stanislav Grof say in a lecture, "Losing the limitations of your mind is not the same as losing your mind."

Paradoxically, this loss is the beginning of our awakening into Truth. When we awaken, we see that our former beliefs were only limited thinking based on inconclusive data. But just as the alcoholic who lets go of alcohol must feel empty and lost for a time, so must we who are addicted to thoughts and beliefs (which is most of us). In fact, the mind must release any addiction before we can heal: it must say and believe, "I no longer need this outer negative influence in my life to feel high." This is true of all addictions, whether to certain ideas, chemicals, sex, or relation-ships. Transformation will always happen first in the mind.

And so to shift from unconscious to conscious living, we must begin with our thoughts. The Buddha taught that we all live in a kind of hypnosis and at some point must all be de-hypnotized. We must become aware that *all* is mind: pain and pleasure; birth and death. Once this is truly seen, the conjurer can no longer function. The mind abandons its assumptions. And what's left over is Truth.

In the New Testament, the name for this change of mind is the Greek word *metanoia*. This refers to the process of repentance, where one is willing to become submissive to a Higher Power's will as opposed to the ego's will. I believe the word "repentance"— which most people today think means "being sorry"—has gotten all mixed up with the concept of sin. Actually, "repentance" originated from the Latin word *repoenitet*, which means "a mental revolt that affects one's whole way of being." It is the "born again" experience many Christians speak of, but it has a much broader context than most people realize. The *metanoia* experience is an ancient and universal concept underpinning *all* true spiritual paths. It is the *felt experience* that accompanies any kind of mental conversion. And this change of mind is also a change of heart. In the words of Jesus, "As a man thinketh in his heart, so is he." We become "a new creature and old things are passed away: Behold all things are become new!" (II Cor. 5:17)

Metanoia is the shift from being intellectual only to becoming filled with the soul-quality of *creativity* or *active intelligence*. Instead of being a passive recipient of others' ideas (a form of codependence), we begin to formulate wisdom gained from our own direct experiences with life, our truth. When we begin to act from this intelligence, we connect with the Mind of our Higher Power. At this stage in our awakening, our soul decides to stand free. The mind opens and says "I am willing!" And we become re-aligned with a bigger and higher Truth that can encompass our whole Self, both our ego and our soul. This is a crucial step in the journey from codependence to co-creation.

The Four Mental Shifts

To access our higher Mind, I believe we must make four basic shifts in our thought patterns. When these shifts first manifest in our lives, we may feel the pain that comes with any death, no matter how necessary. Keep in mind (no pun intended!) that you are moving into a new way of being. I hope the models offered here will guide you. And if you don't feel you are ready to experience *metanoia*, use this section to help you recognize some of the thought patterns that may be at the root of your codependence. The first shift I will explicate can *alone* create transcendence of our old ways, and for this reason it will command most of our attention. The three shifts that follow are spin-offs from the first, but they, too, are vital to our transformation.

Shift Number One: The shift from a dualistic to a triadic model of the Self.

I've noticed that when I can stop for a minute, breathe, and let go of my obsessions, my mind naturally performs a more unitive function: It elevates me above my situation, enabling me to see from the observer self's point of view—that of the "winged bird" I introduced you to earlier. I can see my situation with perspective. And I stop judging the people involved, myself and others; I am lifted out of dualism, the place where we all view things in opposition, where we see others, but mostly ourselves, as the bad self or the good self, the evil or the saintly one.

Many of us with codependence issues live much of our lives in dualism. We try to escape the more ambivalent, gray areas of life by seeing only black and white. We want to be free of pain; we want easy answers. And so we take on a particular set of conditions and roles and become identified, rejecting the other parts of who we are: I'm *this*, but I would never be *that*! This is the beginning of illusion—our loss of Self. This is dualism. A model of this limited self-image would look like this:

Bad Self	either/or	Good Self
addicted		straight
codependent		self-reliant
Don Juanism		moral and faithful
selfish		saintly
neurotic		balanced and appropriate
stupid		always right, sometimes genius

We often see ourselves as either being one or the other. But none of these polarities will ever provide us with growth. For when someone tries to live any polarity, especially trying to be a good self only, that person will have little substance and will behave inauthentically. No one feels comfortable with or trusts these kinds of people. They are always seemingly okay with whatever is occurring, but we never have a clue about what's really going on inside them. Their attitude is, "Well, if you've got a problem with this, it's your problem, not mine. I don't deal with things like this anymore." Later, we hear this person was angry or hurt, but we received only the indirect fallout.

All metaphysical or spiritual teachings speak to this common human difficulty, which is essentially the predicament of the battle of the opposites. And this kind of repression even happens to people we perceive as great teachers or leaders. Many of us have heard about gurus who have a harem or very young lovers, or are beating women into sexual submission. Or we've seen great master teachers put down their devotees with an attitude of contempt or fail to show up at all due to an advanced case of alcoholism. Because these high teachers have denied their shadow, they've been forced to act it out.

For the so-called "bad self" is our impure shadow. And as we've seen, whenever we deny our unwanted parts they go underground, only to be acted out in unconscious ways. Our lives then are spent swinging on a pendulum from good to bad, high to low: we live in dualism, along with all its trappings—competition, all-or-none or scarcity thinking, judgment, perfectionism, victimhood, and so forth. Nothing can ever be resolved when we are in dualism, for we can't even see the real issues that need resolving. Until the pendulum stops and rests in the center so we can align with our Higher Self, we will only re-create our faulty patterns, cycling in them forever. Hence the old saying, "Problems are never solved on the same level upon which they were created." Once we are centered, we can rise above the polarizations in our lives. New possibilities will present themselves to us when we adopt a higher vision and a larger perspective. We need an expanded model of the Self that includes a third party, the Higher Self, our representative of wholeness. We need to abandon the dualistic mode and take on the triadic view of the Self, which looks like this:

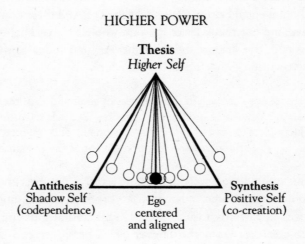

HIGHER POWER
|
Thesis
Higher Self

Antithesis
Shadow Self
(codependence)

Ego
centered
and aligned

Synthesis
Positive Self
(co-creation)

The shadow is the addicted ego, and the positive self is the nonaddicted ego, or the integrated self. It carries forward the healed shadow's substance while simultaneously aligning with the Higher Power's energies we experience as the Higher Self. And if you look above, the Higher Power is honoring the entire process. It's looking down on the horizon and saying, "Hey, all three of you make a team here on earth!" This is why the Triangle is the classic symbol for creativity: It brings together three points and unifies them; *thesis*

(Higher Self), *antithesis* (the shadow, or deficient ego's experiences), and *synthesis* (the positive self, or integrated ego). In creative pursuits, such as designing a new building, the thesis is the original creative design that we *perceive;* the antithesis is there to bring to the surface any impurities that might cause the design to fail and which we must *recognize,* or make conscious; and the synthesis is the culmination of all this well-thought-out planning, which we *declare,* or become a statement of.

From the triadic view, we see through the eyes of our soul, and we note that sometimes we're a partial or phony self but at other times we're real. We see that *both* our ego natures (the shadow and the positive self) reach out into the world to connect and love: one, by being needy and demanding; the other, by simply celebrating Love with all other equal beings. Quite a difference! And these contradictory selves are but two sides of the one whole Self, or Higher Self, which is both the shadow and the light. As Jung said so profoundly in a letter written to his friend, Pere Lachat:

> . . . there is no answer to the question of good and evil; there is only an incurable separation of the opposites. . . . It seems to me the Holy Spirit's task [is] . . . to reconcile and reunite the opposites . . . through a special development of the human soul.

From this unified view we can see our negative patterns and roles with clarity and without judgment. And this, of course, allows us to change our patterns if we so choose. This mental shift empowers us as co-creators. From the Higher Self's perspective, I do not judge my weaknesses and vulnerabilities as "bad"; I simply note them for what they are—with compassion. I see that I'm not perfect. But at the same time, I know that I am also a mature person. I'm doing the best I can and am willing to grow and learn. I quit feeling shame and allow myself to see and honor my childish or threatened self, which just naturally has some character flaws.

As mentioned earlier, I was born two months premature, so tiny I was nearly dead. I can't imagine not loving my vulnerable self and wanting to nurture her with great amounts of parental love. She barely survived her own birth and remembers quite well this precarious state of her barely evident beginnings. I am both vulnerable *and* strong, capable of being both selfish *and* selfless. When vulnerable, I may become needy and act out. When this is occurring, I need understanding, not judgment. I need to remind myself of my strengths, and to see that when I've gotten all caught up in some drama or conflict, I've temporarily forgotten who I am. In the next chapter, when we enter into the ways of the Heart, we'll learn how to better cope with these kinds of upsets when we lose touch with who we are. For now, let's continue with our exploration of the projecting and sometimes uncompromising human mind.

Again, before we can fully integrate our shadow, we need to take a step beyond simply accepting this self; we must recognize its sacred function in our lives. For the shadow is a necessary agent in our awakening and a crucial part of our creativity. Let's look at the Triangle of the Self again in this light:

The Three Arms of Creativity

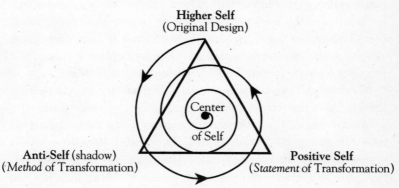

Higher Self
(Original Design)

Center of Self

Anti-Self (shadow)
(*Method* of Transformation)

Positive Self
(*Statement* of Transformation)

From the above, you can see that the anti-self—the addict, the codependent, the possessive and jealous bitch, the hysteric, the shrinking violet, the perpetrator, or the victim—is not who we are; these roles are merely the *method* through which we grow into our wholeness. They are different faces of the misshapen shadow, making up one of the three vital elements of creativity. For the shadow is the "holy grit" that the Higher Self and the positive self rub against to create something (someone) new. It is like all those pieces of clay the sculptor peels away, or integrates, to shape his work of art.

According to the triadic model of the Self, we participate in our own creation. We "art ourselves," as so beautifully stated by Milenko Matanovic in his book, *Lightworks*. And like the sculptor, we explicate our work of art, our Self; we integrate the fragments of ourselves that match our Truth, while casting off the parts that don't. We become our positive self. *And it is the positive ego—the one who lives right here in this dimension and represents our Higher Power authentically—that we call a soul-infused personality.*

From "above," we thank our anti-selves for playing their part, seeing them as sacred agents in our transformation. We honor these little culprits for causing us pain so we could get the point. And recognizing them, we learn to accelerate our energies and spin them all toward more rarified forms, our Higher Power's wholistic ways of being: superficiality becomes authenticity; competition becomes cooperation; judgment becomes nonattachment (although our shadow's ways still may crop up from time to time). From this higher view, the shadow has found its divine intention as part of the human saga and can thereby become spiritualized. From "the bigger picture," its sacred function is laid bare.

In our workshops for professional therapists and others seeking knowledge of the self-transformational process, we sometimes offer a "shadow dance," where the participants come dressed as their most miserable and despised selves. They dance sometimes wildly and sometimes timidly, in whatever way seems spontaneous and real. We've seen everything from a man with big pimples and Band-Aids on his face who goes around all evening trying to elicit sympathy from the women, to a woman walking around in an ugly bathrobe, curlers in her hair and mascara running down her face, oblivious to all those around her. And we've seen that these simple sessions leave participants feeling lighter, calmer, and more complete. They come away, not only feeling that their shadows have been accepted by the others in the group—and that they're not so bad after all—but also with insight into how their shadows may have been useful to them. The oblivious woman saw that her "zoning" behavior had enabled her to balance a busy life full of giving to others; it was a necessary protection. And the pimply man realized he would be accepted by women without constantly reminding them of his weaknesses. Without his shadow, he might not have had this unifying experience.

Once we learn to do this inner work, our shadow will no longer affect us when our backs are turned. We'll see from the observer's point of view how we are both the experiencer and the one creating the experience. We are "both/and," not "either/or." When we transcend duality, even for a moment, we can explicate the positive ego and its shadow and own it all—watching the duality these two selves create *in vivo* while we get the point.

A Note About Positive Thinking

Please keep in mind that what most people think of as positive thinking is not the solution to our dualistic ways. Positive thinking *only* will not bring us truth, for it tries to ignore the painful or negative side, thus creating denial and repression. Positive thinking, as it is commonly practiced, still operates on only one side of the pole. It insists that "everything's wonderful" when it really isn't. When someone's child is diagnosed with a life-threatening illness, someone might say "Oh, isn't this a wondrous blessing? Such an opportunity for growth!" This is a total denial of the terror and agony of potential loss. It is simply nonsense. But it can be dangerous, leading to a deadening of the self.

True positive thinking means focusing in the direction of what is life-giving, even while something or someone is in the process of being negative or even dying. It is about being willing to face every new moment, any circumstance as it unfolds, with the hope and strength to deal with *all* that is occurring—both the terror and the bliss of transformation. In Twelve Step work, this is known as "taking it one day at a time"—and sometimes even one moment at a time. For example, in true grief counseling, a mother whose child is catastrophically ill would be helped to feel all her feelings as they arise. If a block or denial crops up, the therapist would help her focus on the block itself through inner work: feeling her way into it, symbolizing it, dialoguing with it, and discovering its meaning or purpose. For blocks, too, contain keys to the growth. In time, this mother will have a deeper faith in life's processes, having discovered that she has the endurance necessary for the task at hand.

We can never know what strengths and revelations might be on the other side of our fears until we face them and feel them all the way through. *True* positive thinking is the mental stance of surrender, simply trusting the process. We learn to accept what *is*. And we have faith in the bigger picture; even when we cannot see it clearly, we trust that it's always there and that, if not now, someday we'll stand tall enough to see it.

Codependence Is an Evolutionary Function

Codependence is an illness only from the dualistic view. In unitive consciousness, there is nothing bad about codependence. And in order to understand and overcome its dualistic patterns—our separateness from others, how we compare ourselves to them, feel less than or needy for them, or value them more than ourselves—we must switch to the triadic perspective.

As you just saw from the previous diagram, when we are in the triad, codependence as part of our shadow is the very *method* of our transformation—our "grist for the mill." Here we can accept our codependence and stop blaming ourselves for being human. For how can we recognize Love if we never experience unlove? How do we learn our true and purposeful way of loving if we never get to practice and make mistakes? And how do we truly learn to stand in our own power if we never feel the devastation of losing our real selves to another? The triadic model of the Self enables us to embrace codependence as our "teacher"—a means to our transformation rather than a diseased inadequacy. In this light, codependence clearly has a sacred function.

These ageless words from the poem *The Ladder of St. Augustine* by Henry Wadsworth Longfellow come to mind:

> Standing on what too long we bore
> With shoulders bent and downcast eyes,
> We may discern—unseen before—
> A path to higher destinies.
>
> Nor deem the irrevocable Past,
> As wholly wasted, wholly vain
> If, rising on its wrecks, at last
> To something nobler we attain.

This is such a simple concept, and yet it seems to have gotten lost in all the drama and dualism of much of the thinking on codependence.

The shift to the triadic model—and all the shifts in this chapter—will occur naturally once you begin your inner work. When you consciously enter into the healing of your own duality, your mind will literally bring home to you the experiences you need in order to stand in your own Truth—and sometimes this happens even when you're in unconscious denial. For instance, if you believe something erroneous—such as "all men are dangerous"; or "all Asian people are intellectually inferior"; or "all women who get pregnant before marriage are harlots"—the lessons will come home to you in ways you cannot ignore. Your favorite daughter will marry a person of Asian heritage or get pregnant at sixteen. Or, you will undergo some other very painful experience whereby you'll be confronted with your own untruths and be forced to face them head on. If you want to retain your connection with your daughter, or overcome the pain of any such experience, you will have to recognize your mental attachments (or addictions) and surrender them to your higher, more wholistic Self. It's only through the painful lessons of dropping judgment that our "either/or's" become "both/and's."

Codependence, or any other dualistic way of living in the "war of the opposites," eventually causes so much friction in our lives that a brand-new quality is created within us, just as two sticks rubbed together create a flame. For instance, a theme in my life may be the struggle between cowardice and courage: as I fail in my efforts to be courageous, I will eventually develop the quality *bravery* from my very attempts at it. Or if I'm rocking between too much emotionalism and too little feeling, an emotional *steadfastness* is honed as I learn through my relational experiences. Put simply, when we're conscious, we learn from our mistakes. Another example: I have learned that when I'm needy and grasping for love, and my emotions "tell on me," I'm usually rejected instead of loved: people fear being trapped by needy, intense emotional states. Now, I am learning to embrace my neediness and approach people only when I can clearly communicate what I want from them. As a result, my relations are deeper and stronger than ever.

For the triadic view can transform our relationships. In codependence I worship you, my lover or my friend, rather than my Higher Power. In effect, I am asking you to be as perfect as my Higher Power is! And every time you don't live up to the Ideal, I might unconsciously punish you (perhaps even leave you for someone else "more perfect," never realizing the dynamic was my own issue). Or, I might get caught up in glaring steadily at some weakness of yours, and drive you crazy trying to "fix" it—when, in fact, I've got weaknesses and issues of my own calling for my attention. I'm not your Higher Power. Focusing on your faults keeps me stuck in my codependent activity—fixing you! There is no creativity in this. And there's built-in failure in this faulty behavior, for we are never capable of fixing anyone besides ourselves.

But we human spirits just love to throw ourselves into things, to worship and adore! And the Triangle offers us a healthy, growthful way of doing so. Worship means "to be magnified by the image that is pulling you"; our vibration is lifted to the same frequency as that which we worship. This is why we get nowhere when we worship someone on our same level of consciousness. Worshiping others fogs our windshields, and we lose ourselves in one another. It is a misuse of the sacred quality of devotion. But when we send a Higher Power our devotional energy, It reciprocates. In my life, making the Higher Power a viable and consistent Third Party in my relationships brings me Someone I *can* surrender to and emulate. Then I relate to others as true equals, to whom I should never give my power (unless the other is a completely evolved saint with no ego left at all!).

When one of your relationships becomes a triad instead of a dyad, a spiritual purpose begins to unfold. The two of you come together and, behold! a third "something" is created that is bigger than both of you. Sometimes the two of you are involved in meaningful and purposeful life's work that aids humanity and unfolds your future in a spiritual direction. Or sometimes a couple may take the form of two musicians who are jamming so completely, they don't even realize they are creating a masterpiece. For that moment, they have a "sacred marriage," and their audience will feel deeply inspired. This sacred work does not have to be about becoming famous public figures or saving the world; your life's work may be the simple and private unfolding of a loving and meaningful family life that no one ever notices much but you. Yet, a higher purpose will supersede your ego's ordinary ways and become the organizing principle you focus upon: you and your mate's differences or little arguments will lose their drama, requiring less of your energy; instead of feeling anxious, you will feel inspired when working together on your relationship.

I've noticed that this is true for me. Often, I'm just too busy with more important things than to be preoccupied with picking on my partner or noticing how I'm not being taken care of exactly as I want to be. Something more inspiring commands my attention, and things seem to settle down on their own. If I simply choose to watch myself when I want to react, claiming my feelings as my own process, usually by the time I get around to fussing, the issue has resolved itself. For time often has a way of doing this for us. As long as we are willing *to keep our issues conscious* and not go into repression and denial, the concept of triadic relationships can be quite healing. Mentally, the shift looks like this:

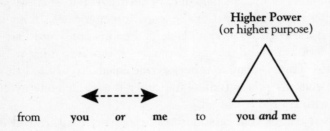

Higher Power
(or higher purpose)

from   **you**   *or*   **me**   to   **you** *and* **me**

Shift Number Two: The inner life determines outer experiences, not the other way around.

In this modern age, most of us are mesmerized by all the tinsel and glamour of appearances and material rewards. We are focused on the outer world. Yet, I want to reemphasize that *the truth of life lies within.* I'm convinced that the outer life that mainstream science honors as *real* is merely where we learn our lessons in living. And the inner way, which, unfortunately, much of science dismisses as "subjective" and hence *unreal*, is actually how we grow.

The mental shift from outer to inner focus places us in direct touch with the Truth of our being. It is the process of shifting from *ego-dominance* to *soul-dominance* I've been referring to throughout the book. Here we are more focused on the *meaning* and *spiritual purpose* of events than we are on getting all tangled up in the content of our lives. In Abraham Maslow's self-actualizing theory, this is the shift from content to process. And this shift clears our vision so that we can recognize our inner spiritual urges—which will ultimately heal our codependent ways.

Intrinsic Spirituality:
We Are Spiritual Beings!

When people tell you they've had a spiritual experience, they do not usually mean a Messiah has arrived in the flesh to take them on a bus to heaven. They are describing an inner event, what Maslow called "peak experiences." And these numinous experiences deeply affect our consciousness. In fact, many transpersonal theorists believe that consciousness is the *razor's edge where spirit and matter meet*. These spiritual events can change our feelings about an outer event, giving it a whole new meaning—or they can even transform our entire worldview. Let me give you an example of what I mean:

One evening during a crucial point in a personal crisis, I was sitting in my bedroom looking out on my deck. I was reflecting on a personal loss and thinking hopelessly that maybe life just wasn't worth it. I was raised a Christian, and as a child I would call on Jesus when I was hurting or lonely. Jesus was an inner personal friend. He would come to me and offer me solace. As an adult, I'd let go of my connection with Jesus, having explored many religions, East and West; I had not thought of Him for quite awhile. In this moment, in my grief, I was staring at a bird feeder hanging on the deck. In the dusk, its outline was an obvious shadow against the darkening sky. As I looked at it through my tears, it began to change. It started moving toward me, and as I looked at it, the hole where the birds feed became a womb, and I saw what I believed to be the Christ Child enfolded in this circular space, a babe *in utero* inside the Mother Mary's body. It came over and merged right into me as I stared in amazement. Later, I realized I'd gone into a trance of some kind and had received a very special blessing. It was as though for a moment I became this Christ Child and It became me! I had a rare moment of being within the purity of Christ's essence. My heart began to lighten tremendously, expanding in compassion and forgiveness. This was a felt experience within my chest; my sorrow was lifted.

This is intrinsic spirituality in action. From these kinds of nonordinary experiences (and the 1987 Greeley polls reported that 67 percent of the people in this country have had them), we develop new qualities: unshakable faith, deep compassion, serenity, wisdom, self-acceptance, and loss of fear of death.

Intrinsic spirituality keeps us able to respond to our inner source or Higher Power. It is a form of religion devoid of codependent trappings; we don't rely on some outside "other" to make our spiritual life work for us. We see that the Truth is within us, and we can get up every morning and say to ourselves, as in the Alice Bailey teachings, "Let Reality govern my every thought and Truth be the master of my life." This is a life-giving affirmation, one that will keep us on the path of awakening. This inner God is the God Imminent of theology, known in Christianity as the Holy Ghost, and It will not violate any religious philosophy that I know of—for all religions believe that God is Truth. As the ancient oral teachings of the Sarmouni Brotherhood (G. I. Gurdjieff's teachers) proclaim:

> There is no God but Reality. To seek Him
> elsewhere is the action of the fall.

People who are in touch with their inner spirituality are known as mystics; they are *knowers*. People who seek the spiritual in the outer world are theologians; they are *believers*. They often study *about* spirituality, rather than experiencing it themselves.

When people begin awakening to inner spirituality, they often find the stiff and unrelenting dogma of externally oriented orthodoxy no longer satisfies their yearnings. For many organized religions actually violate the spiritual teachings upon which they were originally based. In times of personal crisis, churches, ministers, or rabbis may not be there for people and can sometimes let them down, dispelling for all time the romantic illusions many have had about these leaders and their doctrines. They see that these faiths are not the holy panaceas they purport to be. I know of recovering alcoholics who were expelled from their churches when the congregation discovered they had a drinking problem. I also know women suffering from the pain of sexual promiscuity who were told they were beyond redemption for their sinful ways. One of my good friends, who had been a Sunday school teacher for over twenty years, found herself relieved of her duties one day after an ordinary marital crisis hit the rumor mill. She was no longer "perfect" and therefore couldn't be allowed to teach others.

Many people who come to my workshops and lectures confess to me—whispering in my ear—that they have been members of a metaphysical community for years, but cannot share this with friends, coworkers, or even with certain family members. They fear being labeled a heretic or a fanatical "true believer"—even in the 1990s! And they are right. Certain elements of our society are livid about such inner teachings. Even great modern religious scholars such as Meister Eckhart, Teilhard de Chardin, and Matthew Fox have been excommunicated or silenced by their religious institutions for their beliefs in the inner spiritual life.

As a society, we haven't begun to develop guidelines for living in the world as spiritual beings. We've got a lot of work to do. And most of it begins in the mind. For when we *mentally* shift our search for identity inward or upward (for they are the same direction) where we can commune with our Higher Power, we gain a new understanding of who we are. We see for certain that we are not human beings seeking a spiritual experience; we are spiritual beings longing to spiritualize our humanness. And our outer lives gradually will begin to match our inner lives: our codependent relations will clear. For the voice of the Higher Power can reach us in the silence of the inner Self.

The Cross: A Symbol of the Inner and Outer Worlds

According to Joseph Campbell, the cross symbolizes the way in which the outer world and the inner world meet. It has four points, plus a fifth in the middle, which is the transcendent point. In Christianity, Christ is the Savior of humanity, who models how to transcend the opposites by standing steady in the center of the

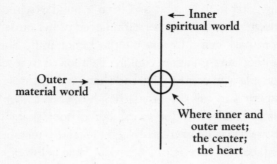

cross, interpenetrated by the energies of both the vertical and horizontal arms—the inner and outer worlds. When we can see this picture in our minds (placing ourselves on the cross), we gain a sense of how we are influenced by both the outer and inner at once.

However, this symbol does not belong to Christianity alone. Anthropologist Angeles Arrien has found in her cross-cultural studies that virtually every culture uses the cross as a symbol for our two dimensions of consciousness, the material and the spiritual. In American Indian cultures, the four points of the medicine wheel are usually expressed as North, South, East, and West. The well-known Celtic cross, which precedes the Christian era, has a circle in the center, symbolizing the surrendered Self. And in the field of psychology, the Psychosynthesis school of thought developed by Roberto Assagioli also uses the cross as a way to distinguish the ordinary from the sublime.

Most people think of the cross as a symbol or archetype for suffering or sacrifice, as it is in Christianity. Hence, in order to truly understand the universal symbol of the cross, we must realize that "sacrifice" is not the frightening concept most of us think it is. It comes from the word *sacer*, which means "to make holy." The word "sacerdocy" actually means "priesthood." In the ancient Greek mystery schools "sacrifice" referred to the portion of a religious ceremony where the neophyte was set apart from the masses and made to stand alone in the temple and listen to his true voice of authority, the God within. This "inner chamber" is called meditation and it is where we are infused with spiritual potency. It is here that we learn through direct instruction how to use our God-given powers in loving relationship to all things.

"Sacrifice" can play a purposeful role in our growth. We just have to know how to do it appropriately. For example, we must relinquish our old ideas when new ones are trying to take their place: we've probably not thought of this as sacrifice, but it is. Letting go of our cherished but limited attitudes and false beliefs is a conscious *voluntary* sacrifice, known in the language of the Twelve Steps as "turning our lives over to a Higher Power" and "living in surrender, one day at a time." This is sacrifice on the vertical arm of the cross, in the inner spiritual realm. And it is the only true form of sacrifice, for it has a higher purpose. We must never sacrifice on the horizontal arm of the cross; it is a dangerous misuse of a holy process. When we focus codependently on others, we are unconsciously sacrificing our beings on the horizontal plane, in the outer world—a form of cannibalism (and a sacrificial rite to be avoided at all costs).

Now I will back up for awhile and explain this misunderstood process further. In the horizontal dimension, we develop *expertise in the outer material world*, while the vertical provides *psycho-spiritual healing and stature*, which happens on the inner side of life. Codependence unfolds on the horizontal arm of the cross, along the time-line of our ordinary daily lives. Co-creation unfolds on the vertical arm of the cross, where our creativity is sparked by our inner source. In co-creation, we bring the knowledge gained from the vertical dimension down into our ordinary realities, and combine it all in the Heart (our center, and the point where the vertical and horizontal meet). The shift from outer merging to inner absorption is food for the starving mystic—and the ultimate cure for codependence and addiction to outer things.

On the vertical side, which corresponds to the triadic view, we can see *in vivo* how our conditions unfold, and we can stop in the middle of an activity and see a bigger picture, for the observer self functions in this vertical dimension. For example, I may be in the midst of bawling out my child, insisting on having my way with great intensity. I might even become emotionally abusive. Suddenly, from within me a greater Self quietly speaks: "Jacquie, what's the big deal? Remember, your love for your child right now is more important than completing this minor task. Something larger is at stake." And through this deeper understanding, I'm momentarily brought out of my robotish unconscious ways, yesterday's "grit": "My mother always made *me* do it, so you have to do it, too!"

In our horizontal lives, we live through the roles we play in our everyday situations: husband, child, mother, lover, boss, hero, helper, friend. These roles are designed by the efficient ego, so that it can feel safe, pleased, or important (the imbalanced lower chakras). And they invite us to fall into the trap of codependently focusing on each other as objects of gratification. Then, we lose sight of the forest from bumping into each tree—each person and event in our lives. We stumble around as though blindfolded, feeling victimized by every unhappy condition. Focusing solely on the outer life eventually gets us down; we become unconsciously caught up in the nitty-gritty, frantic activity of our "fast food/bargain basement" mentality.

According to Jung, when we go inward and activate the vertical arm, we're thrown into a mysterious creative process that spins us into higher levels of consciousness at such an accelerated rate we can't even tell we're moving! Yet we know something is happening; our lives go through amazing changes. We are in a timeless state! Time vanishes because we are completely focused on the vanishing point—the here and now; no part of ourselves is standing outside, diffusing our energies.

The horizontal without the benefit of the vertical is a seedbed for unconscious living. Without the vertical we are lost—for it is consciousness itself! But the opposite is true as well: A vertical focus *only* can lead to the unreality of "spiritual by-pass," meaning we try to transcend our conditions by latching onto spirituality, denying and ignoring our mundane lives. When we live in these two realms at once, we feel balanced and in harmony with our Truth. Like flowing down a river, just enjoying where the various currents carry us, we take each situation in life as it comes, with an attitude that is simultaneously responsible and carefree. Our eyes are wide open as we involve in our outer lives, yet we are meditative and serene inside.

The vertical arm never moves away from the present moment; it only moves up or down. It deepens our experience or lifts us toward higher and more wholistic or *spiritual* ways of dealing with an issue. In fact, from this unified position, most conflicts dissipate in the light of love and understanding. And like a magnet, the vertical arm brings to the surface any unfinished *psychological* business to be felt through, made conscious, understood, loved, and accepted. This is why it's called the *psycho-spiritual* arm of the cross. (I will speak more about this inner work later on in the book.)

When someone learns to live in both dimensions of the Self at once—the ordinary and the spiritual—he or she becomes a "walker between two worlds," one who lives in the world but is not of it, and who inspires others to follow their own inner path. When we make this shift, we become co-creators, leaving behind our codependent stances. We learn to let go of outworn behaviors and thoughts, to follow the *true* dictates of "sacrifice."

Invocation:
The Prayer for Co-Creators

Calling on spiritual resources when we feel frightened, uncertain, or in trouble is what we usually call *prayer*. However, this is often the ego's way of relating to a Higher Power, as "helpless child" seeking truth from "Big Daddy" in the sky. We ask Higher Power to help us because we are feeling inadequate to do the job. Prayer can be merely a reaching outward, seeking an "answer" from outside, from Someone we don't feel a part of. This Greater Someone is often totally beyond us. A prayer usually begins with "Please, dear God, help me. . . ." It is founded upon the notion that we are "creature" and God is "creator," and there is a great big gap in between. Prayer relies on the Higher Power exclusively.

Invocation is another way to pray, and it is much more active. It is a calling out to Spirit to give us our task, with a conviction that we will do *our part* as co-creators to manifest what it is we are asking for. There is a common understanding between "Creator" and "co-creator" that each needs the other in order to do the work of creation. Invocation is founded upon the belief that we are a part of the Creator, with no barrier in between. When praying, the emphasis is on the answer. When invoking, the emphasis is on the call. Both activate on the vertical arm of the cross; but in prayer we are stuck in the vertical, often unable to bring the spiritual down into the material, horizontal world. By invoking we can make the vertical activate in our everyday lives. We ourselves are "Sparks of the Divine."

Jung believed it is crucial that we take responsibility for our part of creation; he felt this was a very important step beyond the "Christocentrism" of modern Christianity. I've noticed that in many cases prayer has become "cosmic codependence," and sometimes even a cop-out: "I waited for God to answer, but since no answer came, I just gave up." The words "I've turned it over" then become empty, as nothing in life ever seems to change. Invocation assumes that we are the hands and feet of the Creator. I believe it is the prayer for a new era, one in which souls are awakening and recognizing that we all have much work to do.

Invoking our spiritual nature moves us further into conscious living. When we feel a relationship is not working, that perhaps we are sacrificing ourselves to another person in codependence, we can intently ask for the right to know Truth, and the vertical arm of the cross will ignite. We can stand in the center of the cross, willing to take responsibility for whatever is revealed. In this manner our unconscious relationships can be exposed to the light of Truth, and even though this awareness is usually quite painful, we learn to co-create a new response. We can invoke a specific quality, such as spiritual discrimination or balanced emotions. But be careful what you decree: for it *will* come into your life! And then, you will be put through whatever you must learn in order to fulfill your demand. When we invoke something, we stand within it while it feeds us its qualities—we take it on.

Here is an invocation that will work—if you feel ready to take on this responsibility right now:

"I Am Willing . . . !"
An Invocation

Begin by reciting these words:

"I am willing to see my codependence patterns, to accept them for what they are, and to no longer allow them to rule me.

"I am willing to become responsible for myself and respondable to my Self from this point forward. I ask for help in this adventurous quest, and with a grateful attitude I will persist until this pattern is dissolved."

Now, close your eyes and visualize yourself sitting in repose in the center of the cross, in the Heart, and feel your chief codependent pattern take you over—the way you lose yourself in someone else or give yourself away. Feel this state of consciousness become your very way of being. . . . *Now, with your eyes still closed, picture yourself rising above it and see it for what it is. Allow it to become a symbol you can observe. . . . When it appears, give it a name. And as you see this symbol you have named, notice that it is* not *you! You are the one observing!*

Now, within your inner mind, see yourself toss this codependent pattern or symbol into a mass of fire. . . . Watch it become aflame and gradually disintegrate into a powdery white ash. Stay with this image until it's completely whitened.

When this is finished, sit in reverent silence for awhile and commune with your Higher Self. (While you are sitting there, stay very close to any feelings you may be having. And listen for any instructions or revelations that may occur from within your mind. Remember to write these down. This is like dreamwork; sometimes the revelations are profound, but they float by rapidly and we may miss them. Even if what is being revealed seems irrelevant or makes no sense, write it down anyway.)

Once you feel you've finished, just go about your ordinary business in your usual ways, and await your next right step. It will emerge at some point as a strong desire or "knowing" that you have to behave differently, some newfound conviction that will emanate from your heart, and at the appointed time, will manifest in your life.

Shift Number Three: Growth is not incremental; it is sequences of death/rebirth cycles.

When we really examine our lives we see that as we travel through time, we do not simply get better and better everyday. Haven't you noticed that no matter what project you are involved in, at some point, even though everything may have been going well, things naturally begin to die? In our groupwork we hear this from people all the time: "I was doing just fine; then I woke up one morning and it had all changed." The relationship (or project) began to lose its potency. Or, "I was at the very top of my profession and should have been content with all the success. Instead, I became depressed and felt my life was over."

You might think the dramatic process of death only happens when we blow up a planet or physically die, but it happens all the time during our ordinary lives. The times when we are failing, or miserably lost, happen cyclically. We all know this intuitively. But most of us don't live as if we know this! We often label these natural deaths "failures" and believe that we've done something wrong or stopped growing. We erroneously think that we are always supposed to be rising—always succeeding at something. Consequently, when we are failing, we beat up on ourselves, blaming ourselves for not moving forward, or at least maintaining. This confusion takes away our potency, giving us low self-esteem. In truth, these "down times" are not only just as sacred as the successful times; they expand our recalcitrant egos and are there-fore even more growthful.

People often want to skip over this death/rebirth process and just become enlightened, shifting from unconscious to conscious living without having to undergo anything to get there. Or they simply want to let go of the past without having to feel anything about all this loss. But as the old-timers in AA say, "no pain, no gain." It is while passing through our most excruciatingly painful times that we allow new truths to penetrate our lives.

This third mental shift reminds us that the very nature of being alive is that we are never stagnant; we are always in constant movement, either toward dying to something or becoming some-one new—waxing and waning, as do all other facets of nature. Human beings are the only living things that tend to judge the death cycles as "bad" or "wrong." It is crucial that we learn to accept that sometimes we are going through a death period, and sometimes we are bursting with new life. As a part of nature, we grow through cycles of dormancy, germination, incubation, growth, blossoming, fruition, and then, a fading into death and dormancy once again. Then some form of rebirth or re-cycling ensues—and the process begins anew (hopefully on higher and higher levels).

When our thinking fuses with Spirit, we begin to honor our natural sequences which include both dis-integrative and integra-tive stages. We learn to relax into the process of becoming whole, realizing we are in the hands of our Higher Self. At certain points we dis-identify with old stages or aspects of our being that we've outgrown. At other points, we are busy re-identifying with some new aspect of our Self that we admire or feel called to become.

Sometimes, even when we've moved beyond it, we are still focused on the death—as we are gaining understanding of what we've just been through. These times don't usually feel very good, for we are half in and half out of a particular stage. The feeling that accompanies this stage is, "I can't go back, but I don't know where I'm going next." We feel that we are enveloped in darkness. In our work, we call this "hanging out in the dangle." We are in a never-never land, either consciously—in surrender to a Higher Power; or unconsciously—feeling out of control.

At other times we are focused more on the renewal part, because we are growing into someone greater. This stage feels considerably more spiritual, and even has been described as "being high." We have peak experiences, or periods of creative insight and energy. We may be validated by others for a talent we have that has manifested in some way. We may meet someone who has the same deep feelings about something we didn't know we could ever share with another person. Or in meditation we receive from our Higher Power a message that we know matches our wishes and hopes about our future. When our inner spiritual longings are validated by some outer expression, we feel blissful and aligned with our mission or purpose in life. This is called "synchronicity," a process we'll explore further later in the book. We feel that we have a reason for being. Lightness accompanies us during this stage.

But latching onto that place just above us has its ways of being painful as well, for our deaths and rebirths happen simultaneously, whether we are conscious of this fact or not. We can never be dying to something without simultaneously beginning something new. This process demands that we peel off old skins that no longer fit but have become part of us; it hurts. Even when committed to this new growth, we may find ourselves at times holding onto something we've outgrown, and then we really do suffer. To make matters worse, people close to us do not always support our changes—even those for the better! They like to keep us predictable. Therefore, as we go through this process, we must always remember that it is through dis-identification and re-identification that we eventually come into our wholeness as fully functioning soul-infused personalities right here in our ordinary world. The growing pains are worth it.

Today's psychologies are beginning to recognize this process of death and rebirth—finally. As I mentioned earlier, the phrase "spiritual emergency" has become important in the field of transpersonal psychology: this concept recognizes that when we are undergoing an ego death—when we are experiencing the natural dark night of the soul of which the mystics speak—and can find no support or validation for this painful inner process, we may feel crazy or be diagnosed as such. Recovering addicts know this as "hitting bottom" (a process we will discuss in detail later on). Dying to something is the beginning of an alchemical process, known by the alchemists of earlier centuries as *dissolution* and *coagulation*, that cleanses us of our illusions about who we are and what we've experienced. This cleansing process happens in our physical, emotional, and mental lives; it is a purification of our lower selves (our first three chakras) that offers us a vital physical vehicle, a limpid emotional "body," and a transformed mind that bring with them new hope and new life.

Codependence has given us our lessons in love. Now we have to face the pain of dying to the old self who got high on people and events. As we die to this self, we may feel that we're right back where we started, having to learn all over again how to relate. Later, we'll see that we have grown, and we are not at all where we were before. But while dying we only feel death. The key is to accept pain as just another consciousness state and to respect these death cycles as positive occasions in our lives.

Nature intended us to become masterful artists, able to both take on and let go. But remember, *letting go is often just releasing the attachment to something and not the thing itself.* Most often it does not mean we have to lose the content of what we are caught up in. For example, contrary to popular belief, money itself is not an "evil"; it is our attachment to money and materialistic pursuits that gets us into trouble, creating an addiction. The only times we absolutely must give up content is when we are addicted to chemicals such as alcohol, to a substance that is truly poison to the physical system, or to people who deliberately deter our growth emotionally or spiritually. Here, abstinence is the only way.

Even if you are in the company of other loving individuals or in supportive therapy, when the process of death/rebirth or emotional purification hits, you're in for a ride. (And so is your therapist, if talk therapy has been your mode!) Sometimes this process is activated within us for no apparent reason—except that it was "time." And other times we create a crisis in our lives—most often unconsciously, of course, with the aid of the shadow. We become so hurt that we take ourselves right to the bottom and "die." Or we may just decide to walk off and leave the situation unresolved. And then, of course, it will have to re-create itself for a later resolution. But that, too, can be our choice.

In any case, a change of mind is needed so that we can learn to include the whole Self—both the waxing and the waning one—in our understandings of how we grow and change. Then, we won't have to label ourselves negatively during those times we are fading, completing, or terminating some aspect of our lives. We need to adopt the triadic view of the Self that will embrace both the down times and the up times as sacred and purposeful. Later we will explore how to find or create a supportive community to help you through this process.

I believe that today we are being urged by our own higher Intelligence to bring forth our mystical nature. For mystics are willing to die to the old to make room for the new; they are familiar with the inner life and know you don't have to leave your body to experience rebirth. Mystics are true philosophers. And Plato said that "all true philosophers make dying their profession." Mystics know that even what they call their "self" is a process, continually dying and being born.

Shift Number Four: Transcendence is not a leaving of life; it is a living of life more abundantly.

Finally, the mind must comprehend the true nature of transcendence, which means "to rise above," as steam rises from a boiling stew. A quote from the Agni Yoga Teachings will lead me to my point:

> Let us remember the myth about the "Origin of Mountains." When the Planetary Creator toiled over the formation of the earth, He gave attention to the fertile plains which could provide people with a quiet agriculture. But the Mother of the World said, "Verily, people will find bread and trade in the plains, but when gold will

pollute the plains whither shall go the pure in spirit to Gather strength? Either let them have wings, or let them have mountains, in order to escape from gold." And the Creator answered, "It is too early to give wings to the people, they would carry death and destruction. But let us give them mountains. Even if some be afraid of them, for others they will be salvation." Thus there are two kinds of people—people of the plains and people of the mountains. (*Fiery World, Vol. II*)

As souls in human form, we all have the power to shift onto whole new levels of being. But for both the "people of the plains" and the "people of the mountains" there are pitfalls to avoid as they go along. "Plains people" get into the myopia of the "wingless bird," and can get all caught up in their conditions. They don't recognize the ways of transcendence or how to change identities creatively. They are stuck in the horizontal realm and are not receptive to a broader view. "Mountain people," however, become susceptible to spiritual by-pass and may try to fly away without dealing with their family-of-origin issues and other conditions of their past. They don't realize that no one can rise above that which one hasn't resolved. They are stuck in the vertical realm. Each one of these stances is faulty; yet they have something to learn from one another. All of us must abide by the wisdom of the Hindu bible, the *Upanishads:*

To darkness are they doomed who worship only the body and to greater darkness they who worship only the spirit. . . . They who worship both the body and the spirit, by the body overcome death, and by the spirit achieve immortality.

As I've already said, people with codependence or addiction issues often fall into the traps of spiritual by-pass; for they are transcenders, unsatisfied with their current lives and searching for a bigger and better reality. They need to be reminded of how to transcend. They must realize that transcendence does not mean a *leaving* of life but a *living* of life more expressive of their full and rich potential.

Transcendence is *an integration* of our warring parts into "both/ and" rather than "either/or." In a sense, it is a culmination and

synthesis of the previous shifts. When we can accept our "negative" traits as valid and sacred parts of ourselves, just as our
"positive" qualities are, we dissolve the tension we've used to hold
ourselves away from these unacceptable selves. Embracing the
shadow releases our energies to move on to higher dimensions of
our Self: this is transcendence. We transcend by enveloping our
shadow in the light of love, by forgiving others, and then moving
on—and up. *Acceptance* is the key to our transcendence.

In other words, transcendence holds us in the present moment,
while simultaneously taking us back into our past to release our
denied emotional pain. Once this is all assimilated, understood,
and resolved it takes us above and beyond our addictions to a
higher, more unified level. When used according to spiritual law,
transcendence is a shift from the personal to the transpersonal life
that unfolds in loving service to ourselves and one another. (We'll
learn more of this process later.) Transcendence is the Law of
Completion.

When we begin to live the mental revelations we just studied,
we'll see how these axioms become the cornerstone of Truth
upon which the Heart stands. They are the foundation for the
Heartwork we'll undergo in the next part of the book. For now, I
want to briefly review the four major shifts, to show you a little
more clearly how they serve as a gateway for the Heart:

1) *The shift from a dualistic to a triadic model of the Self* will now
include the Heart as a viable part of us and our personal transformation. By overcoming dualism, we give ourselves permission
to feel without judgment.

2) *The shift from outer to inner focus* legitimizes the inner
psycho-spiritual life and makes us conscious of the feelings that go
on inside of us, giving them—and the Heart—further validity.
Our Higher Self shows us through our own experience that
everything we feel is our own inner process—*always*—and never
the fault or responsibility of others or life's conditions. The Higher
Self enters through the Heart and removes the projection screen.

3) *The shift that reveals how we grow through sequences of
death/rebirth* is an honoring of the fact that our healing is an

ongoing process that continually happens in the Heart, and that no matter where we are in this process, whether dying or rebirthing, we are still advancing in a spiritual direction.

4) *The shift toward seeing the true nature of transcendence* is an entering into life more abundantly, remaining fully *in* our bodies, rather than thinking only out-of-body experiences are transcendent. It is about completing all our human experiences, not trying to walk off and leave them. This enables the Heart to become a living permanent resident in our consciousness, no longer living in exile. It now will bring the totality of Truth to all our experiences! And we'll *be home* to experience It! If we can stay in our bodies, we can live in the wholeness of mental clarity and emotional truth. Our minds and hearts will be in sync.

The Mystical Marriage of Mind and Heart

According to the ancient art of spiritual alchemy, the marriage of Mind and Heart is the sacred marriage of our masculine and feminine natures. Once we achieve this union, we become whole and no longer seek the Beloved outside ourselves in codependent ways. We may want to celebrate life with one another in true love and sharing, but we will no longer feel possessed by needy love. This is a promise awaiting those who choose to enter the Heartwork section of this book.

Although we may never fully comprehend Its mysterious ways, we know the Divine Feminine is our guide into a deeper, more conscious life. As St. Exupery so poignantly said in his classic book, *The Little Prince:*

> It is only through the heart that one sees rightly. What is
> essential is invisible to the eye.

The concept of "awakening in time" is about this shift in awareness of who we are: from living unconsciously in ego domination to realizing that we are actively participating in the making of our

lives, that we're on the *top* of the creative Triangle, capable of
unifying all apparent oppositions. This shift is about reclaiming
our powers as human souls—and moving away from codependence
toward co-creation. It is the ultimate *metanoia* experience, bringing us the spiritual gifts of imagination, invocation, insight,
inspiration, and illumination from the universal Inner Lovers,
Mind and Heart.

Now that you've seen with the Mind, you must learn to feel
with your Heart: the Mind and Heart must live in mutual respect
for each other's ways. When Heartwork is valued by the masculine
Mind, the Heart nurtures our logical Mind and makes certain that
Spirit expresses in all our orderly activities.

But Heartwork cannot be described; it must be experienced to
be understood. We have begun to see the Truth; now we must take
the next right step and learn to *feel* our way into it.

Work of the eye is done; now go and do heart-work.

—Rainer Maria Rilke

⚜ IV ⚜

Heartwork

The day will come when,
after harnessing the winds, the tides, and gravitation,
we shall harness for God the energies of love.
And on that day,
for the second time in the history of the world,
man will have discovered fire.

—Pierre Teilhard de Chardin

The purse of the heart is identical in all—place
therein the treasure!

—Agni Yoga Teachings

The Heart Is Where
We Heal

Each time we drop our masks and meet
heart-to-heart . . . Each time we are able to
remain open to suffering, despite our fear and
defensiveness, we sense a love in us which becomes increasingly unconditional. . . . Awakening from our sense of separateness is what we
are called to do in all things.

—Ram Dass

The last chapter provided guidance for our rigid, overly
protective minds. This chapter will help guide our hearts,
which now have been given permission to open and bring to life
the ideas of our transforming mind. For Heartwork is how we heal.
It moves us through our painful and illusory sense of separateness
and fragmentation into feelings of unity and wholeness.

The Heart, or fourth chakra, is our Higher Self's feeling nature.
And it is here that the motion of life and the stillness of death
meet. When our hearts are open, we are filled with life; when they
are closed, we feel deadened and our lives seem meaningless. The
fourth chakra governs the anatomical heart and circulates our
blood, or life-force. Hence, the color associated with this chakra
is green, the color of life. The Heart rules the mysterious thymus

gland that governs the immune system; many immunologists today believe the thymus functions best when we are in touch with the energies of love. These doctors have noted that people with immune deficiencies often die when they feel isolated and unloved.

This chakra is the vehicle for communing with our soul. When we truly enter the Heart, we drop our codependence patterns, all our horizontal sacrificing. No longer able to deflect from our true nature, we turn toward the completion of our own lives. At some point we all must enter the fourth chakra and pass through the "Initiation of the Heart" to face both our pain and joy. Otherwise we can never evolve.

For Heartwork is the universal process known as "Initiation" in many metaphysical schools. Simply understood, Initiation means being in a constant process of renewal that leads us closer and closer to our source, or Higher Self. It gives us the necessary trials or lessons we need to grow emotionally, mentally, and spiritually. According to author Joseph Chilton Pearce, "Initiation allows us to enter into the life of the spirit, a life of grace . . . resonate with the Power of God."

Initiates are people with a mystical consciousness who don't just believe, but *know* that the soul, the real Self, never dies: it only takes on new forms. Therefore initiates don't fear transformation and are always open to new feelings, ideas, or paths. The initiatory process is the natural inner process of dying to one limited way of being after another until we are reborn, awakening on the other side of fragmentation into a state of wholeness. It's about learning our lessons in attachment so that we can move to each new level of living and begin again.

In the Dionysian mystery schools of ancient Greece, pageants celebrating the process of death/rebirth were enacted in the streets, and the common people participated in them, learning through these practices that they were immortal (their souls would never die). The Nag Hammadi Gnostic teachings during the days Christ walked the earth taught that death is for those who put themselves to sleep: when we examine death until it is completely understood it will release its hold on us. And in certain Western and non-Western cultures young people were—and in some cases still are—put through difficult "coming of age" rituals to initiate them into adulthood and teach them never to fear transformation or the process of death/rebirth. Most of these experiences belonged to ancient times, and initiatory practices have largely died with the growth of modern Western culture. But a deeper knowledge of the workings of the Heart can help us relearn the process of initiation, so that we, too, can consciously undergo the cycles of death/rebirth and accelerate our spiritual growth. We can regain this knowledge through rituals, spiritual exercises, and an acceptance of how the Heart will just naturally take us where we need to be in order to grow.

But before we go into more discussion, let's deepen for awhile and do some inner psycho-spiritual work. In order to get the most out of this section of the book, we want to open our hearts as much as we can. The following imagery experience can aid in this endeavor. Again, it can be read by someone empathic who will guide you through this experience. Or you can record or memorize the major aspects of this process yourself and be your own guide. Sit or lie down comfortably somewhere where you will not be disturbed for awhile, and begin to relax. You may want to put on some soft, melodic, heart-felt music for this, but be sure it is music with no words.

Opening the Heart:
A Guided Imagery Experience

Gently breathe into your heartspace as you feel your body begin to let go of any tightness or anxiety. . . . Feel your body relax, allowing gravity to hold it up . . . and just let go.

As you focus on your breathing, check to see if you feel any muscle constriction around your chest cavity. Sometimes our hearts feel like they're in little cages. . . . If so, quietly breathe in and out until you feel the constriction begin to dissolve. . . . Allow your heart to become tension free . . . (longer pause).

If any emotion is rocking around inside you, calmly breathe into the body parts being affected. . . . Feel the emotions settling down, becoming still, like a lake with no ripples . . . (longer pause).

Notice if you're having any thoughts or expectations running through your mind. . . . Take some time now to allow these thoughts to dissipate, letting your mind become as clear and open as a cloudless blue sky . . . (longer pause).

Remember that you are not your body . . . you are not your emotions . . . and you are not your thoughts. . . . You are a greater Self, the one who is watching all this. . . .

Now, with the use of your imagination, envision yourself sitting "at the intersection of the cross" in the middle of a Triangle. . . . You are in the Temple of the Heart. . . . It is spacious here. . . . You feel as though you are suspended in a space devoid of content . . . (longer pause).

Now allow yourself to reflect on a personal problem in your life. . . . Take some time to bring this situation completely into your consciousness. . . . See yourself in scenes where this problem is manifesting . . . (longer pause). See the people there with you who are involved. . . . Allow yourself to feel into this difficulty. . . . Bring all your feelings up into full awareness . . . (longer pause). Notice which parts of your body are feeling the feelings . . . and breathe your breath into those parts. . . .

Focus on your breath, and feel yourself beginning to rise up out of the situation you've been imaging. . . . Feel yourself expanding . . . lightening . . . softening . . . (longer pause).

[Begin the heart music here, starting at zero volume and gradually lifting it to a medium, background-music volume.]

Now, you can look down below and see all of that problem and the people who are involved in it with you. . . . You see yourself as well. . . . And from this expanded viewpoint, notice what you all are doing . . . (longer pause). Allow yourself to feel all of it at once! The sadness . . . the love . . . the hate . . . the hurt . . . whatever. . . . If tears want to come, let them . . . (longer pause).

From above, see the meaning or purpose in this situation. . . . See the whole thing—its place in your life, or in the others' lives who are sharing in this situation with you. . . . See the difficulty in its full context now. . . . And let your feelings come . . . (longer pause).

From above now, send down the light and love of understanding to all concerned. . . . Feel your Heart open fully and do this! . . . Surrender your mind into Love. . . . Expand your Heart in forgiveness. . . . Embrace the wound. . . . And love yourself as much as you can . . . (longer pause).

Now, see yourself once again sitting inside the Temple of the Heart. . . . And just allow to come whatever comes for awhile . . . (longer pause). And when you are ready, slowly re-enter your body. . . . Feel yourself coming back into the room where you are. . . . Allowing all that inner process to be still there, coming fully back into this reality as well . . . (longer pause). And take a good long while now to integrate this experience. . . . Remaining in a sacred and quiet space for awhile, you may want to sit silently, to write, draw, move to music, or discuss this experience with your guide.

Identifying and Dis-Identifying with Our Human Conditions

Hopefully, in the above experience, you were able to see your current difficulty through the eyes of the Heart—from a more loving, expanded view—and thereby begin to resolve it. For when we are in the Heart, as we've seen, we are above judgment; we see the big picture. From this standpoint we understand how both the negative and positive sides of ourselves are valid and purposeful. Then we can start to let go, forgive, and move on to a new way of being, clear of our old pattern or situation. This is the process of death/rebirth, otherwise known as dis-identification/re-identification, which happens in the chamber of the Heart. Now that our minds have made room for this concept (shift number three), we can become conscious of how the Heart enacts it in our lives. The following section is devoted to exploring this crucial aspect of Heartwork.

Before we go any farther with our exploration of death/rebirth, we must adopt an attitude of patience. Most of us want to head immediately toward the rebirth part. But before we can be reborn or re-identify, we must die or dis-identify from our old, codependent ways. And this requires hard work, much intentionality, and practice. Things do not resolve simply because we've occasionally meditated on them or invoked solutions once or twice. Only through deep psycho-spiritual work, such as the guided imagery we just did or in other ways I've described of getting to the *heart* of our issues, can we die to a pattern and reach a new level of living. Dis-identifying and re-identifying are a *process*, not an event, and we will spend some time in this chapter looking at the stages of this process. It is the only way I know to truly release our suffering.

For as long as we have a body and a mind, we will have pain, but *suffering* is another matter. Emotional suffering results from holding onto something that needs to be released; yet the mind refuses to do so. It holds us away from our true feelings, thereby keeping the Heart's qualities of openness, spontaneity, freedom, and compassion from coming through and eventually healing us. Our codependent egos only have known a heart that lives in fear of opening. But our mind allows the Heart to function, and when we commit to unfreezing our repressed emotions, allowing ourselves to feel our truth, the Heart's work begins and the following will occur: Whenever it is time to let go of something or someone (as we'll learn in the next chapter) the Heart gathers up our wounds from this relationship or situation and a trigger goes off, a powerful physical or emotional symptom. (For letting go is not a mental decision; it's an emotional or bodily experience.) Once we release our emotions, usually rage or sorrow, *then* the mind can bring us understanding: we can look back at the situation and see it for what it was. But we cannot do this until we feel our feelings. We don't even know what we feel until we let ourselves feel it! Giving our emotions the right of expression isn't anything like suffering, as many people fear; it is an emptying, experienced as *relief*. Afterwards, people say, "I feel a hundred pounds lighter." Or, "I don't remember ever feeling this free!"

As you can see from the above description, the key to

dis-identifying is surrendering in the Heart—and letting go. And this letting go seems to be the hard part, particularly for those of us with codependence issues. We've seen how we become glued to certain people and outer conditions, forgetting who we are in essence. And because of this we must keep re-minding ourselves that in order to grow we *have* to die, over and over again. For following the Heart is the only path to co-creation. As we consciously undergo the Heart's processes, we will be healed of our relational disillusionments and suffering. We will be reborn, re-identified with our soul's intent: the insights, inspiration, and illumination of the Higher Self. Later we'll see that these are the gifts of the higher chakras, levels five, six, and seven. I can promise you that this will happen; but I cannot tell you when or exactly how. If you are willing to open your heart and feel your *true* feelings, you are ready for Heartwork. The rest will follow.

However, you may still need to hold onto your anger, your hurt, or your involvement in a certain plight; you may still be learning something, and you may not be ready to let your negative feelings come up and out so that you can then forgive. In some cases, people feel they cannot forgive a perpetrator or someone else they feel anger towards because to do so would relieve that other person of his or her karmic predicament, or excuse his or her harmful ways. They don't realize that this is never the case with forgiveness. Forgiveness is for *your* sake, not anyone else's. It is the release of your own pent-up energies, which are crying out for a more creative expression. Forgiveness is the resolution of an aspect of your own shadow's pain. The person who harmed you can be released, and your past hurts can be dissolved; but that person will still have to face his or her Maker, or inner Authority, to be healed. And this has nothing to do with you.

Forgiveness is not easy. It is the work of the Heart and therefore requires that a part of us—perhaps a part we've held very close—must die. Forgiveness demands that we relinquish some long-held opinion or judgment that we've valued. We must sacrifice it, no matter how justified it may seem. This means dis-identifying with a lesser identity while simultaneously taking on a greater identity, a more expanded understanding. And remember, it's not only others we must learn to forgive from the Heart; we are to forgive ourselves as well.

A few years ago in one of our workshops, a young woman spoke of her suffering and guilt over an abortion she'd had several years earlier. When she had discovered she was pregnant, she decided hastily to abort the fetus. Having gone through several years of therapy, she thought she was over her pain. In a deep psycho-spiritual therapy process, however, she realized she still was grieving and judging herself harshly for her decision. In the midst of a Heart imagery experience, similar to the one we just did, she ascended up out of her body and met the child she never had. Her child told her of their spiritual connection that was not dependent on form and told her of its love for her. She felt bonded to her unborn child in Love and came out of the experience with tears of joy as well as the relief of self-forgiveness.

This is a wonderful example of Heartwork. Such an experience would not be possible for someone with a closed-off heart who is completely outer-directed. If you told such a person about this happening, he or she would not understand you and would undoubtedly think you'd entered into a never-never land of wishful fantasy. But others who have experienced a "Heart opening" or healing such as the one above will offer you a silent nod of understanding. They know these inner felt experiences deeply affect our psyches and change our lives. They are initiates in the true sense of the word.

As we develop the qualities of *true discipline, spiritual discrimination,* and *rightly-directed intentionality* (described in the chakra chapter and more deeply later in the book), our judgment function dissolves and forgiveness becomes much easier. Judgments are intellectual decisions based on preconceptions of what "ought to be." They are not real distinctions, but are rooted in individual biases, limitations, ignorances, neediness—all the imaginings of the ego. As we evolve spiritually, judgment is replaced by discrimination, an instinctual "knowing in the bones" what is right for us in each moment.

The struggle to separate "the wheat from the chaff" of the Self's true expression, for example, to tell the difference between judgment and *discrimination*, requires that we draw on the qualities of *intentionality* and *discipline*. We must undergo an intentional purification process, a close, disciplined examination of our reactions in everyday life. Notice how you respond to people you meet in the street or interact with at work, as well as to those you live with, love, and depend on. Do you feel constricted and judgmental when someone (including you) steps out of your idea of what is normal or right behavior? Or are you aware of a softening, an "Aha, this is different. How can I communicate with this person or accept this behavior of my own?" Of course, we all step into judgment from time to time, but we need to be sure this is not a frequent state of mind. And if it is, this is probably where we will need to focus our Heartwork.

The Fourth Chakra's Gifts

The Heart's gifts are manifold, for She is creativity itself. Here are Her most well-known qualities: receptivity, recognition, expression, compassion, expansion, forgiveness, childlike and playful spontaneity, lightheartedness, acceptance, nonjudgmentalness, joy, giving, receiving, honoring, worshiping, surrendering, releasing.

These qualities enable us not only to shed our addictive ways, but also to fulfill our destinies as planetary citizens, so that we can give of ourselves to the world around us. They are the qualities of the transpersonal, as well as the personal, Heart.

The Heart Is Where the Personal and the Transpersonal Meet

The Heart merges our egos' longings and pain with the spiritual meaning and purpose behind these sufferings, which belong to the archetypal or transpersonal realm. This is one of the cosmic purposes of personal suffering: It enables us to shift from an egoistic life to one of compassion for others. At the same time, without a connection to our personal life, we would never be able to experience true compassion for "the whole." As so beautifully stated by mystic and spiritual teacher Omraam Mikhael Aivahnov, "We have two natures—human and divine—and they depend upon each other for their survival."

In a therapy session many years ago, I had an experience that illustrates this, as did the example of the young woman above. I was expressing deep feelings of sadness and fear that I was losing my oldest son, now grown, who has had diabetes mellitus since he was two. I'd grieved over his illness many times, yet on this particular day my feelings were amplified as a result of a diagnosis we'd received concerning his kidneys. I felt the pain in my solar plexus, the third chakra. I was doubled up in suffering, crying out "Why him? Why me?" And all of a sudden I went so deep into myself that I lost consciousness of my pain. I felt an energetic shift in my body, which took me into another space. The feeling had left my solar plexus, and I felt a deeper sorrow as well as a sense of being lifted up out of my suffering. This time the feeling was more in my throat and head, where the higher chakras reside. In my mind, I saw all the mothers in the world who've lost children: starving babies at their mothers' breasts in India and mothers receiving news that their sons had died in war. I saw children dying in hospitals and babies being born dead. I even saw the goddess Demeter as she searched frantically for her lost daughter, Persephone, who had been stolen by Hades. This then turned into strong feelings of connectedness to the archetype of the Mother and a profound sense of compassion for all motherly plights.

As all this feeling welled up in my heart, I somehow "got it." I was part of a larger group on this planet that had experienced the same event. And this sense of meaning and connectedness gave me solace. I felt renewed and no longer so alone. Filled with compassion, I wanted to tell others about this healing experience, to offer them hope. The mystical workings of the Heart had activated and brought me a unified experience, both personal and transpersonal.

The blending of our personal hearts with the transpersonal

Heart is what ultimately heals us. For the Heart shows us the whole picture and enables us to reach out into the world for support and deep affirmation. It also provides us with the compassion and insight necessary to help those around us. And I believe this combination is the reason most people enter into service to others. It is one of the underlying tenets of the Twelve Step program: Our experiences with addiction and recovery enable us to "carry the message" to fellow addicts.

However, in order to fully enter the Heart, we need to better accept—even embrace—the cycles It takes us through as we grow and deepen. And we cannot embrace that which we do not yet fully recognize or understand. Therefore, the rest of this section is devoted to getting to know the Heart's cycles, another vital aspect of Heartwork.

The Cycles of the Heart: The Seasons of Transformation

As we've seen, we are always dying, just as we are always being born as someone new. Since we are part of Mother Nature's design, our human nature follows Her laws, and, just like all other living things, we unfold through seasons of change: "To everything there is a season . . . turn, turn, turn. . . ." Human beings have their own way of inwardly experiencing summer, fall, winter, and spring. We begin as dormant, then we germinate, incubate, grow, blossom, fructify, and then fade away—in form only. For, as you probably know by now, I am not talking about physical death but continual transformation, which, ironically, is the only way to become immortal, or truly alive. Despite what most of us may think, immortality is *not* a holding onto our bodies; this is a misconception. It is about learning to maintain a *continuity of consciousness* while undergoing all the stages of our growth—even our demise. When we are able to stay awake through even the most frightening times, we become immortal in the true sense of the word.

Our transformed minds have already taught us that the inner life determines our outer conditions (the second shift of mind). We know that in order to dissolve our codependence patterns, we must be willing to understand the workings of our psyche rather than unconsciously acting out these inner drives in the outer world of relationships. My purpose here is to show you in a deeper, more detailed way how the psyche's processes literally determine our lives. We will see how our feeling states grow out of inner seasons, our summer, fall, winter, and spring. These "emotional seasons," or stages of transformation, when understood and cooperated with, will purify us continually and enable us to live fully. My hope is that this section will alleviate your fears about certain stages or seasons: instead of resisting them, I encourage you to simply recognize when you are in one, and just ride the waves.

For resistance is pointless; the Heart always follows the four seasons of transformation no matter how staid our life may seem. And we experience these seasons over and over in whatever projects we undertake: everything from minor tasks to marriages, careers, even our entire life's destiny. When we look at our anatomical birth process, these four stages become quite evident, as has been noted by medical researcher Stanislav Grof. He discovered four distinct birth matrices that, I believe, track with the seasons described below. In his research, these matrices are called Basic Perinatal Matrices or BPM I, II, III, and IV. The first is the prenatal state; the second occurs at the onset of labor; the third is the struggle through the birth canal; and the fourth is birth itself.

Those of us who have studied with Dr. Grof have found that these stages of birth represent *four distinctive feeling states* that reappear throughout our lives whenever we go through any kind of change or create anything new. These states manifest when we become a parent, move to a new home, begin a relationship, change jobs, and so forth. *Our anatomical birth, we've found, is the prototype for personal transformation.* Whether or not you are aware of the circumstances of your birth (whether you were premature or late, or whether your birth involved drugs or severe trauma), the exact patterning of your birth process conditions how you flow through the four universal stages outlined below, actually coloring how you flow through life. Making your individual birth process conscious—through deep psycho-spiritual work, such as various forms of breathwork, rebirthing, deep-tissue bodywork, or other types of therapy that release cellular memory (see Appendix One)—can bring you a conscious realization of your birthing and rebirthing style. These deep processes can also burst forth spontaneously during times of extreme trauma or dramatic highs such as childbirth, a near-death experience, a powerful sexual experience, spiritual practices such as sweat lodges, deep states of meditation, or lucid dreaming. For our purposes here we'll be looking at the four general stages of birth or seasons of transformation, using a very practical example, something nearly everyone has experienced: the process we go through in an intimate relationship.

Summer: The Reception Stage

When I am in the summer stage of a relationship, I have taken it on. I am busy receiving the direct experience of what it is I'm creating—a new relationship. This is the *thesis* stage of creativity. I'm just floating around in my new creation, loving being connected to this person, and I'm not questioning anything about it. Everything seems ideal: I've chosen the perfect mate, and we are happy. There is no part of me outside of this experience; I am not judging it. I have merged with the state of being in an intimate relationship. And I feel good! The relationship is happening all by itself without much need for processing. Intellectually I may believe that things will need some work at times, but my feeling state is idealistic. This is the "honeymoon phase."

Others in my life may warn me that things might not be as rosy as they seem. But I won't listen. My partner and I may even privately accuse these people of being jealous, or troublemakers. We are preoccupied with each other and won't let anything or anyone interfere. Family and friends are often excluded from our lives at this stage, for most of our needs and desires are being met from within the relationship itself. We believe that this glorious feeling will continue forever. And this period *can* go on for quite awhile, sometimes even years.

This early stage in a relationship correlates with *the prenatal stage* of birth (Grof's BPM I), when all our needs are met in the safety of the encompassing matrix—our mother's womb. At this stage, we are absorbing the essence of our situation or creation. We are *pre-conscious* of any difficulty; we are *being* "the project." I believe this can be the genesis of the debilitating *patterns of denial* we see in codependence and other addictions. It's a stage we long to return to later when the waters become more turbulent, and often we pretend it's still going on when really it is time for us to move on and enter the next birth matrix. But this stage feels so good, we may deny the issues we need to face.

Fall: The Assimilation Stage

When fall hits, out of the blue—and in spite of ourselves—we begin to say and do things that focus on a disturbance. Though we have no idea what we're in for, we are beginning to rock the boat. We are letting some of our differences show. At times, our shadow may even appear. In other words, we're becoming real. It is during this stage that we begin to incorporate the substance of our joint experience as a couple; we are assimilating (learning from) the relationship. But this stage does not *feel* growthful. As a result, we'll fruitlessly try to return to the original summer state anytime something uncomfortable stirs. And when this doesn't work, we'll begin to lose energy—and hope! We'll feel that now *this* stage is the one that will last forever, that it's useless to think things will ever again be the same as they were or that they'll change for the better.

This is the onset of the *antithesis* phase of the Heart's creative process. Things begin to shift from feeling natural and okay to becoming quite depressing. For instance, the relationship might feel strained as a result of one partner giving too much or not enough, and you both are feeling the effects of unmet needs. Now you may notice that your partner has chauvinistic values, and they will become highlighted. Or your own codependence pattern may kick in, and you will begin reacting in dysfunctional ways. Or your partner might begin nitpicking at you, calling you on all your faults. Feelings of mistrust and frustration set in.

These issues need to be confronted, but—codependently—we fear "making waves." Our partner might leave us. We could be abandoned! Or conversely, we might abandon the partner. And we'll never be able to be so intimate again. We may have the urge to quit, but we don't want to process it, or face it honestly—we just want to opt out or disappear. The more we deny them, the more these feelings intensify. This stage correlates with *the onset of labor* (Grof's BPM II). Everything changes, and we don't know what to do about it. We begin to feel trapped by our condition, unable to get out or move on. We feel sick with our "dis-ease." We think we are being acted upon by some outer force, usually our partner, and we fall passively into fear that we cannot express. Victimhood sets in. We feel as though our life-support system is being tampered with, as if we are no longer safe. And we haven't a clue as to what's coming next; we're still half-unconscious and not the least bit prepared. "After all," we'll say, "I was doing just fine. And then *this* had to happen. Why did he have to do this to me? What did I do to deserve this?" And here, if we're not careful, we fold up in our condition and go into denial. We'll feel powerless and therefore hopeless. But really this is the beginning of our shadow's "holy grit" experience, the method of our transformation.

This stage is a seedbed for the codependence pattern of *victimhood and lack of personal power*. It can go on for much of our lives if we don't make it conscious and work through our underlying feelings of despair. We doubt ourselves, blame our mate, or feel shame about what we see as a personal failure. We become completely involved and overcome by our condition, mistaking it for our identity, feeling that our whole life is at stake. We forget that this is a natural part of our journey, so focused are we on the miserable content of this season. And we may begin to act out our misery in patterns of dysfunction. Some of us continually talk about being depressed and hopeless. Others go numb and cannot feel a thing. We may wander around aimlessly, preoccupied with what our partner is doing or not doing, losing more potency every day. Or we will busy ourselves with useless activity in a state of agitated depression. We seek distractions to make us feel better, but nothing works. And we may make up "storylines" that make it worse—such as "He's in love with someone else," "I'm losing my attractiveness," or "This is my last chance at love." We believe we are losing it, and we won't face it head on; it's too scary.

But in fact, all creative ventures must go through this antithesis stage. Those of us in transpersonally oriented communities often recognize these feelings for what they are. We'll say, "I'm stuck in second birth matrix again." And we've learned to laugh at ourselves (a little). This is our worst place in consciousness. I've never met anyone who does not loathe these "second birth matrix" feelings. Even if you have accepted it as natural, this stage often seems unbearable. Perhaps the roadmap outlined in this chapter will help somewhat, but you still will feel depressed and uneasy, worthless, and without hope during the fall season of any transformation. But at least you can learn to be still and wait for it to pass without acting out in a way you'll later regret. For, even though it feels like forever, you eventually move on.

At the crux of this second stage, you will most likely feel cut off from your Higher Power and everything in life you've deemed spiritual. It is the "dark night of the soul" mystics speak of. No matter how great a success you were before this mood struck, you will feel that you are now nothing, that you have a dismal future, and that you will never again be inspired. But eventually you find yourself in the next season, where you become ready to act and move out of the womb, which has now become too small and constricting.

Winter: The Transmutation Stage

The word *transmutation* means an actual change in form or nature. In the third stage of transformation, the winter time, we begin to inwardly activate. Someone within us becomes sick and tired of being sick and tired. We are no longer willing to feel passive and unsafe. We decide we're going to get rid of these feelings—no matter what! And the struggle to be born commences.

During this process, we feel trapped between the opposing forces of life and death. We can't stay where we are; we're too miserable, and we will die. If we move on, however, we're certain we'll die. Finally, we realize we must let go and "sacrifice ourselves" to the unknown. This is the beginning of the *passage through the birth canal* (Grof's BPM III); here both infant and mother enter into a stage of surrender—for their very lives depend upon it. But the unconscious mind experiences this as death. Dr. Grof has found in his research that our psyches cannot tell the difference between birth, death, and sexuality—a provocative idea you may wish to contemplate! Everything feels beyond our control as we struggle through the birth canal. There is no thought, only the raw experience of catastrophe. We feel completely at the mercy of a force greater than we are. Yet we also have the sense that we are finally doing something. And at least *this* part feels good.

In fact, this same body of research suggests that if you were Caesarian-born, you may unconsciously feel that you've missed out on something (because you were simply lifted out), and you may have always had an exceptionally strong need to do things for yourself in order to compensate for this early experience. As a result, you may progress through this winter stage very quickly.

When we are conscious, this stage is filled with both the terror and the bliss of risk-taking—of *acting*. We are dying as one form, while simultaneously coming "toward the light," about to be reborn into a whole new way of being. But if we don't know this intellectually, we just feel the torrential pressures of this inner state, and we may make mistakes. In fact, when we're not conscious, we can do irreparable damage to our relationship or ourselves. We may create chaos in our lives—by treating our partner harshly, getting into an accident, violently reacting to some outside influence, or drawing other dangerous or frightening events into our lives. Moreover, just as our psyches are sexually activated during our physical birth, often our sexual energies are overly stimulated at this stage of the process, and we mistake these inner feelings for the need to act out excessively or inappropriately. Our second chakras are too open. If we're stuck at this level of transformation, we may experience the uncontrollable *urges of love and sex addiction.*

Unlike in the second birth matrix, during this stage we have no difficulty releasing our emotions. We make the shift from withholding feelings to letting them express. Rage, terror, and even exaltation may ensue. The shadow is both explicated and raw. Our old wounds and pent-up energies are seeking release. We want to act, and we want to do it on our own. We are wide open, expressive, and vulnerable—a healing is taking place.

But those around us may not understand these violent energies; our partner or a family member may try to curtail us, to tone us down. Sometimes they even will call us "sick" and try to medicate us. If this third birth matrix pattern is not made conscious and we don't receive guidance, we can become stuck in this matrix's energies for much of our lives, attracting all kinds of highly volatile and disastrous outer experiences. For this reason, when you feel these energies churning inside you, you may want to seek the safety of a therapy session or some other setting where you will not harm yourself or another, and where you can receive support and encouragement. In our Eupsychia workshops, we sometimes have the opportunity to work with Vietnam veterans, people who have been physically and sexually abused, or others who have developed Post-Traumatic Stress Disorder (repressed trauma resulting from terrifying experiences the psyche could not handle at the time of the abuse). During a breathwork or guided imagery session, one of our trainers will occasionally see a person beginning to release these powerful energies, sometimes violently by thrashing about, hitting oneself, or screaming. The trainer will then elicit the aid of others, who will surround the person, allowing all the space and encouragement needed to help him or her release this energy safely and fully.

For at this third stage of our transformation we must pass through all our pent-up emotionalisms around a relationship or event and face them *consciously.* Doing so helps to call forth our observer self to give us perspective and insight. At some point, the depression, hopelessness, sorrow, remorse, guilt, murderous rage, or terror begin to subside—and the body will feel lighter and alive with energy. We will begin to glimpse a bigger picture, and see the meaning and spiritual purpose behind all the pain. In our primary relationship, we will now be able to accept the harsh and angry times as harbingers of rebirth, which is just around the corner. And we can encourage our partner to stay with the process, rather than trying to reach for premature resolution.

Often, in our workshops, incest or physical abuse survivors will relive their hurtful experiences and learn to forgive their perpetrators and unconscious family members, releasing the pain of their past. Once, a Vietnam veteran who had been ordered to bomb a village of unprotected women and children declared loudly to the whole room: "I see now that God sometimes has to kill off whole nations! It's part of the Divine Plan! I feel for the first time since I was nineteen that God loves and forgives me!" We all wept. This kind of release creates a great sense of freedom and brings us to a whole new level of integration and understanding. This is a psycho-spiritual resolution—which brings us to stage four.

Spring: Rebirth

At this stage, we declare a fresh truth, manifesting some unforeseen aspect of ourselves. We may not have all the intellectual answers, but we feel completely free of our old stuff. We're relieved; we can breathe freely at last. This season correlates with Grof's BPM IV. This is the *birth*, or *rebirth* stage.

All the tension of the winter season has dissipated now, and our body is relaxed. We feel as though some new kind of energy is coming through us and into our lives. Doors begin to open—a new creative expression, an exciting new project, or a new possibility within our relationship appears before us. Our hopes and wishes once again show promise of being fulfilled. We feel in charge of our lives.

Here, we are re-minded of who we are, beyond the ego dramas of our relationships. We begin to see our connection to the Higher Self or Higher Power, and we don't feel so threatened by the cycles of change. We recognize the bigger patterns that were holding our anger and hurt feelings in place: we see the whole truth of our situation. And sometimes it's not at all as we'd thought. For instance, instead of being mad at our partner, we find we are angry at our father. Or perhaps we're not angry at our dad but at the cosmic Father. Or we are angry about our own misplaced manhood, as well as at our father. Or we see the real reason we married our mate, which is usually quite different than we'd imagined. Or we see the full value of the breakup. We learn our lesson.

Over and over again, people in our workshops tell us, "The pain was deeper in my psyche than I'd thought." They see that they are indeed bigger than their biographies: larger patterns are holding many of their psychological issues in place. What they thought was their problem was only the "symptom" calling them back to its source. When any of us reach this level, we can see that we have issues and patterns running all the way into the collective unconscious where we still have unresolved birth traumas, reincarnational issues (which people relive in deep cathartic work even when their intellects claim they don't believe in reincarnation!), mythical and archetypal issues, and cosmic or universal issues pertaining to why we're here on this planet in the first place. We see that we are very, very big, connected to humanity's one soul.

At this fourth stage of growth, we are transformed. We know fully who we are. A *codependent pattern may become offset by a positive, life-giving quality,* or some other neurosis will dissolve. We may find that a block in our expression is lifted: we no longer fear being alone, or speaking in public. Or we may manifest a new talent we didn't know we had. Or we may begin to feel differently about the primary relationship that was formerly causing us pain. We will see both ourselves and others differently now, and we will formulate relationships on a higher level. We may never again attract the same kind of people we did in the past. For like magnets, we draw people to us at the level on which we are functioning.

Rebirth always brings us to a new level of being. We never again will be the same. We will attract new lessons and find new challenges, but the part of our past that was involved in that particular transformation is now resolved.

When in the fourth matrix, the true nature of transcendence is completely understood. When we consciously experience this stage, we see how transformation works and how wondrous it can be; we have no desire to leave our bodies or our lives. The Heart has awakened, and we've turned inward. All the mental shifts that we've spoken of in this book become a reality, and we seek to move on in a forward direction. We feel both enthusiastic and at peace. And we believe that this stage is permanent. But it's not! So don't get too attached to this wonderful feeling state. Once this stage of transformation is fully experienced, it, too, begins to fade, and the process will begin all over again—but on a higher level. Remember, *you never arrive: the journey itself is your Home.*

And so the cosmic clock continues running. Transformation unfolds within us one season at a time, always and forever. For this is what creativity is all about; in order to co-create, we must continuously undergo the stages of reception, assimilation, transmutation, and rebirth that renew us. (For those to whom this information is brand-new, I recommend seeking guidance in order to more deeply explore these patterns. As I've said, a whole field of perinatal and transpersonal psychology is emerging now, bringing us new evidence that we run deeper than our biographies.) When we are living unconsciously, we don't recognize these deep patterns, and as a result, we don't understand why we feel the way we do when there may be no outside reason for our depression or elation. We just go along, doing what we've always done, not knowing there is a universal design at work within us. As Jung teaches, *these are unconscious processes that live us until we make them conscious and learn to live them.*

People in adaptive cycles—the "adapters" I described at the

book's opening—grow through these four stages very slowly and
rather smoothly sometimes. Although they undergo the cycles of
death/rebirth, they may have little chaos or change to contend
with. Their entire lives might be devoted to one transformation
instead of many cycles. On the other hand, "transformers," or
people embroiled in transformational cycles, often experience
these seasons quite traumatically, as *rapid* death/rebirth experiences. The process of hitting bottom—where one's whole identity
falls away at once, or an actual near-death occurs—is quite
another matter. Instead of living as if on a quiet lake with gentle
ripples, these people feel they've been caught in a maelstrom in
the middle of a stormy sea.

The next chapter will describe this process of accelerated
transformation. This has been my pattern for most of my life, and
I'm happy to share these experiences with you. I hope they will
help guide you or make you feel less alone if you are presently in
one of these cycles. Some of you may feel no one in your life
understands you anymore, so rapidly have you changed and grown.
And you will be relieved to know that there's a "divine order"
beneath your seemingly chaotic shifts in mood, attitude, or even
lifestyle. Others of you may feel this is not currently your
experience, but you may want to study what follows in order to
prepare for a time when something in your life might trigger such
a rapid shift in consciousness. For even though you may not be
feeling these things now, they are historically a part of the human
evolutionary process. Transformation and deep, powerful *metanoia*
experiences are always just "a matter of time."

The Heart's Accelerated Path

> In such a period of change and growth, *emergence* is often experienced by the individual as *emergency* with all its attendant stress.
>
> —Rollo May

Accelerated transformation is usually experienced as an "involuntary" process resulting from a crisis in one's outer life—such as the break-up of a cherished relationship, the death of a loved one, or a near-death experience. Some people, however, may actually volunteer for this roller-coaster ride to a whole new level of being by consciously choosing to hit bottom—suddenly quitting a job, attending a transformational workshop, and so forth. Whatever the case, when we undergo such an all-encompassing change, our inner seasonal birthing process becomes more accelerated. We begin to rapidly experience dramatic death/rebirth sequences.

It may seem to most of us that accelerated transformation always takes one by surprise. But on some higher level a more knowing part of us often deliberately throws us into the whirlwinds of change, with the intention of taking us deeper into our crisis even when we haven't consciously chosen this path. (That is why I put quotation marks around "involuntary" above.) We'll watch our-

selves saying or doing things that end a marriage or a project, or
that toss a whole way of life out the window. We'll hear ourselves
revealing truths we'd never planned to expose. Yet, even though
our own behavior shocks us, there's a still small voice deep inside
encouraging us: "Go on; this is right. You are pushing to be
reborn."

But, as we've seen, in order to be reborn, we must first die. And
this is the tough part, even though, as people with codependence
and addiction issues, we intuitively know the process of letting go
will *save* our lives, not end them. The following two examples
should help illustrate the death/rebirth cycle, both "involuntary"
and voluntary:

Al's wife of twenty-six years came home one evening and
announced that she was leaving him for another man. Al was
devastated; he felt he'd had no forewarning. However, he later
admitted that he'd known for quite awhile that something was
happening to the relationship. He'd been spending more time with
his friends, which was a new behavior for him. He also had been
taking meditation classes at a local yoga center and reaching out to
people there—another brand-new behavior. It was as though he
knew he needed to prepare for a change. But when he actually
heard the news from his wife, he found himself unable to continue
his regular daily routine. Everything in his life came to a shattering
standstill. He couldn't think; he couldn't go to work; and he began
to do irrational things like showing up unannounced at friends'
houses in the middle of the night and calling his parents in rageful
tears. He could no longer speak coherently; all he could do was cry
and cry. He was aimlessly seeking relief, totally incapacitated with
fear and hopelessness. This involuntary crisis had spun him into
the death of a whole way of life.

Robin was a corporate lawyer who had begun to feel uneasy, flat,
and bored with her high-powered job. She could no longer do the
late nights and the superficial cocktail-party chatter. And she
couldn't even feel excitement when she won a big money-making
case. The magic had gone completely out of her career and her
life. Nothing interested her anymore. Though extremely depressed, Robin was still trying to hold it all together—a ten-year

career, her marriage, and her circle of friends. But she began
fearing her looming sense of despair. Robin had abandoned her
Christian faith many years ago, and though she felt she was
starving for some kind of spiritual renewal, she knew she couldn't
return to her old religion. In response to an ad in her local
bookstore, Robin went to a workshop conducted by a transpersonal therapist. There she underwent a guided imagery experience
that shook her to the core: she felt her body plummet into darkness
and fear, and then in a state of semiconsciousness she experienced
the most blissful feeling she'd ever known. This lasted for several
minutes, though she had no recollection of time. When Robin
returned to her ordinary state of consciousness, she knew that
everything had changed. Though she couldn't intellectually grasp
exactly what had happened, she was certain that she could never
return to her corporate job, not even for one more day.

Without guidance or support, people can have very frightening,
sometimes destructive death experiences: they wind up at the
bottom with no place to go but farther down. This is how some
people never change, going from bad to worse, or even giving up
their lives entirely to alcoholism, the diversions of sex and love
addiction—even suicide. This is the spiritual emergency I described earlier, where ego deaths masquerade as mental illness. If
we listened to the adapters around us, we might respond to our
accelerated process by going into an institution, taking medication, or entering into a therapy that would focus on "fixing" us.
Then we might really begin to question our sanity, for these
treatments cannot touch our deep and direct spiritual experiences.
Fortunately, both Al and Robin had begun to open their minds to
a new way of living before their crises hit them, and therefore,
they were not as vulnerable to harmful outside intervention. And
both of them—Robin in the form of the workshop leaders and
participants and Al with his friends and those in his meditation
class—had supportive, understanding contexts in which to
awaken.

This support is especially crucial because when we are in a state of accelerated transformation, we can undergo a continual flow of dramatic death/rebirth sequences with hardly any time to rest. All of our unhealed life experiences can come up at once. For example, when Robin experienced the death of her career, she inwardly relived several traumas from her past simultaneously. From feeling her job choking her, she actually started to choke, re-experiencing her near-death at birth, feeling the actual umbilical chord tying around her neck. At the same time, she re-lived a near-drowning that happened when she was six years old and her uncle lying on top of her during a sexually abusive incident when she was thirteen—and other times when she felt constricted, abused, or unable to express herself. You might notice that the emotional quality of all these experiences is similar—fear and suffocation. These emotional qualities are the re-minders: the organizing principles holding all this suffering in place within the psyche. Robin was re-experiencing events that had blocked her creative expression. Her second chakra was trying to clear. (We will see later how the healing energy of the fifth chakra will come down and help heal us during this kind of experience.)

As we release these old stored-up hurts, our feelings may change very rapidly—from grieving we go into rage, to fear, to sadness, and so on. The vertical dimension has activated, which means we're accessing things beyond our conscious awareness—all at once. Because the workings of the Heart are not linear or concrete, on the accelerated path we can experience rebirth in the same moment we're going through a death. From below, our psychological unfinished business comes up to meet us, while simultaneously, from above, we may be experiencing numinous, unexplainable mystical feelings or visions of love and light. Robin felt suffocating rage about her uncle's abuse, while seeing in the same instant his deprivation and feeling a deep sense of forgiveness and compassion. We can never logically understand this process. The Heart is truly magical.

Realizations that might have taken years in talk therapy (just think of Woody Allen!)—or more likely might never have come up at all in such limited settings—can come to us in a matter of seconds. Robin realized within moments that she could never return to her job again—and, as a matter of fact, she also had a vision of herself as a legal aid lawyer working with the inner-city poor, using her skills for a higher good. This was her rebirth, as was her forgiveness of her uncle. For others—and this is most often the case—such revelations are more gradual, and the emotional release or rebirth part may unfold over days or months following a spontaneous inner-awakening experience.

The very fact that human beings since the beginning of time have written about and otherwise explored the concept of rebirth is an affirmation that we must indeed accept, even relish, this process. Whether we see it as a gift or curse, psychic renewal is our constant companion. If we are willing to flow with the process and shed our old ways, accepting life's challenges and the gifts of the Heart with courage and a cavalier sense of adventure, we will be reborn more quickly and easily.

The alchemical process of death/rebirth is the universal way we all move from fragmentation to wholeness. Many death/rebirths of varying degrees of intensity may be experienced during the course of one lifetime. Jung believed that the process of individuation consists of a long chain of transformations as we grow from being unconscious to becoming conscious and responsible in our lives. From our clinical work with large numbers of people undergoing accelerated transformations, we've seen that these larger patterns are predictable, usually taking place every seven or every twelve years, though you may have your own predictable timetable. (Take a moment and look back over your life and you'll likely see that this is so.) These painful experiences often usher in major changes, sometimes looked back on as great destiny moves—those momentous times when the "golden thread" of your real life catches hold and pulls you toward another emerging possibility. There may be a lot of anxiety and fear accompanying these changes, and the emergency feeling is real. Sometimes this journey leads us to the very chasm of the Heart where we hit bottom and can no longer go forward in our outer lives. Everything stops, and for the moment we are lost.

Hitting Bottom
in the Chasm of the Heart

When we fall into the chasm of the Heart, we land at the very bottom of ourselves. One day it was one way, the next, all had changed. Again, we often instigate these deaths, even though sometimes we do so unconsciously: Robin purposefully chose to attend the workshop, knowing that she was seeking a new way. Al's "death" seemed to be caused by an outer event completely beyond his control, but on a higher, more wholistic level, he may have had everything to do with it; he'd even unconsciously begun to seek support beyond his marriage. When "our time" comes to undergo a death of some kind, our unconscious mind often takes over our outer life and sets up the experience. We may walk in one morning and quit our job: the words just come out of our mouth, and we're as surprised as our boss. This is different from the harmful acting-out behavior I described in the winter stage of the last chapter. This is the Self's way of making us let go of an outworn attachment. Here's an example from my own life:

Years ago I underwent the breakup of a primary relationship. My partner and I had been in trouble for awhile, but neither of us wanted to face the prospect of losing each other. I had been visiting some friends on the East Coast, who had asked me how my marriage was doing. I'd said, quite emphatically, that we were not breaking up—that I saw hope. And I really believed this: my ego was attached to holding this relationship together. (As we've seen, egos can't stand change.) That same day I flew home, and my mate met me at the airport. The very first thing I said to him was, "I'm ending our relationship. I know that it's over—so we need to talk." I watched myself saying this as though someone was taking over my mouth. My Higher Self was speaking. We went to a restaurant and wept into our coffee cups until the wee hours of the morning. We both knew that the end had come; our relationship had hit bottom. And we grieved openly, for all eyes to see, for months. We were completely lost: both of our lives were thrown into turmoil, and we had no idea what would come next. This is Heartwork. And it usually happens while we're looking the other way.

Just as our shadow can pop up from the unconscious and surprise us with its acting-out behaviors, our Higher Self can "act out" through us when we are paralyzed in denial. Whatever we've been trapped in abruptly ends, and a new way is about to begin—even though our conscious mind may not yet have caught up with the whole truth of the situation.

These unexpected and traumatic "chasm experiences" are often accompanied by symptoms I'd like to describe so you can recognize them in case one happens to you (or feel affirmed if one has already occurred in your life). A series of physical illnesses that are not diagnosable by medical doctors may take hold, in the form of extensive and rapid weight loss, eyesight problems, or drastic change in appearance. There also may be dramatic shifts in the emotional quality of your life, such as being tearful for no apparent reason. You may have been someone who never cried, and now you are blubbering constantly for hours or even days at a time. Or you may have always been known as "being together," and now you behave as though you were lost in space. Your friends think you've turned into a total basket case. And you may temporarily lose the respect of many of your old associates. Just like Humpty- Dumpty, no one can put you together again in your old form. It is simply gone.

This is "hitting bottom," the process so well known to people in recovery from addictions. It's the shift we make from *involving* in something to *evolving* back out of it. We've run it out to the end, while being outer-directed and completely caught up. It is time to dis-identify. We had been busy learning. Now, a voice inside us says "It is finished"—an addiction, a relationship, a career, a role. We know it in our bones; it's over:

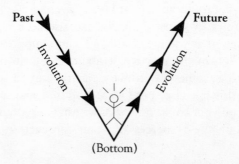

Nowhere to go, no place to hide, we are just there—either stunned or *in* our raw feelings—at the very bottom of ourselves. Like walking off the end of a pier and finding no-thing to stand upon, we've no choice but to await our next right step.

And here is the turning point. Some people freeze on the bottom and go dead inside, terrified of feeling their loss. They never leave the end of the pier, because they've shut themselves off; the next step may come, but they are not open to it. Some stay in this state for years. They walk around in rigid bodies, avoiding everything that could activate their emotions. An example would be someone who dies to a relationship, then vows to never have another. Every time she's confronted with an opportunity to date, her heart constricts and she stiffly declines.

For those of you who choose to move on, you will need to remember the big picture: This is just a condition you're releasing! It's time to call forth your observer self and see your Self still intact. You are greater than what it is you are experiencing. And this "knowing" will allow your deepest feelings to come through and express. A mind that can remain steady and stay in touch with the whole picture—no matter how chaotic it gets, or how badly it hurts while dying to some part of it—will be able to cope with transformation and reach great evolutionary heights. Hitting bottom is a sacred function that enables us to return to the creative void, our source, anytime we need to die to something. And from these depths, we are made new. As so poignantly stated by Dion Fortune in *The Sea Priestess,* "Whoso cannot return to the primordial hath no roots in life, but withereth as the grass. These are the living dead."

For those of you who are feeling stuck and need to return to your source, which is the chasm of your Heart, the exercise that follows might help. You can learn to do this exercise on a regular basis, anytime you feel that you are getting all caught up in some aspect of your life. You might practice it about three times a day for awhile, until it becomes an ordinary part of your daily routine.

As you do this exercise, note what it is that makes your heart contract, within your environment or within yourself, and learn to get clear about these sources of your constriction. They are re-actions! Once you can make them conscious they will no longer rule you. And your heart can remain more open. Likewise, note what it is that causes you to feel expanded, airy, and lighthearted. And you will begin to see what it is you require to express yourself fully and spontaneously—to just be yourself.

You most likely will become painfully aware that feelings are stirring in your gut. Let them come on up—quietly. But really do let them come on up and express—tears or feelings of extreme rage, even of being abandoned or betrayed, can be safely expressed *within your own being—consciously.* (Although those of us with codependence issues often forget this in favor of acting out in the outside world, usually with the people closest to us.) Without repressing them, or going unconscious, *contain these feelings!* You are standing within the tension of "the opposites," between your shadow and positive self. This is how our emotions heal them- selves: We must feel them *as we simultaneously hold ourselves in dominion over them.* Holding dominion over a feeling or idea does not mean stopping it from being; it means merely staying on top of the situation in which it is wanting to express, deciding from a more integrated place what you are going to do about them.

I've found that I can even cry right in the midst of a social activity, with no one but my inner Self knowing it. I let the tears come up into my eyes and heart, and use my breath to connect with them, matching their intensity with the rapidity of my quiet breathing—and staying totally conscious of what's occurring in- wardly as I do this. The times when I usually experience sadness are when something I'm witnessing reminds me of some unfinished business concerning my own losses. There is always a personal connection to the impersonal pain we notice around us; otherwise, we would not relate to it at all. Breathing can help you both realize what it is you are remembering and move on through it. The in-breath fills you with lightness and fresh air (spiritual forces), while the out-breath releases the held-in emotions. You fill up with spirit, and you release negativity. The breath is your best therapist—abiding constantly right under your nose!

Surrender into the Heart
A Guided Imagery Experience

Find a quiet place to sit for awhile. Forget whatever is going on in your outer world and focus on your breath. As you breathe in and out for a moment, notice the feelings in your heart. If you've just become emotionally upset, obviously your heart will be hurting—sore, contracted, or aching. Just notice. Don't judge.

If your heart feels pained and contracted, breathe into your heart. . . . Feel it begin to soften. . . . To relax . . . To drop whatever it is it is holding . . . Just let it go. . . .

Allow yourself to dissolve so that you feel you are merging into the space around you. . . . Feel airy and expanded. . . . Stay with this feeling for awhile . . . (long pause).

Now, from this relaxed state, notice what you are thinking about. If there are still troublesome thoughts, allow the energies of your Heart to reach into your mind and dissolve these thoughts . . . (long pause). Just remain quiet now, until the mind feels free and empty. . . . Then, take some time to sit and rest. . . . And note how much better you feel.

The Practice of
Accelerated Heartwork

Those of you who are undergoing a death of a particular relationship (to a person, thing, substance, career, whatever) or who would like to invoke such a death, the following seven steps are a roadmap to *the dis-identification process.* Most of us truly want to let go of old, dysfunctional patterns and relationships, but we don't know how. We don't realize there are specific steps that can be followed to do so, steps that will take us to even the most remote corners of our psyche. For unless we travel very deeply into ourselves and dis-identify with something completely, we may let the old patterns trip us up again. People in Twelve Step recovery groups can attest to this. And for those familiar with addiction recovery programs, please know that the process you're about to undergo is perfectly compatible, even complementary, to Step-Work.

These steps are already known by your inner Self but need to be brought into your full awareness to become effective. Once made conscious, the process will be available anytime you need it. You can practice these steps in one sitting when you are in crisis and urgently seek to release something (although you shouldn't ordinarily force yourself to let go of something under time pressure). Because they are written in the form of an exercise, it might be useful (as with the other exercises in the book) to tape-record these steps, memorize them, or have someone read them to you when you want to work on them. Eventually, they will become a way of being, an automatic response anytime you're in an accelerated process and need to balance your emotions or seek relief from a codependent predicament.

Releasing the Past
An Exercise

These seven steps will enable you to clear out your old stuff and learn to live within a balanced emotional body. This process is the Higher Power's work and its results will unfold according to the wishes of your Higher Self: we can only prepare, and then stand ready to recognize the changes as they appear. We do not have conscious control over when a transformation actualizes, for timing is always up to the Higher Self.

Be creative. Use these steps any way you wish. It is all the same process, from a tiny "let go" to an all-encompassing death/rebirth. In the descriptions that follow I've given you lots of word-pictures and an intuitive sense of the meaning behind each step. You can shorten these steps into a simple list, or re-create them in your own manner. All emotional release work leads to the same place—to a limpid emotional nature that can reflect balance and true Love.

1. **Surrender.** "I am giving to my Higher Power this aspect of my life [name it], letting go of my preoccupation with it. My ego is powerless over this situation. From now on my mind will be clear of this condition; my emotions and physical body will no longer feel a reaction to it. For I know I am through with this particular condition [name it]. *I release it in love!*" (Even if you don't feel love in the moment, you can *intend* it by saying it anyway. This will activate the release.)

For a moment just experience being in a huge breath of fresh air, expansive . . . and empty . . . with no thought of the subject you just released. . . . If thoughts of this condition or the person involved try to sneak back in, use your will to bring your mind back to the feeling of emptiness. . . . (If tears come, or any other kind of emotional release, let it happen: you are emptying. This means a healing is in progress!)

2. **Recognition.** Reflect now on how this relinquished pattern or relationship has so affected you, and take some time to re-mind yourself there is a bigger picture. *See the whole meaning of this condition all at once.* Maybe you will see the lesson—its spiritual purpose. And perhaps you can sense just how lost (or insane!) you've felt in this situation. You may want to write something at this point, for a profound revelation may come. As you recognize what all this has been for you, you will feel your sanity being returned.

3. **Acceptance.** And now, with total abandon, we are willing to let our will become subsumed under the will of a Higher Power. Take some time now to stand in a feeling of gratitude. You are grateful that such a release is possible—that you can trust your Higher Power to catch hold as you let go. *Being in a state of Gratitude—even for a moment—is the very act of shifting from passive victim to conscious co-creator.* Humbly accept the fact that you are truly a co-creator who, when aligned with a Higher Power, is capable of relinquishing things when you are finished with them.

Realize that you always possess the power to shift your energies to something new. Feel grateful for the lessons you are learning now. Realize how perfect it's all been.

(If you're unable to feel gratitude, please do not judge yourself; just note what you *are* feeling and accept whatever state you are currently in. All of our emotional states—even feelings of being blocked or hopeless—are grist for the mill for a later transformation. Even the nonenergetic states, such as feelings of impotence or of being stuck, can be fully owned and felt through; and then they will release their hold on you.)

4. Sacrifice. Now image what you are sacrificing, recalling fully how it felt when you were attached. Go ahead now and face all that you consider undesirable about yourself or what you are releasing. Let yourself live into what you are giving up. . . . And further, let yourself die to that self who needed this attachment.

Now, gradually begin to feel your way into living without this old pattern. . . . You may feel grief . . . anxiety . . . or loneliness . . . as you move into the unknown—a life devoid of this preoccupation. . . . Pause for awhile now and imagine going through a day in your life without the condition you are releasing. . . . Experience yourself free of it. (Again, you may be overcome with fear or doubt. If these feelings emerge, instead of trying to dodge them, go fully into them. Turn them up to high volume, and feel them all the way through. This is how we heal.)

5. Owning Our Shadow. Visualize a picture or symbol of your shadow—the carrier of these character weaknesses, so mistaken and deformed. . . . Now, very specifically, name each trait or neediness you had that drew this situation to you in the first place. . . . Observe your shadow standing in the warm light of the Heart. See its deformity clearly! Watch as it reveals its shame, and see all its unloving aspects. . . . If you feel that it is hiding, ask it to take off its disguise, and show you more completely who or what it is. . . .

Now, with your imagination, *embrace your shadow.* Enfold your exposed and vulnerable shadow in the warmth of compassion. . . . Be with your shadow until you experience forgiveness, acceptance, or a transmutation. (Your shadow may turn into something different,

more acceptable or whole.) Now, offer this wounded self the
nurturing and acceptance it longs for. . . . As you embrace, feel all
the shadow's defects wash right through and out of you, with no
attachment whatsoever . . . and see them all dissolving in the light
of the Heart's Love. . . . See these old traits becoming light
particles, freed and dancing away to a newfound destiny. . . .
Thank them for having served as your "holy grit," for teaching you
such crucial lessons in Love and unlove.

(If you cannot embrace your shadow, just let it go, wish it well,
watch its image dissipate, and move on to the next step. Also, it
might be helpful for you to process this problem you're having with
your shadow with a friend or therapist. Telling another you trust
what you are ashamed of is often a powerful healing event. And do
not be critical of your progress. Remember, deep healing rarely
happens instantly. Thadeus Golas's saying from his little book, *The
Lazy Man's Guide to Enlightenment,* is helpful here: "Love yourself
as much as you can from wherever you're at.")

6. Balancing of Opposites. This step is designed to completely
remove the attachment from your psyche—to gather up the entire
condition, make it conscious, and move to a state of nonattachment. Reflect now on how this pattern or relationship
you're releasing has been *negatively* affecting you. . . . Feel into
the way it has imbalanced you in the past—too much giving,
too much withholding, too much passion . . . sickness . . . or
passivity. . . . Now, feel into how this pattern or relationship
has *positively* affected you. . . . Note what payoffs you got
from your attachment to it: perhaps it made you feel more
important . . . or distracted you from some fear . . . or helped
you feel sexual, or excited about living. . . . Face whatever it
was that this condition did for you. . . .

Now, feel the pendulum swinging slowly back and forth, from
negative to positive, until it balances in the center. And as it
ceases its movement, feel yourself humbly settle in the Center of
the Heart. . . . Remain sitting in the silence of the Heart for
awhile now, and get used to this calm, serene simplicity. . . .
(Sometimes it takes practice to learn to become still inside—to

experience a feeling of nonattachment. This may be a brand-new feeling for you!)

7. **Living from Center.** As co-creators, we must demonstrate on a regular basis our cooperation with the Higher Power through an ongoing willingness to release our shadow's ways whenever they begin to dominate us. Imagine your ego facing your Higher Self and saying "I am willing!" Then, feel your ego dissolving into the light of your soul, or Higher Self. As you merge into your soul's nature, feel yourself becoming lighter . . . being uplifted. . . . Stay with this feeling until it becomes a felt experience. . . . Now, imagine yourself walking through your day as this Higher Self, going to some of your usual places. Feel yourself as this new, refined, and balanced person. . . . No intensity . . . No attachment . . . Just being! . . . And when you open your eyes, *look around through the eyes of your Higher Self. Imprint this state of consciousness on your mind.* And know that by focusing on this place, you can return to Center anytime you fall off the mark or get hooked in a condition. "Center" is a *feeling* state. We create it with our feelings and imagination. . . . Remember these words of Lao Tzu in the *Tao Te Ching:*

> There is no need to run outside for better seeing . . .
> Rather abide at the center of your being;
> For the more you leave it, the less you learn.
> Search your heart and see. . . .
>
> The way to do is to be.

This is the healing activity of *conscious processing* in action. Thoughts, feelings, attitudes, beliefs, over-reactions—all these responses to our experiences can be worked on within the Heart. Then these reactions dissolve; they are literally melted down to be remade into something more refined. New qualities—such as clarity of vision, calm insight, balanced emotions, and greater physical stamina—are accessed from deep within us. (They were probably just buried underneath all the murkiness we'd collected while we were busy giving ourselves away.)

Later in the book we will go through five more steps, which will help us *re-identify* with higher goals and further us on our path of co-creation.

Healing a Lingering Attachment
A Sacred Ritual

For those of you who want to concretize your process of surrender, the following ritual will increase your powers of dis-identification. But for those of you who are not currently on the bottom and just want to release a lingering attachment, first be sure you are willing to undergo some creative suffering that could possibly take you to the bottom. Rituals are extremely powerful when entered into with a sacred attitude. They tell your Higher Self that you mean business—that you are willing to really let go.

Think specifically now of something you want to give up, something you feel is holding you back. It might be your depression, self-doubt, or fear. Or it might be an attachment to an old relationship you can't seem to release or your attachment to aloneness and your unwillingness to involve. Write it down on a small piece of paper. Be very specific. (Never make it a person! If it's about letting go of a person, label it your attachment to him or her.)

When you are ready, take this small piece of paper and wad it up into a tight ball. Now fill a glass bowl (preferably a beautiful one) half full of water and flower petals. Take a burning candle and put it in the center of the bowl so that it emerges above water level. Now, stand in front of the bowl in reflection, affirming what you want of your Higher Self. And in gratitude, hold the wadded paper ball with a pair of tweezers and light it, being careful not to hurt yourself. As it begins to turn into embers, envision this paper as your relinquished condition. When it is all burned but still in one piece (before it disintegrates completely), drop the burned paper into the water among the flower petals, its burial ground, and look at the shape it takes. Then, feel compassion for this sacrificed "part" you are releasing.

As you stand there, feel as much appreciation and gratitude as you can for the lesson this condition has brought you. See it going back into the cosmos where it can be re-made into something useful for someone else. Nothing is ever lost in this universe—only transformed! This is a loving act, not a destructive one. It is healing you and very possibly others who are involved in what you are relinquishing. Image the power of this process touching those you want it to affect. If you find after doing this that you cannot completely let go or forgive someone, that's okay. Trust that your Higher Power will do the rest. If healing and forgiving is truly your destiny and intention, you will release whatever it is in due time.

Now that we've explored the ways of inner transformation—both slowly through the seasons of inner growth, and rapidly through accelerated growth—we can look at relationships that come from the Heart. For once the Heart is an activated force in our lives, we will no longer relate to one another in the same old outworn ways. The ideas and values we once had about primary relationships will no longer work for us; our old incentives will have shifted. We will hold a new vision of relationships and seek to form them with people who are on the path, becoming conscious and creative.

So let's move on now and learn about relationships with a fourth-chakra quality—people who are learning to "come from the Heart."

Relationships That Come from the Heart: An Interlude

> For many of us today . . . intimate relationship
> has become the new wilderness that brings us face
> to face with our gods and demons. . . . When
> we approach it in this way, intimacy becomes a
> path—an unfolding process of personal and spir-
> itual development.
>
> —John Welwood

In relationships that come from the Heart, couples' lives are sometimes fraught with creative (as opposed to codependent) struggle, for they have often opted for accelerated growth. They're learning to "let it all hang out" together, and they refuse to play ego games. When they hit up against what seems to be an impossible situation, they seek creative solutions and have compassion for each other's unconscious mistakes, rather than simply blaming and judging—or fleeing. They want to truly get to know one another—and thereby understand themselves more deeply. Their primary desire is to remain in the Heart, even when the pain seems unbearable. They know that tasting the true pleasure of living with an open heart is like drinking the sweet nectar of life, a delight so much greater than the drunkenness they've known as

addicts seeking gratification from bottles, pills, glamour, illusions—
and one another! Relaxing into just being themselves is the greatest
freedom.

"Rules for the Road" for Co-Creative Relationships

Many who've suffered from codependence may mistakenly view
primary relationships as being places to escape from the trials of
living; these people have come to view relationships as a drug. They
don't yet see intimate relationship as the spiritual path it is meant to
be, one that is every bit as demanding and growthful as being part of
an ancient mystery school. In fact, as stated earlier, it is often through
codependence and relationship addiction that we actually gain the
lessons we require in order to awaken. We know intuitively that we
belong in relationships—even when we are busy avoiding them!

I know many couples today who are learning to live from the
Heart and, together, are consciously healing their codependence
patterns. Instead of giving examples of their behaviors, I would
like to offer you some of the simple principles and characteristics
of co-creative relationships, a few "Rules for the Road." I have put
the word "rules" in quotes, because unlike most rules, they are not
to be memorized or followed rigidly; they are *living principles*
designed to guide us when our relationships are suffering from
bouts of unconscious living.

But before I outline these "rules," I want to give you the *unifying
principle* upholding all true relating: the law of right relationship.
This one is too big to call "a rule."

The Law of Right Relationship

To unconditionally love and honor each other as equal beings
is the highest freedom.

This is right relationship, a principle we all know intuitively
within our hearts. Right relationship is about each person finding

his or her true place and spiritual purpose within the collective (the relationship and the universe as a whole). We become like individual pieces of a puzzle; when each of us is living as our Truth, taking responsibility for our part, we fill in our own authentic and unique place in the big picture, or the Divine Plan, not leaving any gaps or leaning too heavily into another's rightful space. We are doing "our right part" in co-creating a finished design. And all together we make the statement that *we are members of a sacred transpersonal family of souls, all of equal status. And our nature is Love.* Whenever this revelation becomes part of our daily reality, our relational issues are resolved. We settle alongside one another in right relationship, no longer feeling compelled by constant needs for drama or obsessive focus on others. Our passions and yearnings are no longer directed toward ego games, and we are free to co-create a higher and greater life.

Ten Rules for
Relationships of the Heart

Rule Number 1. Love manifests as freedom to be oneself, not as the bondage of trying to be someone we are not. When you're excited about something other than me, it does not take anything away from our relationship; it only enhances it. If I really value you, I will want for you what you really need—even if I might be threatened by it. If either of us feels that we cannot be our spontaneous selves, we must let the other know, even at the risk of losing the relationship.

All of us are designed to stand alongside each other as spiritual beings, following our bliss. No relationship can fill our lives for us. Letting go of expectation that is rooted in fear and insecurity allows love to flow freely. We then act out of love, not duty. In fact, feelings of duty kill off love. "Shoulds" block the light of our soul.

Rule Number 2. Always tell your partner your truth. Protecting you from my truth is a sickening form of codependence. If I want to be trusted, I must first become trustworthy. But being truthful does not mean I need to be hurtful. If my partner asks me to be honest, I don't need to say, "It's your crooked nose that is bothering me today." This kind of sharing isn't helpful to either of us. But I *can* say in truth, "I'm feeling judgmental of you right now because I'm caught up in my perfectionism." When I communicate from the Heart, I always get to the essence of my truth. In this way, I deepen and become known.

Mature people are not always strong and tear-free. But immature people pretend they are. Playing like we are always strong is an obvious sign of weakness; others notice our shadow acting out even when we don't. Maturity is knowing you can trust that your healthy relationships will remain intact, even when you're down or angry and over-reactive. When I'm "running on empty" I don't have anything to give you. Pretending I'm "there" for you when I'm really not breeds distance and mistrust. If this is my pattern, I need to look at why I fear being honest with you. A codependence pattern may be at work.

Co-creators value just being themselves. They do not always expect to be in a positive state. They know that we are both/and, never either/or. Consequently, they can share from their hearts without judgment—and when they cannot, they own their "stuff" and go do inner work.

Rule Number 3. No one is ever simply "right" or "wrong"; rather, we all receive lessons in how to remain conscious and responsible human beings. Blaming you is a convenient way to not take responsibility for my part—no matter how justified I may feel. Even when I cannot clearly see what my part is, I need to own my contribution to the conflict. I must be willing to discover what that contribution is and then to resolve it. One party never messes up a relationship; it takes a dynamic between at least two. Also, relationship issues that rub me the wrong way usually have something important to teach me about myself. I learn these lessons best by sharing my experiences with you without blaming you or myself. For co-creators are learning to drop blame and judgment. When I am judging you, no doubt there is something about myself that I'm not willing to look at. And when I am judging myself, I'm not giving myself room to change.

Rule Number 4. We all have similar feelings and needs; our storylines are the divergent part. When I'm mad at you, it's my story I'm buying into. When you're mad at me, it's your story that you believe with all your heart. None of us can take others' stories away from them; they are laminated into their brains! When we differ, and heart-felt communication doesn't get us anywhere, it's better to just own that for now, we are in two different universes— mine and yours. And they are both legitimate. For to each of us, our own story is "reality." We can honor each other's stories without having to give up our own. This is a matter of respect for one another's differences and divergent lessons.

Rule Number 5. No one else is responsible for turning us on; getting "turned on" is an inside job. If we are not yet aware that sexuality is part of our life-force, we probably see sex as a body drive that pushes us toward someone else for fulfillment. This attitude might bring us temporary gratification, but ultimately it is an unconscious way of seeking pleasure, and it is not life-giving. And certainly, it is dysfunctional to try to meet our emotional/re-lational needs through the guise of sexual manipulation.

In the Heart, I can experience sexuality as part of my beauty and power, and sex becomes love—a higher emotion. Here sexuality is something within me that I express; it is part of my Self. When I'm tuned in and turned on, my partner will seem appealing to me; when I'm tuned out and turned off, he will not. And he may have nothing at all to do with my response!

The sexual energy that was felt as bondage in the lower nature—attachment to the other for satisfaction—will become transformed into a creative power as we grow in spiritual stature. Saints and sages throughout history have told us that we do not lose the enthrallments of physical sex or emotional romanticism as we spiritually evolve; instead, we learn more healthy and holistic ways of feeling love and loved. Sometimes our sexual energy even increases, along with a newfound discrimination about how to meet sexual and emotional needs. When we begin to rise above egoistic neediness, possessive love shifts to lighthearted play. Once we can function from the Heart, our entire organism becomes as sensual, sexual, relational, and spiritual as we ever desired it to be.

Rule Number 6. Don't let the experience of joy or contentment take you down. Many of us have become so addicted to suffering that we've developed a very low "bliss tolerance." Anytime we begin to experience joy in a relationship, it scares us, and we immediately and unconsciously do something to depress ourselves. We'll revert to an old pattern of dysfunction that will take us back to more comfortable territory. We'll use mental distraction or physical distancing tactics to bring us down; usually it's a negative thought. We don't trust that joy and contentment will last, so why experience it at all? Instead of learning to enjoy the precious moment (without concern for how long it will last), we choose never to live life fully. Co-creators take note of this pattern and make it conscious; then they can work toward expanding their ability to feel bliss. Unless we commit to manifesting the joy in our relationships, we won't recognize fulfillment even when we're right in the midst of it.

Rule Number 7. Aloneness belongs in a relationship alongside togetherness. We must learn how to balance our time so that we can both be alone with ourselves and/or our Higher Power and be involved in activities with friends, family, and partners. Often couples will fight simply to escape the relationship's demands for awhile—just to create distance. For not only do we need our own time, but we also need our own space. Both are necessary in order to breathe and resuscitate. People who say they never need to be alone are simply out of touch with their feelings. Watch how you handle your partner's direct claim that he or she needs to be alone. Quite often, a codependent pattern will be underneath your reaction. We must all learn to aid one another in claiming this vital need for silence, aloneness, and inner work.

Rule Number 8. We grow more from being recognized as having a positive trait than we do from being criticized for having a negative one. When we are recognized by someone as being gifted or doing good, we feel injected with life. This uplift is often the greatest therapist. It helps us rise to our true potential. We want to live up to the compliment, but only if it is something we value in ourselves. Then we feel validated and empowered. False praise never works: we cannot look for these compliments or give them out indiscriminately. But when we do see a genuine opportunity to point out someone's gifts, we must remember to do it. In this way we can help each other real-ize our gifts through the practice of *recognition* (which actually means seeing the essence of people and things—through the eyes of the Heart).

Rule Number 9. Paradox is the name of the game in relation-ship; the more I need, the less I can have. I am responsible for learning what my needs are and then meeting my own basic requirements. No one else can know what I need—ever. Needi-ness and love are incompatible; they cannot manifest within the same space. It's a violation of your integrity for me to pull on you to give me something. Letting go of attachment to "the other" is the Buddha's solution for all suffering. It's usually just our *illusion-ary need* for this "other" and the self-defeating way we go about trying to get that person to meet it that we have to relinquish anyway. When you decide you can do without something you've been insisting on, haven't you noticed how often it magically appears in your life?

As you become conscious you will notice that people we try to hang onto avoid us whenever possible. Anytime you are feeling or behaving *with intensity,* this is your cue that something is your own issue and responsibility—not the other person's. Whenever a fit of neediness strikes, just accept the fact that it's *your* feeling that's up, and it's undoubtedly rooted in loneliness, anger, fear, or anxiety. If you can remember to ask for what you need directly (like a hug, a changed decision, or to be left alone for awhile), you will often get just that. But if you blame the other person or use some other manipulative and indirect means to get what you think you need, you may find that the other party becomes defensive and even less available to you.

Rule Number 10. *In relationships where both people envision ever-expanding love and deepening purpose, the vision becomes reality.* It's more important to share our dreams and visions with one another than to share intellectually what we think we know. When both parties envision a purpose to their lives and work toward becoming more loving and spiritually oriented, their relationship will actually move in that direction. And the two often will find that their coupleship expands into a community of other people who are doing likewise. This lack of exclusivity feeds the relationship and helps it grow, leading all those involved toward right relationship with each other and the world.

Seeing how the Heart works in personal relationships gives us a foundation for understanding all "Heartwork." Again, it is in our primary earthly relationships—with our families, lovers, and friends—that we learn about the mysteries of the Heart, about compassion and the deep workings of Love. And, as you can see from the above descriptions, we are then capable of opening our hearts to all living things.

Now let's move on to explore the powers of the Higher Self, which are accessed through the Heart and which bring our personal relationships to an even higher transpersonal level. As this next section will show us, when we access our "soul powers," these ten rules, as well as the law of right relationship, become internalized, and we move on to "relationships with high callings" that enable us to fully develop our creativity. But first we need to see how these powers manifest in each of us individually, providing a basis for our connections with others and the universe as a whole.

⁑ V ⁂

The Return of Our
Soul Powers

I say these powers will be given to you, but more
correctly, you give them to yourself, for you even now
possess them though you know it not; nothing can be
added from without, all comes from within.

—Will Garver

The Higher Chakras: How We Become Soul-Infused Personalities

There is not an absolute chasm between man and the reality which is beyond him. He can identify with this reality, incorporate it into his own definition of his self, be loyal to it as to his self. He then becomes part of it. He and it overlap.

—Abraham Maslow

Many of us now feel ready to fully embark upon the path to a greater Self. By opening our minds and listening to our feeling hearts, we have already made accessible the powers of the higher chakras, levels five, six, and seven. The object of this chapter is to actually bring these previously hidden or forgotten soul powers down into our everyday lives.

As the last section showed us, when we are aligned with the Heart of our Higher Self, "Heartwork" is automatic and never-ending. We become increasingly *accepting* of ourselves and others and *receptive* to new ideas and paths, making us more and more transparent to our divine nature. In cooperation with the Heart, our observer self recognizes our truth and untruth and notifies us—*in vivo*—when something is on or off the mark. This observing function, as we've seen, is on a higher level than mere intellectual critiquing; it is an inner *felt* sense that something is right or wrong for us. And we cannot violate this sense: When we're off the mark, we experience a "thud"; and when our inner and outer lives are in harmony, we feel a silent and comfortable inner "yes." Those of us who are living from the Heart will never again be able to hide from our true feelings—or anyone else's. In other words, we now are cooperating fully with our inner Self's unrelenting desire to transform. Our Higher Power will now be able to guide us Home.

But the observer self's functions and the open Heart's qualities, as I've described them until this point, are just some of the magical powers we possess. So let's look more closely now at how these and other spiritual qualities can manifest in our lives as soul powers and bring us further toward our destiny as co-creators. Please keep in mind that many of you won't be able to fully manifest all these powers and may occasionally fall back into the ways of your partially imbalanced or uncleared lower chakras. This is only natural—and is part of the growth process. Nevertheless, these higher soul qualities will come through when you consciously invoke them. In fact, simply reading about them may help open your higher chakras and bring out the innate soul powers you've for so long neglected.

The Fifth Chakra: The Powers of Creative Expression

The fifth chakra is that place in consciousness where our creative expression comes alive. This chakra rules the voice, the throat, and thyroid gland. Its color is a clear aqua-blue (more blue than aqua). It is where we access *the powers of imagination, insight, intentionality, and recognition, and then express this wisdom in our own unique way.* This is the home of Higher Mind. And it is here where we learn to "sound our note."

The powers of *insight, recognition,* and *intentionality* enable us to *imagine* and then embody and express our ideals; they empower us to stay with our dreams and see them through. We turn inward and become creative. And this high level of creativity makes us feel good about ourselves and replaces the depression and low self-esteem that accompanied codependence. Through the powers of the fifth chakra we become able to "follow the beat of our own drummer," to express ourselves authentically. Intuitively, we can sense the difference between doing things just to please others and doing what really befits our nature. *Here, the soul blends with the intellect, creating pure intelligence that manifests only in Truth.* These soul powers are crucial—for without them, nothing new could ever be created.

When our hearts are open, our lower and higher minds (chakras three and five) are able to connect. And when they do, even for a moment, we can gain profound insight into and understanding of ourselves and others in our lives. We practice divine thought. For this fifth level of consciousness enhances the ego's intellect, and it gives us the ability to recognize and manifest *Beauty* and *Harmony*. Higher Mind functions like an inner artist. It craves Beauty! And it seeks out Harmony or right proportion in all situations. For example, I may be over-reacting to something in my outer life—lacking clarity or insight about what's really going on inside me—or I may have become too intense about some issue, losing much of my natural ease. When invoked, Higher Mind will observe this kind of imbalance and correct it on the spot, providing the missing ingredients, *insight* and *recognition*. When I step back from the outer situation, I may instantly become calm and see my part, or be able to laugh at myself. Or I might form a mental picture of my condition that gives me the truth of the matter right there on the spot, enabling me to drop my storyline or projection.

Once in touch with these fifth-chakra powers we realize what our spirit wants to manifest and then formulate our lives according to its plans. As the great Yogic master Patanjali taught, we can contact that "raincloud of knowable things" and precipitate divine ideas right here in this ordinary world. We learn to explicate the pearls of life right in the midst of our everyday routines. With spiritual *intentionality* we face in the right direction—upward or vertically, rather than horizontally: We learn to merge with our own creative Source, rather than indiscriminately merging with other people. When we truly let go of our fixation on outer extremes and focus on inner balance and harmony, we begin to see in amazement how much Beauty previously had gone unnoticed. Right relationship becomes an organizing principle in our lives.

At one point in my own life I believed that my home would be made more beautiful if I purchased a multitude of expensive furnishings and antiques. I put my family at risk financially while I went on buying sprees. My house became a copy of other people's materialistic ideas of the latest fashions. Expensive, perhaps, but beautiful? Not really. We've all had the experience of walking into someone's home that is modestly beautiful and creatively designed; we feel uplifted by the simple yet elegant good taste. This illustrates the difference between the third-level "oughts" of trying to impress others and the fifth-chakra quality of taking what one already has or knows and making it into something wondrous.

For the fifth level of consciousness rules the expression of our true talents. It is Plato's level of "good works." When we actualize this level, we often make a lasting contribution to the world. Small or great, these offerings from the Self have the quality of genius. We may not all be Einsteins or Shakespeares, but we each have special gifts to offer the world. When we stop living from the "shoulds" of outer-driven perfectionism, we'll see that we are all creative—even if our creativity expresses through simply planning wonderful weekends or making tasty meals.

At this level of consciousness, we begin to recognize our soulmates and our spiritual communities. We start to feel we are part of a greater family, and we have a strong yearning to share with others our new ideas and creative ventures. Sometimes we rediscover members of our biographical family or old friends we learn to relate to on a deeper level; other times we connect with complete strangers whom we instantly "know" through a mysterious sense of familiarity.

We also attract our life's work at fifth-level consciousness. When we learn to listen for instructions from the Higher Power or our inner Presence (which enters our thoughts during times of mental stillness), we gradually see our chosen work unfold before us. Already designed "in the ethers," it begins to manifest concretely, usually one small step at a time. But again, it's up to us to receive the Higher Power's message; we must have "the eyes to see" and "the ears to hear." For it is the fifth-chakra power of *recognition* that shows us where we are to serve and the people we are to work with. At this level service is no longer the "do-goodership" of the ego, which often aids the doer but not always the one being served. Our egos no longer have a need for the strokes of notice or approval; we "do good" out of abundance, because we are so full we cannot help but spill over!

In addition, because we are learning to focus on our own true expression, we respect each other's differences and divergent choices. This simple shift toward our own unfolding destiny heals a lot of our codependence without much ado; quite simply, we'll be attracted to a higher and totally different kind of relating.

The Sixth Chakra: The Powers of Inspiration and Compassion

Sixth-chakra consciousness is the feeling nature of the Higher Self. In this state, we are infused with true compassion and a desire to serve. The sixth chakra rules the pituitary gland and is stationed in the etheric body at "the third eye," which is between the eyebrows. In Hindu philosophy it's known as "the brow chakra." Its color is a rich, deep indigo blue. This is the place in consciousness where we access *the powers of inspiration and compassion for the whole.*

The sixth chakra complements the second chakra's sexual/emotional center. It refines our earthy passions into the quality of *Goodness*. Our emotional body shifts from being overly reactive and intense to being unattached, yet still passionate and spontaneous. *Here, the soul blends with the emotions, creating enthusiasm and lightheartedness.* We no longer waste emotional energy in the chaos of ego dramas or ungratifying pursuits, for we don't need outside stimuli to turn us on. We are aflame with the energies pouring through us, and we're turned on by our own essence. The future is calling us, and we're listening at last. As stated in the Agni Yoga Teachings, "Fire lives in the hearts of those who love the future!"

When we access the qualities of the sixth chakra, we develop the power of *spiritual discrimination*. This power balances our uneven and sometimes disorderly passions, and replaces our need to act out with a burning desire to serve others. No longer interested in throwing our soul powers away in codependent relationships, or being sexually indiscriminate or emotionally needy, we turn our energies toward more truthful and loving endeavors. Our passion transmutes into *compassion*: we yearn to live lives imbued with meaning and purpose. (I will go further into the concept of Service later on.)

When the qualities of this chakra pour into our hearts, we feel in love with life and those around us, and we no longer seek to harm anyone, even those who may harm us. Having realized the importance of the whole and transcended separatism, we are no longer invested in getting our way. Yet we can stand firm when necessary, because we know who we are and have nothing to hide. We begin to relate to people not as objects for our pleasure or means of satisfying our needs, but as differing facets of one magnificent Diamond, the Self. And we learn to celebrate this diversity of Selfhood with one another. There is now a sense of spiritual purpose in all our relationships. Moreover, when filled with the quality of deep compassion—which is love combined with wisdom—we "gentle down," no longer seeking extremes. We learn to moderate our lives with serenity—even during times of painful growth.

The sixth chakra's energies bring us our loftier emotions. They fuel us with the power of *inspiration*: we become both inspired *and* inspiring, possessing the gifts of leadership and persuasion. For we are magnetic, and draw people to us like moths to a flame. With this quality we can access the future; the divine plan of our lives unfolds one small measure at a time as we gain wisdom about what we love and desire to serve. The urges of altruism have overtaken the urges of instant gratification and excitation.

The Seventh Chakra: The Powers of Illumination and Spiritual Will

Seventh-chakra energy manifests as the will of the Higher Self. Here the ego's will is aligned with that of our Higher Power. The seventh chakra's color is violet, and in certain metaphysical circles this chakra is known as "the Violet Flame" or "the Seventh Ray," believed by many to be the ruling energy for the coming New Age. In the East, it is called "the crown chakra." Its station is the top of the head and it rules the pineal gland.

This chakra responds to light that enters "from above." When open, our seventh chakra connects directly with the vertical dimension, serving as a bridge to a higher order beyond this reality. Most spiritual systems teach that this is the highest level of consciousness human beings can experience. It is the place where we access *the powers of illumination and spiritual will.* When we tap into seventh-chakra energy we are literally standing in the light of our soul. We are one individual statement of humanity's Higher Self. This is what unitive consciousness is all about.

At this high state of consciousness, *the soul blends with the body, making it sentient.* Our abused, numbed-out bodies become sensual and alive. They can now register true pleasure and pain, and can pick up on the vibrations of our surroundings. We are able to feel in our bodies the truth of just about any situation; this is seventh-chakra awareness par excellence. But it is a detached awareness—with no resemblance to the hyper-sensitivity of the maddened and intoxicated addict. For at this high level, we are no longer attached and can identify and dis-identify at will.

When the doorway to this level of consciousness opens, the Higher Power comes through and overshadows us, choosing us as Its instrument of expression. We thereby learn the *true discipline* of the dedicated disciple who submits to higher law. The seventh chakra teaches us the right use of will. Here, we stand in authentic "beingness," fully aligned with our true nature and purpose. Those imbued with this quality have a very potent presence. They carry with them a quiet authority—a "knowing" that comes from having learned life's lessons well. Standing steady with spiritual stature, they are the bearers of Truth.

The seventh chakra's "Violet Flame" is of a very refined quality while also strong and forceful. It was from this level of consciousness that the Christ spoke when He said: "Think not that I am come to send peace on earth: I came not to send peace, but a sword." In fact, the symbol for this level of consciousness is the Sword of Truth. Some refer to it as "the destroyer ray." Its spiritual purpose is to dissolve old forms and usher in the new. It makes us staunch, forthright, and demanding—but always loving.

The old codependent urge we had to control others and to be the boss finds its proper expression when level seven unites with our body/ego. We are no longer unconsciously codependent. The lower needs of the first chakra may not vanish completely and will sometimes try to overpower us, but they no longer rule: instead, we rule them. Our potency now manifests in our ability to *lead* our own lives. We now function according to our ego's refined *Truth*, in addition to Goodness and Beauty. And we draw these qualities out in others as well.

This seventh-chakra energy also balances our first-chakra feelings of isolation and fear of annihilation, which is really the fear of being separated from our Source. How can we feel unsafe when we *know* that we are immortal—and never alone? All the separation anxieties we experienced when we were born vanish when we re-connect to the powers of our crown chakra. In this lofty state, we realize we are a part of the One.

The qualities of this chakra belong to the *practical* mystic or sage, who participates actively and intelligently right here in the world wearing "plain clothes." People at this level would prefer not to be in the limelight—though sometimes their life's work will take them there. They are so grounded that to "do their being" requires no effort at all. Whenever you experience those great feelings of being "together" and whole, you are tapping into this energy. It is the state of Self-realization.

When we find ourselves seeking to resolve a relational conflict, this can be a sign of the seventh chakra at work. For this level of consciousness pulls us toward integration and synthesis. Hence we desire to rid ourselves of dualism and merge into the oneness of spirit behind the content we're caught up in. Moreover, our codependence patterns of people-pleasing are dissolved by this energy. We no longer fear others' judgments. We are open and clear in our communication, and we know where we are headed. We can locomote ourselves away from wrong relationships or ineffectual activities without laying "our trip" on anyone. We just tell the truth. Or if that truth is not welcomed, we simply act as our Truth.

The seventh chakra is a synthesizing energy that brings together all the energies of the higher chakras. We now embody the powers of the fifth, sixth, and seventh chakras and are well on the way toward our unfolding destiny. We are full of spiritual purpose. At this level there is no "other"; there is only "the One." But paradoxically we have a strong sense of "otherness," a sensitivity to the feelings and plights of all peoples. Our selfishness has transmuted into Self-ness.

Becoming a Soul-Infused Personality

I hope you now can see how the soul's nature merges with the ego's three-layered structure—its body, its emotions, and its mind. When our hearts are clear and open, the lower chakras become imbued with soul qualities: the codependent first chakra's involuntary "urge to control" now will be directed upwards instead of wasting itself in futile attempts to always control ourselves and other people. You'll have a body that can safely register the soul's sensuality, its true feelings, yearnings, and desires.

Moreover, the second chakra's involuntary urge to excite will transform into balanced emotions that are enthusiastically primed and fueled with compassion. You will be filled with newfound hope, liveliness, and inspiration—the true pleasures of creative force that are far more fulfilling than the temporary thrills the imbalanced second chakra seeks.

And you will no longer obsessively need to merge your

identity in with the people you feel close to; you will be secure in your life and in your own humanness. For you now realize that you are eternal and part of a bigger plan. Your third chakra will balance. You'll have a mind that can receive impressions from the Divine Mind and resonate with higher ideals and inspired thinking rather than indulging in the judgments and fears of the damaged lower chakras. These transformations are the makings of co-creators who see through the eyes of their soul.

Because these powers have always been within you, when you arrive at the gateway of the Heart and the higher chakras, you feel as if you're coming Home. You've returned to a familiar place that you never really left, and you recognize a "fragrance" that had dissipated, yet somehow is still remembered. This mystical perception was always underneath all your codependent urges. It was the drive underpinning your addictive searches for highs and other nonordinary dimensions of Reality. The inner and Higher Self is the root-consciousness from whence you've sprung. The inner Artist, the Mystic, the Divine Builder, and the Co-creator make up your true identity. When we commit to a higher purpose, these "Rods of Power" are returned to us one by one. Just like young King Arthur, we are able to lift the Sword of Truth right out of the hardened stone of our conditions.

These mystical inner forces have driven the human soul for ages, although as a people we seem to have collectively and temporarily forgotten how to use them. Today, a return to the inner life of the Self, or soul, is an imperative. We must bring a sense of meaning and hope back into this materialistic world, or our desired future will remain a veiled and dormant dream. We must use these powers to create societies that are more attuned to our spiritual natures. As said so beautifully by Dominican priest Matthew Fox, "Mystics must come out of the closets, must gather to share their stories that we might set fire again to our tired and cold civilization."

And remember, these qualities do not belong just to saints and sages; we *all* have the ability to merge with our Higher Self and the powers of the soul latent within us. But we must be willing to do the inner psycho-spiritual work necessary to clear out our minds and hearts so that we can recognize these spiritual gifts—to receive them, and then have the courage to act on them.

It's also important to remember that you do not move in a linear progression through these chakras. The Heart opens the gateway for *all* of these higher, more refined energies to pour through you and out into your life. They are invoked by your commitment to them, which initially means you must *act as if you are them,* practicing these qualities and powers until they become second nature. As with any new behavior, do as they say in Alcoholics Anonymous: "Fake it till you make it." These powers are your birthright. You only feel separate from them while you are undergoing your ego development. Once you commit to turning inward and upward, these high qualities are yours to wield right in the midst of your ordinary lives.

In the next chapter, we'll explore relationships that contain these higher chakra energies and mystical powers. For rarely do we manifest these high expressions in isolation: it is through inspired relating that we change ourselves and our world.

Relationships with High Callings

> In communing with himself he finds not deadly
> boredom and melancholy but an inner partner,
> more than that, a relationship that seems like
> the happiness of a secret love, or like a hidden
> springtime when the green seed sprouts from the
> barren earth, holding out the promise of future
> harvests.
>
> —Carl Jung

Most of you have realized by now that the Higher Self is not separate from us; It *is* us! It is our "other half," the true Beloved all lovers seek and that never leaves us—not even for an instant. You need not crave another for intimacy and a deep sense of mission or purpose; you need only to awaken to your Self. For you are already complete, fully equipped with everything from sensual bodily pleasures to numinous spiritual delights—just as you are. The path homeward for all of us is to unite once again with this inner Beloved, to fall madly in love with ourselves and our lives.

In this chapter we will see how people awaken when they return to their Beloved, bonding with their inner Self. And we will watch them enter into right relationship with all whom they encounter.

Both, or all, parties in these couples or groups are becoming *individuated*—meaning they express their true natures alongside and in harmony with one another. They do not lose themselves in their relationships. They are no longer codependent; they are co-creative.

Relationships with high callings can develop in any facet of life. Their hallmark is this: Two or more people come together and create a third (or fourth or fifth!) "something," which is inspired and serves more than their egos' desires. On a deep level, they are committed, not only to each other, but to *materializing the spiritual world*. (And some might see themselves as vehicles for *spiritualizing the material world.*) These inspired relationships can take the form of romantic couples, or family units (householders, as Buddhists call them). But these are not only love or family relationships. In fact, they are often most evident in the expressive arts: masterful duos in figure skating, dance, music, acrobatics, or athletics. They also manifest among business people, politicians, scientists, religious leaders, teachers, students, therapists, coworkers of any sort, or among friends. These relationships don't always look "spiritual," for the people involved are most often not ministers or great missionaries, nor do they frequently have an obviously high goal: they can be gardeners, clerks, or next-door neighbors.

As you read about the specific ways these relationships materialize, try not to get caught up in the glamour of how they appear. If you get hooked on the *outer* form of a relationship, it will become a codependent one; you will become addicted to it. If you remain aware that I am describing an *inner* dynamic, and that the relationship is always with your Self—even though the varying bodies and faces may change—you are becoming a co-creator. However, it is not unusual to become fixated on one of these relationships, growing overly attached to the other person rather than holding steady in the high *process* you two (or more) are co-creating. This common confusion has existed throughout human history, and was the subject of much of Carl Jung's work. People often are seduced by the plethora of myths about "soulmates" and "Twin Flames." And they can base their entire lives on illusion, believing their inner masculine, or animus, and inner feminine, or anima (soul), comes in only one outer embodied form (when really this is the exception rather than the rule).

Nevertheless, all high and purposeful relationships do have an archetypal tone or feeling to them. Some people in romantic relationships may genuinely feel they are Ideal Lovers. In such cases, their outer mates match with their Inner Ideal—at least for the moment, or from time to time. The danger is in expecting this feeling to last forever, or to serve as a panacea for all of life's pain.

When people enter into one of these high-powered relationships, they recognize this fact in the silence of their hearts, for words are too limiting to describe this exalted dimension. The minute we try to speak about it, the relationship usually lessens, fragments, or changes. Moreover, people who have a constant need to remind you of the spiritual nature of their relationships or their lives are always talking from the ego. (Egos love to masquerade as the Higher Self and will not let you forget how "holy" and "evolved" they are.)

It is also crucial to stand back and look at these deep or archetypal connections before acting on them or trying to materialize them. Many couples who feel bonded are not meant to be romantic mates—or even necessarily to relate concretely in any fashion. They realize they are related *in essence,* and they know that no outer condition can truly affect their sacred bond. For example, true soulmates would never break up a functioning marriage in order to be together, loudly proclaiming their eternal love. This kind of nonsense is a form of spiritual by-pass. Real eternal mates have no need to tear up their lives for physical love. Instead, each lovingly honors the other's current involvements. However, they might find they can do something together that will serve a higher goal, or they may find some other way to share their lives that is harmless to others in their world.

When romantic relationships are imbued with the quality of high Love, there's no doubt that they are purposeful and spiritually directed. And as a result, there is seldom any drama. Unlike in ego-driven relationships, there is no jealousy, competitiveness, or longing for some new mate. There is an eternal bond that is strong and fulfilling to the soul. In spite of the trials of living—or even separation, if the two are living apart—the couple will feel perfectly mated from the inner side of life. They share each other's visions and dreams. These Love partners and soul brothers and sisters share a deep and wordless understanding, going about their high business, knowing intuitively that their love is not to become a drama—nor is it to be denied.

The Psycho-Spiritual Dynamics of High Relationships

Co-creative relationships are triadic, for they are dedicated to that third "something," which is the will of the inner Beloved. They are colored by the transpersonal qualities of the higher chakras: Control needs are now met by the true authority of the Self; over-excitation is grounded in worship, devotion, and high spiritual love; and that old codependent urge to merge and disappear into someone else is now inwardly directed toward our true Beloved—the soul. And the soul, like a flame, reduces to ashes anything within us that blocks us from turning *all* our relations into loving ones.

I've found that there are four basic components of high relationships: 1) an ongoing commitment to psycho-spiritual inner work; 2) a desire within each person's heart to serve a higher calling; 3) an openness that enables them to recognize this life's work as it unfolds; and 4) a willingness to direct their energies toward this inner calling. Because co-creative people are in touch with their spiritual purpose, they often become lights or guides for others. But this does not mean that they model perfection! This would be an illusion of the ego. They are simply willing to be fully present, relaxed, and truthful.

However, it is important to remember that co-creative relationships are not always functioning at high levels. The people involved are not living saints in the way we commonly define them. They merely draw down soul powers spontaneously from time to time, to be used for unselfish purposes in some manner or other. These relationships may even still have a few dregs of codependence that crop up when they are under stress, requiring vigilance from the observer self; but they lack the debilitating lifelessness of imbalanced lower chakra relationships. For there will be little need to overly focus on the other, to feel separate from, or to argue: the two (or more) of you will be able to overcome differences through communication that is respectful, caring, and attentive.

Now I will explore in more detail different kinds of co-creative relationships. These are ideal states I will be describing, but if we are committed to manifesting them, we can access these levels of consciousness and our relations can become purposeful and full of love. While describing each chakra I will also illustrate the kind of inner work, or Yoga, one can do to tap into these high levels and the spiritual by-pass that can occur if we're not careful. Spiritual force is potent! Many can become consumed by it and fall into the negative patterns of using spiritual powers for the sake of ego gratification.

As you study the descriptions that follow, you may realize that some of your favorite relationships have high callings—you just hadn't noticed. Or you may become better able to visualize the kind of relationships you want to develop. But again, try not to think of these higher chakra relationships in a linear fashion. These high powers are really just essences we tap into at certain points in our lives, often without our recognition.

Relationships with a Fifth-Chakra Quality

People in these relationships have intellects that have merged with the Higher Mind (which as you remember, always makes room for the Heart). They are traveling together on a path of Self-understanding, what Hindu philosophy calls the path of Raja

Yoga, the Yoga of Self-knowledge. Relationships with a fifth-chakra quality function largely *at the mental level,* meaning these people learn best through concentrated thought. They often unite through a creative sharing of ideas and visions. Their keynote is active intelligence, for they *understand* and then they *practice* what they know. Because their third and fifth chakras have united, their intellects are being trained on the inner side of life, and they have a passion for exploring philosophical worldviews, which they feel are the hope of the world. For they see that most of our sorrows today result from the lack of a proper philosophic base. They seek knowledge about how divine and human laws really work and how they can cooperate.

Sometimes these people literally become the thinkers for the human race. For instance, two or more people may write a book together that changes how many people think. Or they may create an ideal model that changes how an institution, government, or political group is run. Or, if they live a simpler life, they may study great literature together, or meditate collectively for the troubled world, or hold discussion groups for people who want to learn to think more clearly and share their ideas.

There are many fifth-chakra groups and couples heading up service institutions, ministries, grass-roots organizations, or centers of philosophy and education that stand for spiritual truth and are propelled by this quality. These groups can see how larger patterns unfold beyond the ego's intellect, and they can concretize and express these archetypal patterns. Fifth-level archetypes are the mental geniuses of the race. And since archetypes are principles only, they manifest in one way—through *us,* when we live as these qualities, when we take them on.

Fifth-Chakra Forms of Spiritual By-pass

It is not uncommon for people to misuse these high mental energies. They may become enamored with their wisdom or myopic in their thinking and decide they have the answers. They mistake these egoistic ideas for spirit's work and set about implementing their idiosyncratic desires. And without realizing it, they contribute to the ruin of the planet—all for what is really personal gain. They have lost sight of the whole. Their third chakras have become imbalanced, contaminating their mission.

We must all guard ourselves against spiritual arrogance. Our codependent urge to merge can easily dominate our intellects and projects, causing us to lose objectivity. For example, two great Nobel scientists might decide their discovery is the only one that can save humanity; they believe they are "special" or "messengers from God." They've lost all perspective and are using the spiritual power they gained from their discovery to satisfy their third chakras' imbalanced urges. We must learn to stand back from our projects or missions and redirect ourselves when we feel we are slipping into this fifth-chakra pitfall.

Relationships with a Sixth-Chakra Quality

This chakra takes our animal passions and transmutes them into a type of "sexuality" that seeds whole new creations, such as artistic expressions, new religions, new philosophies, or new psychologies. In these high relationships, passion, sexuality, and emotion are the cornerstone; the people involved are functioning from their *feeling nature.* They can *feel* Truth and learn to balance the precarious energies of their sexual/emotional nature. They are following a path of the Heart, and their keynote is devotion. These potent people sometimes have an awakened kundalini, an Eastern concept that means the sexual center has fully opened and become an inner spiritual force spreading throughout the body and no longer contained only within the erogenous zones. Sixth-chakra energy is essentially a heart-felt, intense ecstacy or compassion, which manifests as worship of the inner Beloved and as a path of service in the outer world. This process is beautifully taught in the Sufi tradition; in our work, we sing a Sufi song, written by Zuleikha, that describes this heart-felt compassion:

Rabia, Rabia, the people asked.
Why are you weeping?
And Rabia replied: I am sorrowing.
But Rabia, Rabia, they said to her,
Why are you sorrowing?
And Rabia replied:
I am eating the bread of this world,
While doing the work of that world.

Other spiritual traditions also teach this path of the Heart. Bhakti Yoga is the Hindu practice of high worship and devotion. And the Hindu and Tibetan Buddhist, Chinese Taoist, and Kashmir Shaivism schools of Kundalini and Tantric Yoga teach methods that balance the sexual/emotional energies.

People in these high relationships often together become healers, spiritual leaders, or creative artists and craftspeople. Two inspired surgeons saving a life would be one example. Another would be several talented musicians "jamming" together, when suddenly their creativity becomes so passionate and exhilarating that the audience bursts into spontaneous applause. Their "high love" is contagious; it spreads to all who participate in their masterful artistry. But sixth-chakra relationships are not limited to lifesaving activities or to the expressive arts; as I stated earlier, co-creators are *all* artists and muses of the soul—regardless of their occupations! A man and a woman lovingly coming together to create a child is also an example of ignited sixth-chakra energy, as is two people joining together to create a relationship that models mutuality, openness, and deep caring.

People who function at this high level have mastered the passions and emotions associated with the lower rungs of the evolutionary ladder: their sexual and emotional natures now obey a very high spiritual law. The same energies that once manifested in the lustful desires of codependence through an imbalanced second chakra are now inwardly directed, inspiring divine co-creative activities that can help liberate others.

But, once again, releasing our patterns of codependence does not mean we must lead lives devoid of pleasure and desire. I recall feeling doubt about this when I first embarked upon "the path." I used my fear of losing my sexual self as an excuse for remaining stuck in certain romantic illusions. I would constantly warn myself that I might become so heavenly that I'd have no earthly pleasures. However, I gradually learned that nothing human need ever be lost on the evolutionary path—although it can be augmented by a finer quality. Sometimes we may even bounce between the energies of the second and sixth chakras as we grow in spiritual stature and learn to balance our passions.

Sixth-chakra energy in its highest form is known as "the Christ Consciousness" of compassion. In metaphysics it is sometimes called "high Heart." Although this level of high love has only been modeled in pure form by saints, prophets, and sages, we are all capable of embracing this selfless love and spiritual function.

Sixth-Chakra Forms of Spiritual By-pass

If our second-chakra imbalances are severe, they may contaminate these highly charged energies. We then can misapply them either emotionally or sexually; we may become sexually indiscreet, or fall into some kind of romantic illusion. As I said earlier, egos often misuse the "soulmate" or "Twin Flame" ideal to glamorize a lower chakra relationship and to rationalize their materialistic urges toward romance, sexual acting out, or interfering with each other's committed relationships. These types of activities become dysfunctional quite easily, often containing painful lessons, or "karmuppance" as Ram Dass humorously calls it—meaning that there are cosmic "just desserts" when we misuse potent spiritual forces for the sake of the ego only.

Once a beautiful young woman told me she had given her baby boy up for adoption because her "Twin Flame" had come into her life and asked her to work with him. He couldn't be distracted with raising her child because "in a former lifetime he had committed to being childless this go-round." Years later, long after the "Twin Flame" had left, I heard she was contacting adoption agencies, vainly trying to find her child. Moreover, a man I knew in college has left at least four women since I met him—each one, serially, became his long lost "Twin Flame." (Once, all his exes got together and had a big laugh!)

The second-chakra "romantic love" addiction likes to march around pretending to be high love. In romance addiction, we try to make our outer mate permanently and perfectly match our inner Ideal mate. But it doesn't work. In our ignorance, we either leave the person for someone who seems to better match this Ideal, or we try to manipulate our mate into changing. We are often addicted to "unrequited love" (*safe* love!). And disenchantment rules our lives. We fail to realize that our inner Ideal, our true Beloved, is something only we can manifest, and it can be present no matter what relationship we're in (unless, of course, our relationship is irreparably dysfunctional).

A Warning About Kundalini Awakening

Kundalini awakening is a true spiritual path and is experienced legitimately by many people, in the East and West alike. A universal process, it is known in Hinduism and Kashmir Shaivism as "the rising of the serpent power" or the "Shakti force" of the Divine Feminine; in Japan, it is called *ki*; in Chinese, *chi*; and in Christianity, it is known as the Holy Spirit. But there has always been a lot of glamour associated with this potent and enlightening spiritual force.

The rising of the kundalini is an actual biophysical awakening wherein all seven chakras are systematically opened, sometimes all at once (which can cause a "spiritual emergency"), but more often gradually through proper training and practice. (I won't go into these Yogic practices here, but there are many books on the subject and I've included some in Appendix Two.) When the kundalini is awakened, the soul powers that live in the physical body rise up the spine and travel through the chakra centers, awakening them, filling them with light. If each chakra is clear, there will be little disturbance. The light will shine through, and the energies of that particular quality will be released into our lives. If, however, we're holding onto some unfelt experience, Shakti, as she comes through, will invite us to complete these issues—and sometimes not very gently. We may be jolted by the force of kundalini, and an imbalanced emotional state may ensue until the energies resolve.

In Eastern cultures, where this phenomenon is more widely known, kundalini energy is known to purify all the chakras like an inner spiritual fire. Once this type of awakening occurs, the person is never again the same. People with awakened kundalini energies usually produce great works. Their creative force is awakened.

However, kundalini awakenings are not fun—and they're not romantic. In fact, they can be dangerous if a person has not worked through most of his or her lower chakra imbalances. Moreover, people who are in a spiritual by-pass sometimes unconsciously use the symptoms of this inner awakening (which can be physically and emotionally painful, and even bizarre) to rationalize the pain of their unprocessed family issues. No one should attempt Kundalini Yoga practices or other spiritual methods that activate the chakras unless he or she is prepared to undergo an accelerated process that can be quite excruciating and unless one has the support of others. If opened fully, the energies are dispersed in ways that provide light and high love. But the half-awakened "serpent" can ignite the well-known dangers of the kundalini power, such as imbalances in the nervous system or physical illnesses for which doctors can find no medical cause. Sexual promiscuity can also result.

Eventually the energies run to the top of the head, bringing forth full spiritual clarity. Then, many believe, it comes over the head and back down through the chakras until it settles in the belly, safely balanced in the center of our being. Its host is now blessed with an enlivened sexual/spiritual force to use for the sake of the world. Gopi Krishna reminds us that

The aim of the evolutionary process is to create a more noble, more sober, more far-seeing, more sensitive, more compassionate, and more loving individual.

But warns that

> Those who think that their . . . spiritual discipline has come to
> fruition or that their kundalini has awakened would do well to assess
> their progress by a critical examination of their own thoughts, acts,
> and behavior to know how far their evolution conforms to the
> standards set in the great religious scriptures of the world. (*Kundalini
> for the New Age*)

Relationships with a Seventh-Chakra Quality

People who embody seventh-chakra energies are working toward
manifesting spiritual values in the outer world. They may be
members of groups that are attempting to design whole new
cultures for an emerging Age. These relationships are functioning
from *the physical level*—the level of concrete activity. The people
involved in these relationships learn best by *operationalizing* their
ideas and values and correcting them as they unfold. They know
the true essence of discipline, and are attracted to a "path of the
will," such as the practice of hatha-yoga, which disciplines the
physical body through orderly postures that align it with spirit.
This Yoga often includes the practice of healthy diet and nutrition
as well. Agni Yoga, the Yoga of fire, is also attractive to people
who are learning to use their spiritual radiance in the world of
form. For our nature is fire—and requires much discipline and
understanding. People involved in relationships of this category
are "walking the mystical path with practical feet," as transpersonal teacher Angeles Arrien says. They are able to express the
will of the Higher Power in this world.

This chakra is so divine and aligned with spiritual purpose that
egoistic relationships become impossible at this level. Those
involved are not living the personal life at all, unless it has totally
blended into planetary work. For the seventh chakra empowers
only high work. Joseph and Mary, who birthed Jesus, would be
archetypes of this quality. Shakti and Shiva, the spiritual founders
of the Hindu tradition of Kashmir Shaivism, would be another

example. This seventh chakra is the much-esteemed "Violet Ray" of metaphysics, as mentioned earlier, that comes in during times of global transformation and spiritualizes every new Age. Many believe we are currently in one of those transformational times. And even though most of us probably don't have the ultimate high destiny that our beloved archetypal models have, we co-creators all seek our high work, a notion I will develop in the next section of the book.

Seventh-Chakra Forms of Spiritual By-pass

When people are still gripped by an egoistic need to control or manipulate their surroundings, they will misuse their fiery natures. And they can become "black magicians," people who utilize spiritual force for the sake of ego gratification and aggrandizement, caring naught about how their actions might affect others. To avoid falling into this trap, it is crucial to learn the practice of surrender, to place ourselves at the mercy of our Higher Power. We must learn to walk a path of true spiritual discipline. When in doubt about the effect of actualizing our spiritual powers, we choose not to act. When we are truly guided by the Higher Power, we will know it, as such actions will feel loving and wise and will never lead to the domination or manipulation of another human being.

A misuse of seventh-chakra energy is a misuse of the will. However, we must be patient with ourselves. When we first begin to utilize this high energy, we may "come on too strong," until we get used to being authentically powerful.

Now that we've seen how the inner Beloved teaches us the ways of the Higher Self and allows us to manifest our soul powers along with those around us, we are ready to move on to more fully explore the concept of Service I've been referring to throughout this section. For Service is how we maintain and manifest our soul powers in the inner and outer worlds. And in the next portion of the book, we'll also learn that we are involved in a universal evolutionary process, not only with those we are in relationship with, but with an undiscovered community of like-minded people, who are learning their own unique way of Service in the world, and who can become members of our new co-creative families of choice.

But before we move into this final section, let's do some inner work. The following imagery will give you the opportunity to meet your own inner Co-creator, a living Principle and Truth within your unconscious mind. You will reach into your future for this identity, while at the same time allowing your past to pull you back to complete your old identities—and to say good-bye.

The Co-creator:
A Guided Imagery Experience

Find a quiet place to sit for awhile, close your eyes, and take a few minutes to relax. Gently breathe in and out until you feel yourself settling down. Be especially aware of your breath and how it feels as it enters, fills, and leaves your body. . . .

Now, let your body be infused with sensuality. . . . Feel the deadness leaking out, and notice how the sensuality feels as it fills your body . . . (long pause).

Allow your soul to slowly overtake your emotional body now. . . . Let your feelings merge completely with the Heart's love. . . . Pause for awhile, and really feel what is occurring within your heartspace . . . (long pause).

Now . . . shift your focus to your mind and feel your head filling with pure, crystal-clear intelligence. . . . Note what this feels like inside your mind. . . . And then allow your mind to explore what you know you are capable of. . . . Reflect on your talents and experiences for awhile. . . . And now be filled with inspiration! . . . (long pause).

As you sit there with your eyes closed, feel yourself breathing in the light of your higher identity—the Ideal that you wish to become with all your heart. . . . Breathe in this new Self . . . and feel yourself becoming it . . . (long pause). Allow the old parts of you that were excessive and are no longer needed to melt away, as this new Self emerges. . . . Let yourself feel the tension between the pull of past hurts and the pull of future joys. . . . Become aware of what is there right in between this feeling of hurt and joy (while feeling them simultaneously). . . . Find the point in the midst of the tension. . . . And let this place become your whole being . . . (long pause).

As you do this, note how your inner Self shifts your stance—your body posture and positioning. . . . See how It wants to sit. . . . And how It wishes to present Itself. . . . Now, just let It be . . . (long pause). With your eyes still closed, imagine that you are looking out at the world as this new Self . . . as your Higher Self. . . . Notice how your perspective is changing. . . . Feel this transition happening, right now . . . (long pause).

As you slowly open your eyes, imagine that you are staring into a mirror. . . . You are seeing the clearest, most beautiful Being you've even seen! This is yourself, as Whole, in all your glory! . . . For this is You! . . . And You are glorious!

≫ VI ≪

Co-Creation: A Shared Human Destiny

What is it in the end that induces a man to go his own way, and to rise out of unconscious identity with the mass . . . ? It is . . . called vocation [which] acts like a law of God. . . . Anyone with a vocation hears the voice of the inner man: he is called.

—Carl Jung

Service Is "Doing Your Being"

> I feel that if one follows what I call one's "bliss"—
> the thing that really gets you deep in the gut and
> that you feel is your life—doors will open up. . . .
> Through your own inner experience, the divine
> mystery is revealed.
>
> —Joseph Campbell

At one point during the well-known *Power of Myth* television series that featured mythologist Joseph Campbell, journalist Bill Moyers asked, "And you tell people to 'follow their bliss,' Dr. Campbell. What exactly does this mean?" The great man looked into the camera, childlike, innocent, and *blank*! After a short silence Mr. Moyers laughed and said, "Well, Dr. Campbell, I guess you just *do* it, don't you?" And a look of relief melted Joseph Campbell's face as he beamed and said, "Yes! Yes, Bill, I do!"

Following our bliss is something no one can teach us. It is co-creation in action. And it happens when we begin listening to our inner voice and following our spiritual urges. Then our life's path unwinds like a golden thread, and we take on the life of the Co-creator. We have a new sense of purpose that enables us to wear a quiet smile as we go about our outer activities, even during the hard times. Following our bliss is soul's work; it is the simple act of "doing our being."

Co-creators live in a state of bliss, although at times they may go unconscious and become attached to their conditions (which happens to all of us from time to time). However, people not yet on the path don't even understand or recognize the consciousness of bliss. For them bliss is still confused with happiness. And happiness is an ego state only, still dependent on outer gratification. In fact, happiness is seldom truly rewarding, for it is temporary, often vanishing as quickly as it appears. People who spend their lives seeking happiness feel good when they have it and flat or miserable when it eludes them. The search for happiness can itself become an addiction.

Bliss, on the other hand, rises up from within us, not depending on anything outside. And it exists right at the midpoint between the tension of "the opposites" I described earlier. While feeling the *pain* of a human condition, such as the death or loss of a loved one, we simultaneously feel the *joy* of its meaning and purpose, the "high ritual" this loss signifies. No longer can we react to an event without seeing its deep significance. We are *both* human *and* spiritual at once. We experience the *fullness* of the Heart, of which the mystics speak. Like Rabia in the Sufi song, we are "eating the bread of this world, while doing the work of that world"—a conscious walker between two worlds.

Then there's another side of bliss, when we are not going through any kind of predicament. During these times, there is no intensity, and we just walk through life, doing our being, "taking time to smell the roses." We aren't needy or weighed down by tension or worry; we dance like rapidly moving light particles. This is the *emptiness* of the Heart, of which the mystics speak.

Bliss can bring us either state: We are either uplifted by total freedom and expansion, or by the intense emotion of a situation, both its pain and joy. Again, bliss is the center point—between the pain of the past we are purifying and the joy from the future we are becoming. It is the feeling of being awake in the fullness of each moment.

Co-creators see that *their addictions are mere "freeze-frames" in time*, taken on while they identify with some condition fully (so they can "know" it). And *creativity is the flow through time* that dissolves these addictive patterns and leads them to their next emergent step. Although co-creators are *very* feeling creatures—completely in touch with their physical, emotional, and mental bodies—they are not attached to their emotions. They allow their unfinished feelings from the past to brew consciously within their minds and hearts. Like a rich stew left on a back burner to simmer while the cook goes about other chores, the emotions no longer command priority, making their host act out.

Co-creators know how to let go of suffering and they know the power of *gratitude*. This soulful emotion helps hold them in a state of bliss. When they feel its quality entering their hearts, they can turn away from feelings of victimhood (the past) toward feelings of expansion (the future). They become willing to see "their part" and the purpose behind every plight, with gratitude even for the extremely painful lessons. Anytime you feel your past threatening to consume you and your mind beginning to fixate there, open your heart and go into a state of gratitude, while asking to be shown the Truth. In this way, you make the shift from victimhood to empowerment as a soul. Your *ego's intensity* will transform into the *soul's intentionality.*

As you read about bliss, the Co-creator, and other aspects of our Higher Self, don't think that I am merely dreaming. By now, I've met thousands who are entering these stages of awakening. The higher archetypal "personalities" I've been discussing are every bit as real as the inner child, the shadow, the codependent, the clown, the addict, or the family hero that you've heard so much about. The only difference is that these higher selves are a part of *your future,* not your past; and if you want to come into your *full* identity, you must give them as much attention as your more familiar selves. Until now you may not have known to focus on your future; you've been too mesmerized by your past! You may have feared not measuring up to your Ideal, feeling safer in your limited identities. But the result is that you've been hiding from the Higher Self.

Codependence is a challenge we must face at the very core of our being-ness: it is an evolutionary crisis, as I stated earlier. And it is a hurdle we must move beyond in order to drop our attachment to the situations and relationships we've outgrown. We learn to love, forgive—and leave, if something is finished (and we always know when it is). As we become masters at dissolving attachment, we'll see that this has always been our natural way to travel. We were never intended to hang onto anything in form—for we are *spiritual* beings! Therefore, we don't stop anywhere for long; the journey is our home.

If you feel yourself resonating with much of what I've said, you undoubtedly are taking on your identity as a conscious co-creator. And the principles below will become your reality, guiding you anytime you stumble:

The Co-Creator's Pledge

- *I am willing to stand steady in my truth, even when the price is high.*

- *Any feelings of victimization I fall into, I will immediately replace with a commitment and willingness to stop and see "my part."*

- *I seek to deepen into the existential and transpersonal realms of my consciousness, where the principles of wholeness can be accessed.*

- *I am constantly willing to sacrifice "the lesser" in me for "the greater."*

- *I am willing to empower others as co-creators, with the utmost respect, providing validation and support for other seekers like myself.*

- *I can honor others' differences, enjoying the richness their diverse interests and expressions bring into my life, and will aid others in seeking and discovering the oneness behind all diversity.*

- *I pledge to serve humanity in my own unique manner, offering my gifts and talents whenever opportunities present themselves. I know now that it is my own level of commitment which creates such opportunities for service.*

- *I will offer my philosophy and work to others through the principles and powers of attraction, not promotion—and never coercion.*

Service

Service is the outstanding characteristic of the soul, just as desire for ego gratification is the outstanding characteristic of our lower nature. As we've seen already, we reach a point in our evolution when ego pleasures are no longer that interesting to us. Nor is our own personal growth. It's not that we don't like having the thrills of a gratified ego or focusing on our own exciting process of awakening; it's simply that a more expanded life is now attracting us. We yearn to put our lives in order and turn them into ones with meaning and high purpose. As our reality enlarges, we are called by the archetype of Service, which invites us to take responsibility for what we create and to be willing to do so in alignment with our Higher Power. We use our own ongoing growth process as a model and basis for co-creating a healthy world. As co-creators, it is up to us to bring into being a different scenario, one in which it is possible to have growthful relationships (and where all people have an equal opportunity to do so).

As the great spiritual leader Krishnamurti once said, all human problems in the world today are a matter of consciousness. Because we are conscious beings, continually seeking our Selfhood while simultaneously working toward awakening our culture is the highest expression of Service. Many have a mistaken notion that we become enlightened (fully conscious) and then commit to "the work" of teaching, healing, and serving. Not so! It's the other way around: We commit to "the work" (which also means Service) and it, in turn, enlightens us.

Co-creators are the muses of the soul. They are the world's "pleasure junkies" who channel all their passion into co-creating a more beautiful reality. They are busy "arting" themselves and their surroundings, their institutions, their cultures, their societies. From the gateway of the Heart, co-creators merge with the World of the Ideal (fifth-level consciousness) and together, they can manifest our visions and dreams. This is the shift from codependence to co-creation.

When you've committed to Service and begin unfolding your life's work, you will find that your ability to dis-identify and release

your old "stuff" will happen naturally. The seven steps of dis-
identification that we studied in the chapter called "The Heart's
Accelerated Path" will become second nature to you. Every time
you note that you're getting all caught up in something, you'll
intuitively begin the process of "let go." Or, if you feel you're
having trouble releasing something (or someone), you can perform
the Sacred Ritual that I described on pages 186–187, or some other
spiritual practice you yourself have created.

And then the final stages of Heartwork described below will
begin to take hold in your life; you may want to review the first
seven steps on pages 182–185 before going on. All twelve steps
will strengthen your stance as a co-creator and lead you toward
your unique expression of Service. You will be "doing your being."
The following five steps are not meant to be accomplished in one
sitting; the process will unfold according to your own "inner
clock":

8. Finding Your Soul Group. From the first seven steps you
experienced in the chapter on the Heart's accelerated path, you
learned about your willingness to let go and forgive. This attitude
of humility, you will discover, lifts you to a new level of relating.
If you've felt deep existential loneliness much of your life, never
feeling you've belonged, you are in for a great surprise: "Your kind"
are about to show up in your life! Let yourself feel this anticipa-
tion. Prepare yourself by invoking a willingness to recognize these
true soulmates and coworkers when they appear. They will likely
surface in your life when you start to long for a life larger than your
personal melodramas. Members of a soul group usually recognize
each other instantly—there's a familiar "aroma" these relationships carry. When you meet them, you catch on fire with
love—and joy! You will share with them a deep and abiding
nonattached love and understanding—a quiet "knowing."

9. Manifesting Your Life's Work. Now that you are learning to
keep your relationships honest and to associate with people more
aligned with your truth, you will begin to know a new kind of
freedom. Your whole outlook on life will shift. You are expanding;
consequently, your world will also expand. As you deepen your

commitment to do "your part" to remain clear, your life's work will become apparent—if it hasn't already. This will be your unique area of Service, an expression of your true talents as a soul-infused personality. As you simply go about "doing your being" you will find that *you already are in your work.*

Many believe they must give up the familiar and start all over again with some special kind of project that seems "spiritual." But this is rarely the case: your life's work is what you already know best and have always been in training to do and be. If you are someone who's never been satisfied with your work and have been desperately seeking your true calling, you can rest assured that your past training—in careers or at home—as well as your natural talents and desires—the things you do most easily—all will be used at some point for spirit. You only need to recognize these opportunities when they appear and act on them; Higher Power does the rest.

You may have given away your power so often that you've temporarily forgotten what you came here to do or complete. Connecting with your true talents, hopes, and dreams will re-mind you of what this work is. Sometimes you may need to go back in memory to the place of childhood, where some of us were already sure of "what we were going to be when we grew up." It is important to relax into this process and let go of outcomes. Your time will come. Your Higher Self is already guiding you toward your next right expression. Remember, it's while literally "hanging in the dangle," in the creative void, without the vaguest hint of what is coming next, that we usually re-connect with our true expression and awaken to something new.

10. Radiating Through the Heart. By now, the Heart is busy magnetizing you! This means you are capable of invoking Heart-love any time you wish: you can settle back, go inward, and allow the Heart to show you what real Heart-love feels like. There may be times, of course, when your heart is closed and you are not in the mood. But when you *can* feel loving, turn that love outward toward others, even those whom you may feel have harmed you. See each of them receiving the light of the Heart. This higher love transcends the boundaries of roles, such as "the lover," "the parent," "the confidant," or "the provider." It's all of these and more.

When you are "in" this Heart-love, others will feel drawn in and embraced by you. In your presence, they will glow. And when anyone in your life cannot stand "the heat of love," that person will leave your energy field. Love is a state of consciousness that we enter and exit, usually involuntarily—but with training, we can do so at will. At first, your ego may "get high" on the fact that you are magnetic. But after awhile, you will settle down and realize that Heart-love is the work of the Higher Power.

You will learn that spiritual development is an ongoing, here-and-now process. You can no longer allow resentment, anger, or any other negative emotion to build. Instead you remain conscious and promptly own your errors, speaking your truth when you see that you've gone unconscious and fallen off the mark. This willingness will keep your heart open and Heart-love pouring through.

11. Transmitting Through the Mind. As you become a co-creator, your authenticity begins to show. You will begin to carry out the plans of your Higher Power on a regular basis. Integrity is now a must for you, for untruth will literally make you sick. You know now that you can access a higher Mind by going into the inner silence of meditation. Your physical brain has the ability to connect with insightful and illuminating ideas, phrases, or important messages that are not only for you, but are universal truths. You will begin to express inspired and creative thought *through your own intellect.* For you are now capable of consciously tuning in and resonating to a higher mental vibration. This is the awakening of fifth-level consciousness. As you develop this spiritual power, you will find that you are able to remove the barriers between your intellect and Higher Mind; you will become an emissary for Truth.

From now on, it would be advisable for you to carry a notebook around with you wherever you go. (I keep a small one in my purse at all times.) For you never know when your wee brain will suddenly become filled with inspired thought, more profound than your ego could ever create on its own. This is how all my books have been written; they began as ideas that at first had no structure. When I would look back over what I'd written every several months, I would begin to see a pattern or a message I felt compelled to share with others through the written word or by giving talks. No one at first believes he or she is an inspired communicator. Every great writer has begun like this: by being a willing but amateur receiver and transmitter of divine Truth and inspired Ideals.

Some people call this "channeling." But be careful not to fall into the glamorous illusion that only special people channel and are channeled. Channeling is most often a connection between the one Higher Self and each personal and aligned ego's intellect—and we are all capable of this at a certain stage in our awakening. But it will only happen when we are aligned with our Higher Power and are living in surrender. Otherwise, we might misuse this divine right. If we fall into the illusion of our own self-importance, this power will be carefully and quietly withdrawn.

12. A Return to the Self. Now, if you are willing, take a moment to shift from who you thought you were to who you realize you are now. And you'll see that you're already changing. You are becoming someone who knows and is involved in both an inner and outer world. And you are learning to accept the transformational cycles both we and our world must go through. You may even be ready to create a whole new life for yourself, or aid in the healing of the earth.

For this to happen—as with all change—your mental life first must be set into motion. As we've seen, whatever the mind dwells upon will begin to manifest. Our imaginings will always set the stage for something new to appear in our lives. So even if you've only planted a seed in your mind, you are beginning to create it. (You've probably begun this process by simply reading this book.) And you will bring these new creations and teachings to others by your very way of being. Why? Because, as is said in AA, you're learning to "practice these Principles [of co-creation] in all your affairs." You are becoming one who, in the Dalai Lama's words, is dedicated to "the importance of love and compassion, and a clear recognition of our shared human status."

The Four Pillars of Service

Now, I would like to elaborate on the concept of Service I've referred to in this chapter. What may surprise some of you is that Service is not just about your outer work in the world. Outer work is whatever projects, community work, or ideals you commit to, but in order for this work to be truly effective, it must express your inner Self. For Service with a capital "S" is your very way of being; it's not only what you do. As Ram Dass says in his book with Paul Gorman, *How Can I Help?*:

> Service, from this perspective, is part of [the] journey. It is no longer an end in itself. It is a vehicle through which we reach a deeper understanding of life. Each step we take, each moment in which we grow toward a greater understanding of unity, steadily transforms us into instruments of that help which truly heals. . . . We are constantly given, for example, the chance to experience the inherent generosity of our heart.

Service is about being conscious no matter where you find yourself in life: you can be alone out in your garden caring for one precious plant, you can be giving a keynote speech to thousands in a public gathering, or you can be working in your local soup kitchen. Bringing consciousness to whatever you are doing in the moment is your Service, and is what co-creation really means.

I feel that in order to travel this path of co-creation, we must commit not only to the projects we select in our outer service, but also to maintaining an inner clarity—a healthy body, balanced emotions, and mental stability. For if we are not in harmony with ourselves, we will bring our destructive ways into all our endeavors. To remain clear and balanced, we must utilize what I see as four aspects of Service, and we must do so in right proportion, never overemphasizing any one. These four pillars are: *meditation* (going within), *inner work* (psycho-spiritual catharsis, integration, and expansion), *study* (alignment with the truths that have come before us), and *outer work* (the daily practice of our inner principles in the world around us). For each person, this balance will manifest uniquely, depending upon one's preferences, temperament, and intention. If these areas become imbalanced, our bodies and emotions will begin to show signs of stress, which is our cue that we may be overusing or underusing any one of these pillars of Service.

Meditation

First of all, meditation is not always about sitting in a lotus position on an Indian pillow under a Boddhi tree. Meditation is whatever one does to make conscious contact with a Higher Power. It can be anything from running a fast mile to spinning and whirling in a Sufi dance. Some people feel they are too active for sedentary modes of meditation. Others are more mentally oriented and prefer to contemplate something such as a candle flame, a word, or an idea to focus their minds while meditating. Others have no trouble sitting for long periods of time in silent meditation, their bodies still and their minds empty. It's important to know you have options, as many people erroneously believe they are incapable of meditating.

As I saw written on a bookmark once, "Meditation is not what you *think.*" Whatever your preferred mode, meditation turns off the thinking mind for awhile so you can hear the voice of the deeper Self from within the Heart. Many people meditate without realizing they are doing so, for it happens during those periods when time vanishes and you're lost in the moment, when you've been doing something (or have ceased doing something) for hours and it feels like minutes, or no time at all. But in order to meditate on a regular basis, it is crucial that we develop a conscious method.

You might seek out a teacher, or discover a method on your own, but in either case you must begin to practice. And this requires discipline. At first begin practicing for very short sessions, about five minutes or so. Then, as you get better at it, you can increase the time to twenty minutes. Remember to be patient. In the early seventies, I recall hearing Ram Dass once say that as a new meditator, he sat for ninety minutes and achieved only one minute of meditation! As a brand-new meditator myself, his story encouraged me and kept me going during my early struggles.

It's through meditation that we receive our "instructions" from a Higher Power. Or, if not direct instruction, we receive the blessing of peace and serenity. This is considered "Eleventh Step work" in Twelve Step recovery programs. And in Christianity, it's the contemplative life.

Moreover, meditation stabilizes our physical appetites, emotional reactiveness, and mental confusions. Eventually, its practice will transform us; we'll act primarily from the higher chakras, leaving the imbalances of our lower chakras behind. Meditation brings us to our center, the undisturbed, immovable place where we already know peacefulness. We go into the silence and sit in the very midst of our inner Self. And from here, we learn commitment, concentration, perseverance, and patience; we build up inner strengths. In addition, this process teaches us to stand in the light of our own being. Before, we were looking for the light. Now, through meditation, we see that we *are* the light! And meditative practice keeps that light glowing.

Inner Work

In the psycho-spiritual dimensions (the vertical arm of the cross), spiritual work is not superior to psychological work. For our repressed issues and emotions stand in the way of our pristine clarity as spiritual beings. And for this reason we must do the psychological work necessary to resolve our past and present conditions. Both the spiritual and the psychological are aspects of the inner life and when worked on simultaneously, they take us to a deeper (or higher) and more wholistic identity.

Here's how my own inner work often takes place: When I'm emotionally activated, some stimulus is reminding me that I'm repressing something. My symptom will increase until I decide to go within and work on it. That throbbing headache becomes a massive migraine! Or the little feeling of disappointment I'd carried in my chest for days turns into rage. Now I'm losing sleep or going through my days obsessing. As the symptoms accelerate, I realize I have to express whatever truth is trying to come through. Perhaps I'm scared, angry, or feeling guilt and shame. There is likely an old pattern or storyline based in remote childhood fears or misconceptions that is being ignited by some current event. I must go within, access my feelings, and allow them to come on out in some appropriate manner.

If there is no safe place to let these feelings out, to cry, scream, or rage in solitude, then journaling—writing it all down—will help. If I'm at home, I may go into my room, put on some music that befits my mood, and begin to move as it plays. If I'm angry, I will play loud, chaotic music, and just allow my feelings to express. If I'm hurt and feeling sad and vulnerable, I may play music of women chanting, or some heart-felt melodic piece to awaken more of my heart feelings. I might cry, moan, dance, chant, do rituals, or curl up in a fetal position and nurture myself. I just go with whatever wants to happen, letting the energy move me. I've realized that spontaneity is often my teacher. Later, I can better see what was going on. But usually not before: prior to expressing the energy, I have a storyline going in my head that is not grounded in reality.

If after working on myself my pain is still present, I'll seek out a therapist or friend and ask her or him to listen to me for awhile. If it's a relationship issue, my partner and I will seek a third party to help us communicate "heart to heart" and not from "below the belt." Any therapy or healing method that invites us to be receptive to spirit or the inner life, rather than merely listening to the advice of others or being talked to by outside "experts," is helpful for processing emotional issues.

By doing inner psychological work, you will see concretely how you repeatedly undergo the "seasons of change" described in the Heartwork section of this book. And you will no longer fear or resist these well-grooved inner psychic processes and patterns. They will become familiar turf.

A Word About Synchronicity

As you become more practiced and disciplined in your inner work, there's one aspect that remains light, spontaneous, and lots of fun: *Synchronicities begin to occur all around you.* When signs manifest in your outer life, reminding you that you're on or off the mark, you are experiencing synchronicity. Synchronicity is actually a principle that ties archetypal events to outer activities. The connection between the inner and outer event is acausal (seems to be coincidental), yet is rich with a meaning that you alone give it.

Here's an example that occurred recently in my own life: I was riding in a crowded car with friends one evening, debating about whether or not to speak on the topic of Infinity for a group the following day. As we got out of the car, I stepped on a string that was in the shape of a figure 8, the infinity sign in mathematics. We all stopped and stared in amazement. I gave the talk, and it was very well received. Or here's another: On the evening I first spoke with my editor at Bantam Books about the possibility of publishing this book with them, just as I hung up the phone a tiny toy rooster my friend's child had left behind fell off a table and hit me on the foot. (The rooster is Bantam's logo!) I signed with Bantam a few weeks later.

Another incident of synchronicity occurred years ago when I was in a restaurant with friends, processing a disagreement I'd had with a former boss. (I'd just quit my job.) Just as I made a thundering proclamation reeking of righteous indignation, the music playing in the background began building until it became evident to us all: It was the ending of a dramatic John Philip Sousa march. It seemed as though the Higher Power had been orchestrating the background music to reflect my rising aggravation! My friends and I had a "cosmic chuckle"—a truly healing experience for me. A synchronistic event such as this can lighten intensity, reminding us that we're all connected and, on some level, above it all.

The examples above are rather lighthearted and humorous. But sometimes synchronicities can be even more profound. For example, in one of my recent workshops, I was equivocating about adding a certain type of ritual to our psycho-spiritual work. I took the risk and tried it. The energy was high and holy, and the participants seemed to gain a lot from the experience. Afterwards, several members of the group called me to come see what was in the foyer: The indoor lights had made on the wall a design in the form of a perfectly shaped six-pointed star. It was beautiful! A security guard walked by as we stood there staring and said he'd never noticed that star before. We all stood in awe, feeling we had received a "sign" that the new work had been accepted by the universe. These types of experiences reveal the Higher Power in action.

Synchronicities become a major part of our inner work when we learn to recognize them: they're the threads of our bliss we can follow by watching carefully and taking note. When we do recognize them, there is often a feeling that "something spiritual has happened," and a sense of purpose, no matter how slight, is added to one's life. Like little spiritual landmarks, synchronicities keep us moving toward our future destiny.

Scientists do not honor synchronicity as "real" quite yet, because they cannot tie these occurrences to an observable chain of cause and effect. These "chance" happenings, however, never seem like chance to conscious co-creators; they see synchronicities as Higher Power's scientific law of cause and effect! Jungian theorist Jean Shiboda Bolen says of these high experiences, "Every time I have become aware of a synchronistic experience, I have had an accompanying feeling that some grace came along with it."

Study

When we study the inspired ideas of the world's great masters and read their stories of awakening, our creativity is often ignited and we feel connected to a larger whole. By merging our own intuitive ruminations with these great ideas, we carry forward inspired thought and can create our "next right step." What we choose to study should track with our own inner work, and reflect or verify

what we learn *through our direct knowing*. Otherwise, study becomes an empty exercise, for ideas cannot nurture us if there's no
tilled mental soil in which to plant them.

Many tell me that connecting with ideas and authors through
study soothes their life-long sense of isolation. Indeed, literature
from throughout the ages can help illuminate and validate our
heart's true interests, especially when we are having trouble
finding people who understand our deeper longings. We can
sometimes even discover our life's work through the writers,
leaders, or philosophical ideas that fascinate us. Study helps align
us with our "soul group" of coworkers, fellow travelers, and
teachers who have felt a similar purpose.

For instant, after reading books by people such as C. S. Lewis,
Ram Dass, or Gary Zukav, you might feel called to help re-shape
our culture's ideas about spiritual life. Or perhaps the field of
psychology or some of the new sciences, such as subatomic physics,
may become your passion. The world needs people to serve as
bridges for the emerging "new-paradigm" philosophies that unify
the findings of science, psychology, and religion or spirituality.
Therefore, study is essential for the future of the planet.

If you want to serve as such a bridge, you will need to study
"old-paradigm" and "new-paradigm" religion, education, philosophy, psychology, and science. This way you can discover for
yourself the changes that are necessary in the coming Age. You
needn't become an expert in any one of these fields (unless you
want to master or teach one of them specifically), but you can
absorb the principles and implications of these evolving theories.
(I've listed in Appendix Two some of the books I've used to make
these shifts in thinking. I recommend them to you, but in no way
am I suggesting that these are the only ones, or even the right ones
for you.)

Those of you interested in psychology should know that the
bridging of "old" and "new" psychology is occurring now, and
transpersonal or spiritual psychologies are at the leading edge. New
ways of thinking and research concerning the wholistic functioning of the Self is currently gaining wider acceptance. (This book
falls into that category.) As you study the new paradigm in all areas

of thought, you will see a major shift in emphasis from outer to inner focus, from relying on outer "experts" to developing inner empowerment.

Today, subjectivity is once again being honored, after having been nearly dismissed by scientists and psychologists for the past hundred years or so. Many believe, along with Bill Moyers and Joseph Campbell, that "we are at this moment participating in one of the very greatest leaps of the human spirit, to a knowledge not only of outside nature but also of our own deep inward mystery" (*An Open Life*). Many new-paradigm thinkers believe such internal processes as meditation, visualization, breathwork, dreamwork, movement therapy, process hypnosis, and other psycho-spiritual methods soon will become standard tools in the field of psychology. This is an important shift, indeed. For the mysteries of the unconscious mind are treasures, containing the building blocks we seek for creating a new and better world.

Outer Work

For conscious co-creators, effective outer expression of one's Service is the goal of all meditation, inner work, and study. I will not focus here on specific areas of Service, as I am exploring the *being level* we each bring to bear on whatever causes and projects we take on. I would like to point out, however, that these areas do fall into the healing and teaching categories within the fields of psychology, medicine, social work, religion, education, and philosophy; into grass roots political work and special-interest projects; and into various forms of business, where there is plenty of opportunity to help bring about positive change. You all will feel attracted to different areas of Service, based on your personal character traits, talents, and interests. Some of you are best at leading and implementing systems; some make great inspirers, while others are most effective at maintaining daily operations and detailed functions. *In planetary Service, all work and workers are equal.* Some may look more valuable, stand out more, or appear more glamorous, but all Service leads to the good of the whole. And it is through high-level beingness that we become not only effective in our own work, but guides for others who also seek to serve.

The previous three pillars of Service enable the co-creator to remain conscious and balanced when involving in his or her work. Regardless of your particular area of interest, the ongoing process of personal transformation is crucial to your larger life of Service. All of us who work with others are constantly coping with imbalanced energies, individual differences, feelings of discontent, sticky problem-solving responsibilities, difficulties with implementation, and other particulars that on the surface often appear impossible to resolve. Co-creators seek to bring about a unified viewpoint—to help others continually re-focus on the "big picture" anytime dissidence occurs. And since transformational energies are contagious and empowering, many people are affected by co-creators' commitment to work on themselves while helping to heal various segments of society.

Whenever co-creators start to feel emotionally re-active themselves or otherwise ill-prepared to deal with outer circumstances, they connect with their observer self and go inward to steady themselves. Meditation calms their emotionalisms and aligns them with the Higher Self. Inner work provides them with ongoing intuitive understanding concerning where their personal issues come from and how they might be affecting their work. And study gives them potency, a sense of confidence and correctness in their knowledge and relationship to the specific areas they've chosen to involve in.

Moreover, co-creators are grounded and cooperate with the "laws of the land" when doing their work. They are careful not to fall into the traps of "pie in the sky" thinking, such as believing that if it's a spiritual cause, all things will just naturally work out through prayer or positive affirmations. This is a fallacy currently being corrected in many "New Age" circles. I was once at a meeting devoted to bringing a well-known speaker to a city. At one point, one of the members (the owner of a wholistic healing center) offered to pay for the publicity fees through his constituency. He said, "Spirit will guide my people to pay this bill. Don't worry; they are good people." When we questioned him further, asking if this meant we could give him the $200 bill to handle, he became irritated, giving us a lecture on prosperity consciousness and demanding that we be patient and have faith. Another member of our group wound up paying the bill in its entirety! Co-creators do not dichotomize the laws of materialism and the laws of spirit, realizing that, at least while living on planet earth, *sound business principles and practice provide the integrity essential to doing "good work."*

As you turn toward your expression as a co-creator, you will notice that all four of these pillars of Service begin to preoccupy you. You'll see that you are probably already practiced at one or two, but lacking in the others. In order to balance your stewardship, I suggest you begin attending to those at which you are least adept.

People who focus purely on meditation become "top-heavy" without the balance of the other three pillars. They may mistakenly seek spiritual perfection rather than spiritual wholeness; they often try to fly right over their "all-too-human" urges. Often, meditators tell me they feel they live from the heart up; this often means ignoring their "lower" natures and failing to work through their emotional issues with family members or aspects of their biographical past in the ordinary world.

Similarly, inner work can become overwhelming if co-creators don't take time for meditation, study, and outer work. They may never allow their emotions to settle and therefore may fail to gain insight from their processes or resolve their conflicts. When we continually bring things up and never integrate them, we are very vulnerable to addiction. Without the balance of the other pillars, we can become entangled and overly stimulated by the ups and downs of emotional release.

People who overuse study or try to think their way onto the path of Service often end up sidestepping inner work and meditation, or they may participate in outer work with an imbalanced disposition. Then, they will "carry harm." They might be intellectually brilliant, and even become astute judges or analyzers of others' process, but they have little personal experience or spiritual growth to give substance to their knowledge. This is the difference between knowledge and wisdom. These people are living in their heads, from the neck up.

And finally, people who turn to outer Service without honoring the other three pillars have no way of remaining steady in their own sense of Self. They are often exclusively outer-directed, and may become easily caught up in the dramas of professional codependence. In fact, many people try to avoid their own issues by throwing themselves into "do-gooder" roles "for the sake of others." We've all experienced such self-serving do-gooders who think they're helping others, but really are getting in everyone's way. These people are unprepared and improperly trained for true Service.

However, you must not believe for a minute that you have to be fully healed in order to serve. In my experience, no one is ever completely healed while inhabiting a human body! In fact, in the field of mental health we've noted that "wounded healers" often make great therapists. Traditionally, shamans (true medicine men and women) were known to continually wound their hearts in order to stay attuned to humanity's suffering. Being willing to own one's wounds or "stuff" and take full responsibility for one's self is all that is necessary for stewardship to begin. Your continual healing is a crucial part of your service, making you more real and easy to relate to. No one likes being around "perfect people." As Carl Jung reminded us: People with no shadows also have no substance. As co-creators, we do the best we can to stay balanced; and when we're not, we promptly admit it, own our part, and set about taking care of ourselves.

The more we practice the four pillars of Service, the more our daily lives will begin to reflect this balance. And the degree of inner balance we attain will determine the degree and sphere of our influence in the outer world. As we grow inwardly and gain spiritual stature, our field of influence will grow, for we will be able to handle more and more of society's imbalanced energies without falling apart ourselves or misguiding others with fanaticism or lack of mental clarity. We'll live with a sense of quiet joy, for we'll feel meaningfully employed and good about ourselves. And people will notice. For we are not just talking the talk; we're walking the walk, as is said in Twelve Step programs. And we begin to see that changes are really happening in our consciousness: In harmony with both inner and outer worlds, we are learning to follow our bliss.

Let's stop again for awhile and do some inner work. This guided imagery will help you connect with an important archetype that sits way out there in the cosmos, as a Star in the sky, and that can merge with you now that you are committing to serve. This imagery will bring you under the influence of this Great Being's energy and teach you how to hold the "Rod of Service" during this planet's chaotic time of transformation.

The World Server
A Guided Imagery Experience

Imagine yourself sitting outside on a beautiful starry night, looking up at the deep indigo-blue sky. Feel the breeze blowing gently across your skin. . . . You are in a state of peaceful contentment. . . . Experience this feeling for a moment. . . . Make this scene real in your mind.

As you look upward into the night sky, a particular Star begins to draw your attention . . . beckoning you. . . . You feel compelled to rise up toward it. . . . As you come closer and closer to this Star that is drawing you, you begin to feel Its powers enfold you in Love. And you realize this is the archetype of the World Server, the blueprint for Divine Love and Wisdom, for Service . . . (long pause). As it merges with you, feel it enter your mind, clearing out the cobwebs. . . . And now entering your heart . . . filling you with blissful serenity. . . . [If emotions come up at this point, let them come until they settle on their own. Then continue.]

Gently now, feel your mind and heart begin to merge into oneness. . . . And listen quietly in inner Silence to the message this Great Being imparts. It may guide you toward finding your life's work . . . or tell you which area of Service you need to focus on. . . . Receive this message now. . . . [Allow several minutes of silence.]

Now, accept a gift from this Great One. . . . Visualize a symbol of this Being to place within your heart so you can carry It with you always. Accept this gift (long pause).

Take some time now to honor your Higher Self in gratitude for what has just transpired . . . (long pause). And now, gradually feel yourself beginning to descend back down to the place you were sitting under the starry night sky . . . (long pause).

Become aware once more of your body. . . . And the room in which you are sitting. . . . Take some time to integrate this experience. . . . You may want to write down the message you received, draw a picture of your symbol, or sit in quiet reflection for awhile.

Transformational Groupwork: Communing at the Edge with Co-Creative Families

> In living organisms . . . new forms of behavior
> emerge at critical points. . . . [They] exchange
> their individualistic behavior for a collective one.
>
> —F. David Peat

At certain points along their journey, people begin to crave a larger context. And for many, now is one of those times. They long to be in the supportive and joyful company of others who are seekers like themselves. I believe there are so many people looking for this kind of community that a new culture is beginning to take form: the seeds of a new communal life have been planted. And just in time. For as I've said, without the context and validation community provides, we cannot safely transform.

One of the first signs you're becoming a soul-infused personality is that you begin to long for and sense you are part of a larger family of spiritual adventurers, even if you haven't found them yet. And when you actually do meet these fellow travelers, you'll feel a deep sense of familiarity and aliveness: you'll fall "in Love." This is an expanded kind of Love, beyond codependence—the possessive and exclusive nature of "special relationships." There is a sense of shared purpose and there's room to love a whole lot of people all at once. You are part of a "soul group."

Those who've grown up in addictive or otherwise dysfunctional families who choose to clear the wounds from their past have a special need for validation and support to help them through the rapid changes they are beginning to undergo. Otherwise, they are likely to become too lonely or afraid, feeling disoriented and unsafe, just as they did as children. This is even more of a danger if they embark upon an "accelerated path."

Groups that include a Twelve Step recovery philosophy can create a new sense of belonging, serving as a balm for the hurt many of you experienced in your biological families or during your addictive days. This new level of intimacy tends to strip away one's old sense of isolation—almost instantly! These gatherings enable people to co-create whole new families of choice that make up for their dysfunctional families of origin. I often hear people describe their experience in these groups by saying they feel as if they've come "home." "Home," of course, is not a place; it's a state of communal consciousness.

And because of the prevalence of this consciousness, people in metaphysical circles call this coming Age "the cycle of conferences." Self-help groups and psycho-spiritual groupwork are spontaneously appearing in answer to our call "to convene." But actually, they are not a new path for humanity: they are an ancient path dressed in new clothing, a synthesis of the various Ageless Wisdom traditions from both the East and the West. They hark back to the camps of Sufis, who came together to dance and sing and share from their hearts, and the ancient Greek mystery schools, where novitiates were cloistered together with protective priests and priestesses until they were strong enough to withstand the pressures of the ordinary world. This groupwork is being sought because it provides a context large enough to meet both the ego's needs and the soul's transpersonal yearning to serve. Combining social, psychological, and spiritual ingredients, these groups are safe places to share emotional hurts while awakening to the fact that we are "more than what we look like."

Although these communities are highly transformational and spiritual in nature, they do not promote worshiping "gurus" or revered teachers. For this would be a violation of the spiritual function of individual *empowerment*, a primary goal in all group-work. Moreover, there is no sense of cultism and elitism. These are free-floating groups; people from all walks of life enter and leave by choice. They are drawn in through attraction, not promotion or coercion of any kind. And they learn from each other as they share their life stories, feelings, visions, and dreams. Together, they learn to release dysfunctional ways and dis-identify from old identities, while awakening to a new and healthier sense of Self.

The Co-Creator's "Laboratory"

I felt this longing for community in the middle 1970s, and am now an experienced leader of transformational groups that take people into their issues in an accelerated, immediate way. I've seen that as people's identities as co-creators broaden, they are drawn to intense psycho-spiritual work, which includes deep emotional catharsis and healing and usually requires professional leadership and a safe methodology. Many people bring up old memories and emotions and actually re-live them in the moment. To facilitate this process, transformational groups meet for much longer periods of time than do the majority of self-help groups, usually a weekend, a week, or sometimes a whole month. These meetings often take place in retreat settings so that group cohesiveness can be especially strong, enabling individuals to feel safe in a rather short period of time.

I would like to share with you what I'm learning about both the purpose and the power of what I call "new-paradigm groupwork." But let me first say that what follows are only my descriptions and opinions, based on my experience. I do not mean to imply that the groups in which I'm involved are the only kind of new-paradigm groupwork now coming into being. Any gathering that taps into the inspired energies of transformation will have similar healing effects.

The purpose of this groupwork is to provide an enhanced therapeutic milieu for people to safely undergo ego death/rebirth sequences. In my first book, *Becoming Naturally Therapeutic*, I sensed this need was emerging when I said people were going to require "a safe place to come and express their feelings of pain—feelings of anger or grief that may have driven them to drink, to take drugs, or to act out in other harmful ways at some point in their lives. This safe place is a cleared-out human heart."

New-paradigm groupwork sets up such a space. It is a container or "net" for Heartwork. Here all religious and psychological schools of thought are honored. No one is ever told to change their beliefs, or if someone is under psychiatric care, one's current medication or treatment plan is never tampered with (unless the medication is a type that blocks the process, in which case the attending physician's permission is sought.)

People come from all walks of life to share their woes, terrors, longings, visions, and dreams with one another: doctors and other healthcare professionals, lawyers, clergymen and women, carpenters, CPAs, corporate personnel, mental health workers, celebrities, homemakers, artists, and musicians. Some are recovering from various addictions and mental illnesses; others who are simply searching for like-minded seekers.

Together they release their most painful feelings and share their deepest secrets. At the same time they play like children, dance, sing, drum, and chant; often they create spontaneous, high-spirited rituals out in nature, like happy little muses! The freedom they feel from releasing their constricted energies and issues is what creates this climate of "high spirits." For music and other forms of artistic expression play a large part in our groups. And so do various methods of accessing the unconscious, such as meditation, breathwork, vision quests, sweat lodge experiences, contemplation, ritual, and mythic-poetic storytelling.

Both ordinary and nonordinary states of consciousness are honored, as long as they are brought on by the process and are not drug-induced. Following the flow of these inspirited groups is quite intoxicating without any artificial aids. We jokingly call ourselves "the roto-rooters" of the health-care system; we go very deep into our personal processes and often clear out old material never before accessed through ordinary therapies. Like a hothouse, this new transformational groupwork brings with it an enhanced energy field where accelerated transformations take place. And it offers support and validation for these experiences, which might otherwise be spiritual emergencies. Together, the participants commit to continue doing inner work, as well as study, meditation, and other spiritual practices, when they return to their everyday lives.

Seeking More Fertile Ground

Many people today feel they've outgrown their families of origin, or have decided their families are so beyond repair they'd rather work to enhance their created families instead—the ones formulated in adulthood by choice. But whether or not we want to release our biological families, we still need the nurturing, support, playfulness, and community that can be found in group life.

In these newly created families, our individual spiritual growth is not only supported, it is enhanced. Psychological healing and spiritual transformation are one and the same: the journey from fragmentation back to wholeness. Both lead us to our Source and toward the expanded, unified Self. And as such, we can then move on toward a greater life. I believe many people are seeking such a greater life and are finding many who share their ideals and visions. Perhaps it's "in the stars" or in our genetic code that at some point we'll find our group and begin the journey Home. I certainly know that it feels that way to me. And I'd like to share with you a profound metaphor for this "merging into wholeness" influencing many of us today:

Of all creatures in nature, the lowly little slime mold colonies pattern for us most clearly this amazing process of expansion and evolution. As described by F. David Peat in *Synchronicity: The*

Bridge Between Matter and Mind, slime mold spores feed on the forest floor as individual cells, until at some point they totally demolish their food supply. Then, an "emergency bell" goes off in one of them, and they all come together to form one conglomerate—a "sluglike creature." Then, as one entity, the slime mold travels through the forest, searching for a new feeding ground. Once firmly positioned in its new food haven, this little amalgamated character changes into a spoutlike shape and shoots out into individual spores once again. And off each creature goes on another "adventure in consciousness," separately and together, happily nourishing themselves in their new-found home!

And this, I believe, is our story, too. As we begin to wither in our arid, materialistic environment, we are becoming desperate for the fresh air of spirit. Many of us are now being called to go back to the Self and collapse into our Source for further instructions. And from here, we can learn to reunite with one another at home base. Jung called this return "going into the deep well." And Plato believed that we are constantly feeling pulled to reunite with our original blueprint. Perhaps this root-consciousness from which we've sprung, this ultimate human design, is truly our connection to God.

Like our little slime mold friends, perhaps we are seeking a new "feeding ground"—more spiritual sustenance—so we can thrive once more. Transformational "family clusters" made up of soul brothers and sisters of equal status can provide this nourishing experience. Together, we help one another release our long-held constrictions, garner our strengths, and recognize and express our unique and specific purposes on earth. When we find our soul group, the personal life of relationships unites with the impersonal life of Service; combined they make up the path of co-creation.

Home!

Nothing under heaven can arrest the progress of the human soul on its long pilgrimage from darkness to light, from the unreal to the real, from death to immortality, and from ignorance to wisdom.

—The Tibetan

Today something is happening to the whole structure of human consciousness; a fresh kind of life is starting.

—Pierre Teilhard de Chardin

I'd like to share something I received in the mail recently from one of our groupwork leaders. She has a professional background in addiction treatment, and now, after four years of intense work on herself, has become a seasoned and inspired teacher, though just thirty years old:

I've Come Home

I am so full of joy and love! But a new feeling pervades my body, a feeling of peace, and contentment; not an anxious excitement, but a subtle certainty of my purpose, my place here on this planet. The simpleness of who I am rather than the fragmented self of days and lives gone by. The slower pace at which I embrace life and its lessons. The broader base at which my reality expands.

I have come to know simple truths that before were so disguised by my complexity. I have come to know the inner vision that sees with so much clarity. I've come to know me, the gentleness of my spirit as it may express through love and tenderness. I've come to know power in a way that's personal and creative: My personal power of choice. I've come to know love; love of self and others is the same. I've come to know the oneness of all who walk the planet in an attempt to journey home.

—Greta Metcalf

When our blissful nature is acknowledged by ourselves and those around us, it begins to resonate with nature's abounding patterns of light and shadow at play in the world, as has so clearly happened for the teacher above. And then we really turn on! For we feel called to share in the spiritual uplifting of the planet, and we begin to dance together in right relationship, immersed in the rapture of being alive. *This* is the recovering addict's dream, for it's really "living it up"! And this state of consciousness and enthusiasm for life is, of course, the healing of addiction. Turning toward each other in Love is the absolute cure for codependence and unconscious living. And it feels wonderful—better than any outworn addiction every could. It ignites our soul.

We've heard most of our lives that "Home is where the Heart is." But now we recognize this as a Truth rather than an empty platitude. Like our little cousins the turtle and the snail, we carry our Home with us wherever we go, no matter what we're up to. Once again, the journey is our Home: because we ourselves are consciousness and our nature is light, we have no *destination*, only a *function*. Like little lightning bugs, we glimmer and glow, lighting things up as we go along our way. Eventually we can become guides for others, not because we're smarter, but simply because we're a little more experienced—and awake.

Today, co-creators are emerging all over the world with their heads in the clouds and their feet placed firmly on the earth. They are here to participate fully in life—and because they are practical mystics, they serve humanity as they go. I believe humankind is truly returning Home to the Heart, through such avenues as the Twelve Step movement, concern for our weakening environment, and the deep empathy and responsibility we have felt from our involvement in the Persian Gulf crisis. We're finally awakening to the essence we've always been underneath our differences, as is evidenced by the following statement from one of my students, who is also a teacher:

> In this environment of seekers I've been able to battle and befriend the dragon, to walk through the cavern of darkness, to struggle with the known and paradox, to encounter and trust internal wisdom, to be a vehicle through which Love's never-ending energy expands and flows—to cry, to laugh, to be vulnerable and in this to find strength, to watch another grow and be transformed, to marvel at God's manifestations through each one of us.

The process of learning about one's nature and then finding the courage to *be* this nature is something human beings must do over and over in every Age. I hope this book has helped some of you begin or further the unfolding of your true nature, your own inner Self. For each of us must reinvent the wheel and undergo the spins of transformation on our own, even if we have the support of guides, writers, or teachers. This way Truth can become *our* Truth, not merely borrowed from other's experiences. For we learn from our own direct experiences only—no one else can do our growing for us. And as I've said, when we awaken, we can see that our own codependence patterns have been perhaps the greatest teacher of all.

When the four mental shifts we've studied in this book become living principles in our lives, we will be able to manifest the following great axioms of spirit, leaving the pain of addiction behind:

1) **Remembering** that you are a triad and never a duality, you will always create from a position of *true perspective:* You will be creating an aspect of Truth.

2) **Realizing** that the inner determines the outer will keep you *rightly focused*, so you can connect with your Higher Self.

3) **Knowing** that we grow through death/rebirth cycles—and that both are necessary and legitimate—we learn to *remain steady* while undergoing rapid change or shifts in consciousness.

4) **Recognizing** transcendence as the "pull" we constantly feel toward *being more than we are* will enable us to settle down at last to find our particular path of Service. For this urge to merge with a godlike nature keeps us on track, pulling us in an ascending direction, toward wholeness.

Following this inner path is our way out of codependence and into the ways of co-creation. The urge to transcend is our lifeline Home, a reminder to return to our Self. For the Self is the one who always calls. And the Self is the one who always responds. Once we realize this, we will no longer feel the need to seek our Self in others. We'll be Home, living and sharing a life of our own.

> To all the Pilgrims upon the Path of Life: "*Know thyself*" is the first great injunction, and long is the process of attaining that knowledge. "*Know the Self*" comes next, and when that is achieved, man knows not only himself but all selves; the soul of the universe is to him no longer the sealed book of life, but one with the seven seals broken.
>
> —The Tibetan

APPENDIX ONE

Glossary of
Transformational
Resources and Methods

F or information concerning qualified methods, practitioners, and programs of personal transformation in your area, consult your local metaphysical or New Age bookstores or centers for wholistic health, human potential, or personal growth.

For information concerning any type of Twelve Step addiction programs or meetings, you can call your local Council on Alcoholism or Alcoholics Anonymous. These resources are usually listed in the yellow pages of the telephone directory under "Alcoholism Information."

If you need help with spiritual emergencies or other types of personal crises, or workshops and training in this type of work, write or call the following:

Eupsychia, Inc.
P.O. Box 3090
Austin, Texas 78764
512/327-2795

Pocket Ranch
P.O. Box 516
Geyserville, California 95441
707/857-3359

Spiritual Emergency Network (SEN Central Office)
c/o Institute of Transpersonal Psychology
250 Oak Grove Avenue
Menlo Park, California 94025
415/327-2776

Spiritual Emergency Network (SEN Rocky Mountain Office)
4301 North Broadway
Boulder, Colorado 80302
303/444-9537

The following descriptions are not intended to be scientific definitions of the listed methods, therapies, and techniques for personal transformation. This listing is merely an informal guide for those of you who may be attracted to some of these methods.

Acupuncture/Acupressure. Acupuncture uses small sterile needles at meridian points throughout the body, based on Chinese medical technology. This highly skilled form of bodywork is performed by medical doctors, East and West. Acupuncture enables the body's energies to flow according to its natural pathways, which can heal physical disease. Acupressure utilizes the same energy pathways, but practitioners are not usually M.D.'s, and the balls of the thumb and fingers are used instead of needles.

Bodywork and Massage. There are so many forms of bodywork; I will only describe it generally. This work is a form of touch therapy, sometimes used in conjunction with other psychotherapies, that releases emotional blocks, alleviates stress, and balances the body's energies. Some examples are: Bioenergetics, Esalen Massage, Feldenkrais, Reichian Bodywork, Rolfing, Shiatsu, Structural Integration, and Trager Integration.

Breathwork. Various forms of breathing methods have been used throughout the ages for personal transformation and spiritual awakening. Deep breathing, often combined with meditation, music, or Yogic exercises, opens the psyche to wholistic levels of consciousness, and also releases pent-up emotions. Breathwork accesses the existential, perinatal, and transpersonal bands of consciousness, taking people beyond biographical memories into deeper realms of the human unconscious mind. Some of the most common forms of breathwork in the West are rebirthing, bioenergetic core breathing, Yogic breathing, holotropic breathing, and Eupsychia's integrative breathwork process.

Chanting. Chants or mantras are words or phrases expressed repeatedly for several minutes or hours, taking one into a trance state that balances the nervous system and integrates emotional instability. The word or phrase used can invoke high states of consciousness.

Contemplative Prayer. A form of Christian meditation, its practitioners are trained to focus on an inner symbol that quiets the mind and trains it to concentrate on the inner life. When practitioners become skilled at this method of meditation, they undergo a deep trance state, similar to auto-hypnosis.

Dreamwork. There are many forms of dream analysis and interpretation. Jungian and Gestalt dreamwork are two of the most common. The purpose of all dreamwork is to access the decoded messages from the unconscious mind to gain a deeper understanding of one's day-to-day problems or the major events in one's life.

Focusing. Eugene Gendlin's focusing technique is a form of psychotherapy that accesses the body's exact emotional needs by concentrative methods of body-talk that speak directly to the mind through precise inner felt experiences.

Guided Imagery. Guided imagery is a form of creative visualization utilized and explained in this book. (See page 58 for description of this method of inner work.)

Movement Therapy. Dance and movement are ways the whole body can participate in one's expression. The body, when allowed to be spontaneous, never lies; our movements will demonstrate our characteristics and our statement; and the movement itself—usually done to music—releases pent-up emotions, inhibitions, and blocked physical energies, rendering the body and personality more flexible and expressive.

Movement Meditation. Slow and precise body movements can also be an effective form of meditation. Tai Chi is one of the most well-known forms. Through a series of systematic movements, the body and mind are stilled, and the person's vital energies are enhanced by this art form. Movement meditation is known to relieve stress, balance the body/mind, and sometimes even heal physical disease.

Nutritional Balancing. Trained nutritionists or herbalists can aid in finding the diet and nutritional supplements uniquely required for one's body. Good nutritional counseling can help balance the body's emotional energies and heal physical illness.

Process Hypnosis. Hypnosis puts the conscious mind "to sleep" while accessing the subconscious mind. Process hypnosis works with the material that comes up in a therapeutic manner; the client participates in one's own subconscious work.

Psychosynthesis. This is a system of psychotherapy that legitimizes both the ego and the Higher Self. It seeks a personal synthesis of the body, emotions, and mind. It then moves practitioners on to deeper levels of spiritual or transpersonal synthesis once a high degree of ego integration is evidenced. The person moves from personal, to interpersonal, to transpersonal healing. Creative visualization and various forms of meditative exercises are combined with psychotherapeutic intervention. Psychosynthesis was developed by Italian psychiatrist Roberto Assagioli, a student of Sigmund Freud.

Rebirthing. Brought to the United States by Leonard Orr and furthered by Sandra Ray, rebirthing is a form of breathwork that accesses the perinatal band of consciousness, enabling participants to relive their anatomical birth physiologically. Rebirthers vary in style: some utilize deep breathing in water to simulate the birthing process, some use music or affirmations during the process, while some work only with the breath.

Ritual. Ritual and ceremony bring mental abstractions and symbolic interactions down into structured, concrete statements, grounding the Self's psychological and spiritual intentions in the ordinary world. The purpose of ritual is explained in more depth in this book. (See pages 186–187.)

Sweat Lodge. Constructed of various types of hot stones and other methods for heating a small enclosure, "sweats" take small groups of people into nonordinary states of consciousness with a trained shaman or medicine man or woman as a guide for this deep spiritual process. The intense heat and guidance can cause visions or other profound forms of spiritual experiences. Sweat lodges are a part of the Native American tradition.

Suggested Readings for Bridging Old and New Paradigm Thought

Psychology and Transformation

Imagery in Healing. Jean Achterberg. New Science Library, Boston, 1985.

The Call of Spiritual Emergency: From Personal Crisis to Personal Transformation. Emma Bragdon. Harper & Row, San Francisco, 1990.

The Unfolding Self. Molly Young Brown. Psychosynthesis Press, Los Angeles, 1983.

The Aquarian Conspiracy. Marilyn Ferguson. J.P. Tarcher, Inc., Los Angeles, 1980.

What We May Be. Piero Ferrucci. J.P. Tarcher, Inc., Los Angeles, 1980.

Creative Visualization. Shakti Gawain. Bantam Books, New York, 1982.

Focusing, Eugene Gendlin. Bantam Books, New York, 1981.

The Stormy Search for the Self. Christina and Stanislav Grof. J.P. Tarcher, Inc., Los Angeles, 1990.

The Adventure of Self Discovery. Stanislav Grof. State University of New York Press, Albany, 1988.

Beyond The Brain. Stanislav Grof. State University of New York Press, Albany, 1985.

The Search for the Beloved. Jean Houston. J.P. Tarcher, Inc., Los Angeles, 1987.

Toward a Psychology of Being. Abraham Maslow. Van Nostrand Reinhold Company, New York, 1968.

The Farther Reaches of Human Nature. Abraham Maslow. Penguin Books, New York, 1976.

Lightworks. Milenko Matanovic. Lorian Press, Issaquah, WA, 1985.

The Courage to Create. Rollo May. W.W. Norton, New York, 1975.

Opening to Inner Light: The Transformation of Human Nature and Consciousness. Ralph Metzner. J.P. Tarcher, Inc., Los Angeles, 1986.

Magical Child. Joseph Chilton Pearce. Bantam Books, New York, 1980.

Grist for the Mill. Ram Dass with Stephen Levine. Celestial Arts, Berkeley, CA, 1987.

Yoga & Psychotherapy: The Evolution of Consciousness. Swami Rama, Swami Ajaya, Rudolph Ballantine. Himalayan Publishers, Honesdale, PA, 1976.

Sri Aurobindo, or the Adventure of Consciousness. Satprem. Harper & Row, San Francisco, 1968.

Transformers: The Therapists of the Future. Jacquelyn Small. DeVorss & Co., Marina Del Rey, CA, 1982.

Beyond Ego: Transpersonal Dimensions in Psychology. Francis Vaughan. J.P. Tarcher, Inc., Los Angeles, 1980.

Journey of the Heart: Intimate Relationships and the Path of Love. John Welwood. Harper & Row, San Francisco, 1990.

No Boundary. Ken Wilber. Shambhala Publications, Boulder, 1979.

The Spectrum of Consciousness. Ken Wilber. Theosophical Publishing House, Wheaton, IL, 1977.

Healing

Minding the Body. Mending the Mind. Joan Borysenko. Addison-Wesley, Reading, MA, 1987.

Healers on Healing. Richard Carlson, Ph.D., and Benjamin Shield. J.P. Tarcher, Inc., Los Angeles, 1989.

Beyond Illness: Discovering the Experience of Health. Larry Dossey, M.D. Shambhala Publications, Boulder, 1985.

Living in the Light. Shakti Gawain. New World Library, 1986.

Shaman, The Wounded Healer. Joan Halifax. Thames & Hudson, New York 1988.

When the Twelfth Step Happens First. Barbara Harris. Health Communications, Deerfield Beach FL, 1992.

Teach Only Love. Gerald Jampolsky, M.D. Bantam Books, New York, 1984.

Joy's Way. Brugh Joy. J.P. Tarcher, Inc., Los Angeles, 1979.

The Realms of Healing. Stanley Krippner. Celestial Arts, Berkeley, 1986.

Who Dies? Stephen Levine. Doubleday, New York, 1989.

Black Butterfly. Richard Moss. Celestial Arts Publishing, Berkeley, 1986.

How Can I Help? Stories and Reflections on Service. Ram Dass and Paul Gorman. A.A. Knopf, New York, 1985.

The Mind of the Cells. Satprem. Institute for Evolutionary Research, New York, 1982.

Love, Medicine, and Miracles. Bernie Siegel, M.D. Harper & Row, San Francisco, 1986.

Becoming Naturally Therapeutic: A Return to the True Essence of Helping. Jacquelyn Small. Bantam Books, New York, 1989.

Religion and Spirituality

How I Believe. Teilhard de Chardin. Harper & Row, New York, 1969.

The Coming of the Cosmic Christ. Matthew Fox. Harper & Row, New York, 1988.

The Mark. Maurice Nicoll. Shambhala Publications, Boulder, 1985.

The New Man: An Interpretation of Some Parables and Miracles of Christ. Maurice Nicoll. Shambhala Publications, Boulder, 1984.

The Road Less Traveled. M. Scott Peck. Simon & Schuster, New York, 1980.

Spirituality in Recovery. Charles L. Whitfield, M.D. Perrin & Tregget, Rutherford, NJ, 1985. Available by calling 1-800-321-7912.

The Seat of the Soul. Gary Zukav. Simon & Schuster, New York, 1989.

Science, Medicine and the New Physics

The Tao of Physics. Fritjof Capra. Bantam Books, New York, 1987.

The Turning Point. Fritjof Capra. Bantam Books, New York, 1987.

Quantum Healing. Deepak Chopra. Bantam Books, New York, 1989.

Space, Time and Medicine. Larry Dossey. Shambhala Publications, Boulder, 1982.

Recovering the Soul: A Scientific and Spiritual Search. Larry Dossey, M.D. Bantam Books, New York, 1990.

The Wholeness Principle. Anna Lemkow. Theosophical Publishing House, Wheaton, IL, 1990.

Synchronicity, The Bridge Between Mind and Matter. F. David Peat. Bantam Books, New York, 1987.

The Universe is a Green Dragon. Brian Swimme. Bear & Co., Santa Fe, 1984.

The Secret Life of the Unborn Child. Thomas Verny, M.D., with John Kelly. Dell Publishing, New York, 1981.

Natural Health, Natural Medicine. Andrew Weil. Houghton-Mifflin, New York, 1990.

Parallel Universes. Fred Alan Wolf. Simon & Schuster, New York, 1988.

Taking the Quantum Leap. Fred Alan Wolf. Harper & Row, New York, 1988.

The Reflexive Universe. Arthur Young. Robert Briggs and Assocs., Mill Valley, 1984.

The Dancing Wu-Li Masters: An Overview of the New Physics. Gary Zukav. Bantam Books, New York, 1984.

Codependence

Reclaiming the Inner Child. Jeremiah Abrams, ed. J.P. Tarcher, Inc., Los Angeles, 1990.

Codependent No More: How to Stop Controlling Others and Start Caring for Yourself. Melody Beattie. Harper & Row, New York, 1988.

It Will Never Happen to Me. Claudia Black. Mac Publishing Co., Denver, CO, 1981.

Bradshaw on the Family: A Revolutionary Way of Self-Discovery. John Bradshaw. Health Communications, Deerfield Beach, FL, 1988.

Healing the Shame That Binds You. John Bradshaw. Health Communications, Deerfield Beach, FL, 1988.

Homecoming. John Bradshaw. Bantam Books, New York, 1990.

Leaving the Enchanted Forest: The Path from Relationship Addiction. Stephanie Covington. Harper & Row, New York, 1988.

The Adult Children of Alcoholics Syndrome. Wayne Kritsberg. Bantam Books, New York, 1988.

Gifts for Personal Growth and Recovery. Wayne Kritsberg. Health Communications, Deerfield Beach, FL, 1988.

The Flying Boy: Healing the Wounded Man. John Lee. Health Communications, Deerfield Beach, FL, 1987.

I Don't Want to Be Alone. John Lee. Health Communications, Deerfield Beach, FL, 1989.

Witness to the Fire: Creativity & the Veil of Addiction. Linda Schierse Leonard. Shambhala Publications, Boston, MA, 1989.

Affirmations for the Inner Child. Rockelle Lerner. Health Communications, Deerfield Beach, FL, 1990.

Emotional Incest Syndrome. Patricia Love. Bantam Books, New York, 1989.

Facing Codependence. Pia Mellody. Harper & Row, San Francisco, 1989.

Shame and Guilt: Masters of Disguise. Jane Middleton-Moz. Health Communications, Deerfield Beach, FL, 1990.

Codependence: Misunderstood—Mistreated. Anne Wilson Schaef. Harper & Row, New York, 1986.

Escape From Intimacy. Anne Wilson Schaef. Harper & Row, New York, 1989.

Is It Love or Is It Addiction? Brenda Schaeffer. Harper & Row, New York, 1988.

Power Plays. Brenda Schaeffer. Hazelden, Center City, MN, 1986.

Signs of Healthy Love. Brenda Schaeffer. Hazelden, Center City, MN, 1986.

Codependence—Healing the Human Condition. Charles L. Whitfield, M.D., Health Communications, Deerfield Beach, FL, 1991.

Healing the Child Within. Charles L. Whitfield, M.D. Health Communications, Deerfield Beach, FL, 1987.

A Gift to Myself. Charles L. Whitfield, M.D. Health Communications, Deerfield Beach, FL, 1990.

Jungian Theory and Philosophy

The Body as Shadow. John P. Conger. North Atlantic Books, Berkeley, 1988.

The Creation of Consciousness. Edward F. Edinger. Inner City Books, Toronto, 1984.

The Gnostic Jung and the Seven Sermons to the Dead. Joseph Hoeller. Theosophical Publishing House, Wheaton, IL, 1982.

The Way of Individuation. Jolande Jacobi. New American Library, New York, 1965.

Inner Work. Robert A. Johnson. Harper & Row, San Francisco, 1986.

Memories, Dreams and Reflections. Carl Jung. Random House, New York, 1989.

Descent to the Goddess: A Way of Initiation for Women. Sylvia Brinton Perera. Inner City Books, Toronto, 1981.

Projection and Re-Collection in Jungian Psychology: Reflections of the Soul. Marie-Louise von Franz. Open Court Publishing Co., La Salle, 1980.

Addiction to Perfection. Marion Woodman. Inner City Books, Toronto, 1982.

The Pregnant Virgin: A Process of Psychological Transformation. Marion Woodman. Inner City Books, Toronto, 1985.

Kundalini Awakening

"Kundalini, the Awakening and the Unfolding," *Darshan*, Vol 41/42, 1990. P.O. Box 600, South Fallsburg, NY 12779.

Kundalini for the New Age: Selected Writings of Gopi Krishna. Gene Kieffer, ed. Bantam Books, New York, 1988.

Kundalini: Energy of the Depths. Lilian Silburn. Suny Press, New York, 1988.

Kundalini: Yoga for the West. Swami Sivananda Radha. Shambhala Publications, Boston, 1978.

Kundalini: Psychosis or Transcendence? Lee Sannella. Integral Publishing, Lower Lake, CA, 1987.

Mythology

An Open Life. Joseph Campbell with Michael Toms. Larson Publications, Burdett, 1988.

The Hero with a Thousand Faces. Joseph Campbell. Princeton University Press, Princeton, 1968.

Myths to Live By. Joseph Campbell. Bantam Books, New York, 1984.

The Power of Myth. Joseph Campbell with Bill Moyers. Doubleday, New York, 1988.

Mythology. Edith Hamilton. Little, Brown & Co., Boston, 1942.

The Mythic Imagination. Stephen Larsen, Ph.D. Bantam Books, New York, 1990.

The Goddess Re-Awakening. Shirley Nicholson. Theosophical Publishing House, Wheaton, IL, 1989.

Metaphysics

Theosophy Simplified. Irving Cooper. Theosophical Publishing House, Wheaton, IL, 1956.

Brother of the Third Degree. Will Garver. Borden Publishing Co., Alhambra, CA, 1894 (reprinted 1964).

Lectures on Ancient Philosophy. Manly P. Hall. Philosophical Research Society, Los Angeles, 1942.

Initiation. Elisabeth Haich. The Seed Center, Palo Alto, California, 1974.

Reincarnation. An East-West Anthology. J. Head and S.L. Cranston. Theosophical Publishing House, Wheaton, IL, 1968.

To Order Books by Alice Bailey (The Tibetan):

Lucis Publishing Company
866 United Nations Plaza, Suite 566–7
New York, N.Y. 10017–1888

Education in the New Age. Alice Bailey. Lucis, New York, 1954.

Ponder on This. Alice Bailey. Lucis, New York, 1971.

Serving Humanity. Alice Bailey. Lucis, New York, 1972.

Glamour: A World Problem. Alice Bailey. Lucis, New York, 1950.

To Order Books on Agni Yoga:

Agni Yoga Society
319 W. 107th St.
New York, N.Y. 10025

Agni Yoga. Helena Roerich. Agni Yoga Society, New York, 1980.

Heart. Helena Roerich. Agni Yoga Society, New York, 1975.

Infinity Vols. I & II. Helena Roerich. Agni Yoga Society, New York, 1980.

Aquarian Educational Group
P.O. Box 267
Sedona, AZ 86336

The Science of Becoming Oneself. Torkom Saraydarian. Aquarian Educational Group, Sedona, AZ, 1969.

Talks on Agni. Torkom Saraydarian. Aquarian Educational Group, Sedona, AZ, 1987.

Recommended Periodicals

The Journal of Transpersonal Psychology
P.O. Box 4437
Stanford, California 94309

The Quest, A Quarterly Journal of Philosophy, Science, Religion & The Arts
Theosophical Society in America
P.O. Box 270
Wheaton, Illinois 60189-0270

Gnosis Magazine
P.O. Box 14217
San Francisco, California 94114

Darshan
SYDA Foundation
P.O. Box 600
South Fallsburg, New York 12779

ReVision Journal
4000 Albemarle Street, NW
Washington, DC 20016

New Dimensions Newsletter
P.O. Box 410510
San Francisco, California 94141

The Common Boundary: Between Spirituality and Psychotherapy
7005 Florida Street
Chevy Chase, Maryland 20815

Changes Magazine: for and about Adult Children
Enterprise Center
3201 S.W. 15th Street
Deerfield Beach, Florida 33442-8109

Index

Abandonment, 102, 163
Abuse physical/sexual, 67–68, 76, 96
Acceptance, 144, 182–83, 199
ACOA (Adult Child of an Alcoholic), 46
Active intelligence, 116, 215
Acupuncture/acupressure, 260
Adapter, 11–13, 19, 169–70
Addictions
  alcoholism, 173
  to beliefs, 115
  disease-oriented treatment approach, 24–27
  inner life and, 9, 115–16, 128
  in utero influence, 67
  Jung and, 30
  projections/storylines as, 49
  sex and love, 84, 166, 173, 219
  spiritual quest and, 36–38, 143–44, 228, 245
  See also Hitting Bottom
Addicts, 27
  and spirituality, 36–38
Adrenal glands, 76
Adult Child of an Alcoholic (ACOA), 46
Affirmation, 130, 175
Agni Yoga, 99, 221
  books by, 272-273
  Teachings, 107, 113, 142, 147, 204
Aivanhov, Omraam Mikhael, 109, 158
Alcoholics Anonymous, 5, 25, 26, 29, 30, 139, 209, 235, 259
  Jung and, 30
Allen, Woody, 174
Allport, Gordon, 34
Aloneness, 193

Amulets, 63
Archetypes, 18, 34, 157, 168, 212, 215, 221, 229, 231, 240, 247
Arrien, Angeles, 132, 221
Arthur (King of Britain), 208
Assagioli, Roberto, 28, 132, 262
Assimilation stage, 163–64
Awakening in time, 145

Baby-Doll syndrome, 78
Bailey, Alice, 130
  books by, 272
Basic Perinatal Matrices (BPM), 160–69
Beauty, 100, 201, 206
Becoming Naturally Therapeutic (Small), 111, 252
Behavioristic therapies, 27, 29
Beloved, 210, 216, 219, 222
Bhakti Yoga, 217
Birth process, 32, 160–69
  birth, 167–69
  Caesarean, 165
  onset of labor, 162–64
  passage through birth canal, 164–67
  prenatal, 161–62
  See also Basic Perinatal Matrices
Black magician, 222
Blaming. See Projection
Bliss, 228, 256
  following your, 92, 227
  tolerance, 193
Blue (and fifth chakra), 200, 203
Body as Shadow, The (Conger), 53
Body ego, 69–70
Bodywork, 260
Bolen, Jean Shiboda, 241

Brain
  left, 94, 101
  right, 101
Breathwork, 166, 179, 261
Brow chakra, 203
Buddha, 18, 114, 115, 194
Buddhism, 21, 99, 211, 214
  Hindu and Tibetan, 217

Campbell, Joseph, 37, 45, 66, 91–92,
    131, 227, 243
Center, 185–86
Chakra(s), 31-141
  1st, 75–83, 206, 207, 208
    gift of (Truth), 82–83
    healing, 80–82
    issues of, 77–80
  2nd, 83–94, 166, 203, 207–8
    gift of (Goodness), 93–94
    healing of, 90–93
    issues of, 84–90, 211
  3rd, 94–103, 111, 115, 158, 215
    gift of (Beauty), 100–101
    healing of, 98–100
    issues of, 94–98
  4th (Heart), 109, 111, 149–50
    gifts of, 157
    Initiation of the Heart, 150–51
    relationships from, 187, 188–95
  5th, 200–203, 234
    archetypes, 215
    relationships with, 214–15
    spiritual by-pass and, 215–16
  6th, 203–5
    relationships with, 216–18
    spiritual by-pass and, 218–19
  7th, 205-7
    relationships with, 221–22
    spiritual by-pass and, 222-23
  chart of, 71–72
  ego and, 72, 74, 82–83
  Higher Self and, 72, 91, 105, 155,
    200–209
  kundalini awakening and, 219–20
  medicine and, 73–74
  system, 6, 69–75
Channeling, 235
Chanting, 261

Character armor, 44–45
Chasm experiences. See Hitting bot-
    tom
Chi, 219
Childhood issues, 70, 76
  first-chakra (survival needs) imbal-
    ances
    and, 76–79, 81
  second-chakra (emotional needs)
    imbalances
    and, 84, 87–88
Chinese medicine, 72, 260
Chogyam Trungpa, 31
Christ, 131
  Consciousness, 218
Co-creation, 5, 11, 17, 109, 116, 133,
    155, 186, 227, 245–47, 254,
    256–57
  "The Co-Creator: A guided Imagery
    Experience," 223–24
  The Co-Creator's Pledge, 230
  groupwork and, 251–53
  and relationships, 189–95, 211,
    213–23
Codependence, 1–7, 17, 20, 160, 163,
    211
  books about, 4–5, 269–70
  childhood patterning of, 66–69
  definition of, 3–4, 5, 10, 25, 55, 229
  as evolutionary function, 124–28,
    141, 168
  first-chakra issues and, 77–79
  healing, 128–38, 155
    cross symbolism and, 133
  in utero predisposition to, 67
  limitations of label, 5
  naming and claiming, 26
  Schaef, Anne Wilson and, 10
  second-chakra issues and, 83, 86–
    90, 166
  shadow self and, 42, 55–58, 69, 70
  spiritual by-pass and, 143
  symptoms, 4, 5
  treatment programs, 24–27
    negative example, 26
    urges of, 71, 77–79, 86–88, 95–
      97, 101, 206
  Whitfield, Charles and, 10
Codependents Anonymous, 25, 29, 82

Collective unconscious, 30, 34–35, 115, 205
Coming of age, 151
Coming of the Cosmic Christ, The (Fox), 38
Compassion, 204
Conger, John, 44, 45, 53
Contemplation, 238
Contemplative prayer, 261
Corinthians (II, verse from), 116
Crane, Stephen, 41
Creation spirituality, 38
Creativity, 100–101, 103, 116, 157, 161, 228
    fifth chakra (World of the Ideal) and, 200–203, 231
Cross, 131–35, 136
    diagram, 132
Crown chakra, 205, 206
Cycle of conferences, 250

Dalai Lama, 235
Death, 150
Death/rebirth, 35, 138–42, 144–45, 151, 153–57, 165, 170, 171–75, 258
    examples, 172–74
    See also Dis-identification; Rebirth; Re-identification
Defenses, psychological, 70
Denial, 20, 31, 42, 49, 53, 55, 111, 124, 125, 128, 162
Depression, 162–64
Descent of the Goddess (Perera), 29
Destroyer ray, 206
Discipline, 8–82, 156, 205, 221, 222
Discrimination. *See* Spiritual discrimination
Dis-identification, 153–56, 230, 231–32
    "Healing a Lingering Attachment: A Sacred Ritual," 186–87
    seven steps, 180–86
Divine Feminine. *See* Heart
Dreamwork, 261
Dualism, 117–128, 144, 207, 257
    diagram of, 118

Eating disorders, 88
Eckhart, Meister, 38, 131

Ego, 26, 27, 31, 33, 44, 102, 105, 212, 229
    body-ego, 69–70
    chakras and, 69–75, 207–9
    emotional/relational nature of, 83-94
    Heart and, 110-13
    mental/intellectual nature of, 94–103
    physical/instinctual nature of, 75–83
    death and, 140, 173. *See also* Death/ rebirth
    definition of, 18
    dominion over shadow, 55
    Higher Power and, 205–6
    integration of, 31, 119-20, 143–44
    psychology and, 30
    stages of development of, 69–103, 207–9
    transcendence, 31
Emerson, Ralph Waldo, 100
Emotional incest, 68, 87
Emotionalisms, 51, 166–67
Emotional seasons, 160–69
Emotions Anonymous, 82
Empowerment, 251
Engulfment, 102
Enlightenment, 30, 115
Ereshkigal, 28
Eupsychia, 9, 32, 259
    workshops, 156, 166, 167, 168, 240–41
Exercises, 181
    "Releasing the Past," 181–86
    See also Guided imagery; Ritual
Existential psychologies, 34
Experiential
    data, 67
    therapies, 81–82, 92
Extroverts, 52

"Fair witness, the," 21
Ferguson, Marilyn, 34
Fetishes, 63
Fiery World (Agni Yoga Teachings), 143
Focusing, 261
"Following our bliss," 92

Forgiveness, 155–56
Fortune, Dion, 178
Fox, Matthew, 38, 131, 208
Frankl, Victor, 34
Franz, von, Marie-Louise, 46, 102
Freud, Sigmund, 263
  therapies of, 27, 29
Fry, Christopher, 3

Garver, Will, 197
Gendlin, Eugene, 92, 261
Gestalt therapy, 26, 261
  "Open Seat," 81
Gibran, Kahlil, 56
"Going into the deep well," 254
Golas, Thadeus, 184
Goodness, 93–94, 206
Gopi Krishna, 220–21
Gorman, Paul, 236
Gratitude, 183, 186, 229
Greek mystery schools, 132–33, 150, 250
Green (and fourth chakra), 149
Grof, Christina, 32
Grof, Stanislav, 32, 34, 115, 160
Group(s)
  therapy, 44–45
  transpersonal, 33, 138, 249–54
Groupwork. See Group(s), transpersonal
Guided imagery, 58–65, 154, 166, 173, 262
  "The Co-Creator," 223-24
  "Healing the Emotions," 103–4
  how to practice, 59–60
  "Meeting Your Shadow," 60–62
  "Opening the Heart," 151–53
  processing, 62–64
  "Surrender into the Heart," 180
  "Visualizing Your Higher Self," 65
  "The World Server," 247–48
  See also Exercises; Ritual
Gurdjieff, G.I., 130

Hatha-yoga, 221
Healing, readings in, 267
Heart (Divine Feminine/Fourth Chakra), 109–13, 144–46, 209, 219

chasm of (hitting bottom), 176–79
cycles of (seasons of transformation), 159–69
gifts of, 157
healing and, 149-170, 185
high (high love), 218, 233–34
marriage with Mind, 145–46
"Opening the Heart" (guided imagery), 151–53
personal and transpersonal in, 157–59
qualities of, 154
radiating through, 233
relationships from, 187
sitting quietly in, 185
"Surrender into the Heart" (guided imagery), 180
Heart (Agni Yoga), 113
Heartwork, 112, 113, 144, 146, 147, 149–53, 156, 176, 195, 199, 252
  accelerated, 180–86
  steps, 180–86, 232–35
Hero's journey, 30
Higher Power, 9, 11, 25, 33, 46, 80, 91, 98, 101, 105, 116, 122, 126–27, 130, 135, 164, 168, 182, 183, 187, 200, 202–3, 221, 231, 233, 234
  defined, 17
  ego and, 205
Higher Self, 9, 19, 20, 21, 30, 31, 36, 37, 64–65, 74, 99, 101, 139, 143, 144, 155, 168, 176–77, 185, 186–87, 199, 233, 258
  chakras and, 73–74, 199–209
  creative expression of, 200–203, 233
  definition of, 18
  ego, merging with, 207–9, 210
  feeling nature of, 203–4, 229
  feminine aspect of (Heart), 109–113, 144–45
  guided-imagery experience ("Visualizing Your Higher Self"), 65
  initiation and, 150–51
  masculine aspect of (Mind), 112–13, 144–45
  ritual and, 186
  triadic view of, 119–28, 133
  will of, 205-7

Hinduism, 219, 221
Hitting bottom, 7, 13, 32, 141, 170, 171, 173, 175, 176–79
  symptoms of, 177
Holy Ghost/Spirit, 130, 219
Home, 22, 208, 250, 255–58
  journey, 30, 169, 249–50
Houston, Jean, 34
Humanistic psychology, 29
Hypnosis, 262

Illumination, 205
Immune deficiencies (and fourth chakra), 150
Inanna, 28
Individuation, 175, 211
Initiation, 150–51. *See also* Heartwork
Inner life/work (spirituality), 128–38, 144, 160, 236, 238–39, 244, 245
  See also Cross
Inspiration, 204
Intellect. *See* Mind
Intentionality. *See* Spiritual direction/intentionality
Introverts, 52
Invocation, 80, 135–38
  "I Am Willing . . . !", 137-38
Ishtar, 28

Jacob's ladder, 73
Jesus, 18, 101, 116, 206
Joseph, 221
Jung, Carl, 18, 20, 30, 34–35, 41, 42, 46, 47, 53, 78, 102, 115, 120, 134, 136, 175, 210, 211, 225, 246, 254
Jungian philosophy, 6, 9, 261
  readings, 270–71

Kashmir Shaivism, 217, 219, 221
Ki, 219
Krishnamurti, 231
Kundalini, 217
  awakening, 30, 216, 219–21
  readings in, 271
Kundalini for the New Age (Gopi Krishna), 221

Lachat, Pere, 120
Ladder of St. Augustine, The (Longfellow)
Lao-tzu, 185
Lazy Man's Guide to Enlightenment, The (Golas), 184
L'Engle, Madeleine, 100
Letting go, 141, 155, 182, 194, 232.
  See also Death/rebirth; Dis-identification
Levels of consciousness
  one, 75–83
  two, 83–94
  three, 94–103
  four, 109–13
Lewis, C.S., 242
Life's work. *See* Service
Lightworks (Matanovic), 122
Little Prince, The (Saint Exupéry), 145
Longfellow, Henry Wadsworth, 125
Love, 56, 124, 145, 184, 190, 195
  addiction, 84, 91, 97, 166, 173, 219
  eating disorders and, 88
  high, 212–13, 218, 249–50
  needy, 50–51, 82, 145, 194–95
  second chakra and, 87, 90, 166
  shadow and, 184
  soulmates/Twin Flames, 211–12, 218–19
  unconditional, 189
  See also Heart; Relationship(s)
Love, Patricia, 68

Mary (mother of Jesus), 221
Maslow, Abraham, 1, 9, 34, 128, 129, 199
Massage, 260
Matanovic, Milenko, 122
Materialism, 95–97, 245
May, Rollo, 171
Medicine, readings in, 268
Meditation, 45–46, 52–53, 140, 236, 237–38, 244, 245
Metanoia, 116, 117, 146, 170
Metaphysics, readings in, 272
Metcalf, Greta, 256
Metzner, Ralph, 24, 28
Miller, Alice, 96

Mind (archetype; Big Mind; Higher
    Mind), 112–13, 116, 117, 234–35
  fifth chakra and, 200–203, 214–15,
    234
  meditation and, 234
Mind (intellect), 114–15
  definition of, 114
  four mental shifts, 257–58
    one, 117–28, 144
    two, 128–38, 144, 160
    three, 138–42, 144–45, 153
    four, 142–44, 145
  marriage with Heart, 145–46
  unconscious, 46, 176, 243, 252
Monkey chatter, 99
Mother-hen syndrome, 78–79
Movement
  meditation, 262
  therapy, 262
Moyers, Bill, 227, 243
Mystic thought, 36, 38, 90, 99 105,
    130, 140, 142, 164, 206, 208, 228
Mythology, readings in, 271
Myths to Live By (Campbell), 66

Nag Hammadi Gnostic teachings, 150
Narcotics Anonymous, 25
Near-death experience, 32
Needy love, 55–56
Neumann, Erich, 28
New Age adherents, 244–45
New-paradigm
  groupwork. See Groups, transpersonal
    religion, 242, 243
New physics, readings in, 268
New Testament, 116
Non-reaction, 52
Nutritional balancing, 262

Observer self, 21, 54–55, 178, 199–
    200
Obsessing, 84, 239
Oneness, 206, 253
Open Life, An (Campbell), 45, 243
Origins and History of Consciousness,
    The (Neumann), 28
Orr, Leonard, 263
Osiris, 28

Outer world/work, 236, 243–45
  cross symbolism and, 132–35
Overeaters Anonymous, 25

Paranoia, 80, 89
Passive-aggressive behavior, 52
Past (personal), 42, 46, 69, 105, 125
  blaming, 49
  healing wounds, 102–3
  "Releasing the Past" (exercise),
    181–86
  working through, 11, 49, 88, 104
  See also Childhood issues
Patanjali, 201
Peak experiences, 129, 140
Peat, F. David, 249, 253–54
Pearce, Joseph Chilton, 150
Perera, Sylvia Brinton, 29
Perinatal psychology, 67, 263
Periodicals, recommended, 273–74
Perls, Fritz, 34
Peter Pan (puer aeternis) syndrome, 78
Pineal gland, 205
Pir-O-Murshid Inayat Khan, 105
Pituitary gland, 203
Plato, 142, 202, 254
Positive self (positive, purified ego),
    20–21
Positive thinking, 123–24
Post-Traumatic Stress Disorder, 166
Power of Myth, The (Campbell), 227
Prayer, 135–36
  contemplative, 261
  See also Invocation
Process hypnosis, 262
Processing
  conscious, 185
  guided-imagery experiences, 62–64
Progoff's Journal methods, 81
Projection, 46–49, 58, 201
  codependence and, 55
  examples of, 47–48
  in relationships, 56–57, 191–92
  steps to clear, 57
Projection and Re-collection in Jungian
    Psychology (Franz), 46, 102
Prophet, The (Gibran), 56
Psyche, 30, 33, 35

Psychology, 30
  abnormal, 34
  expansion of, 34–36
  normal, 34, 35
  readings in, 265–66
  See also Transpersonal psychology
Psycho-spirituality, 24–38, 208–9, 238–39
  therapeutic approach of, 6, 29, 151, 154, 156, 161, 167
  See also Transpersonal psychology
Psychosynthesis, 28, 132, 262–63

Raja Yoga, 215
Ram Dass, 34, 149, 218, 236, 237, 242
Ray, Sandra, 263
Rebirth, 32, 167–69, 175
  See also Death/rebirth
Rebirthing (breathwork), 263
Reception stage, 161–62
Recognition, 42, 55, 101, 182, 194, 201, 202
Red (and first chakra), 76
Reflexive Universe, The (Young), 73
Reich, Wilhelm, 44
Re-identification, 153–54, 155, 186
Reincarnation, 33, 168
Relationship(s)
  1st-chakra imbalance, 79–80
    discipline and, 80–82
  2nd-chakra imbalance, 86–90, 166, 211
    spiritual discrimination and, 91–93
  3rd-chakra imbalance, 95, 97–98
    spiritual direction and, 98–100
  4th chakra (from the Heart), 187, 188–95
    law of right relationship, 189–90, 195
    ten rules for, 190–95
  5th chakra (co-creative), 214–15
  6th chakra (co-creative), 216–18
  7th chakra (co-creative), 221–22
  addiction, 3, 4
  codependence and, 55–58, 95, 211–12
  conflict resolution, suggestions, 57, 206
  dis-identification, seven steps, 180–86

  dysfunctions, 27, 163–64
  with high callings (co-creative), 210–24
    four components of, 213–14
  negative aspects of, 9–10
  right relationships, 189–90, 195, 210–11
  seasons of, 160–69, 239
    assimilation (fall), 162–64
    rebirth (spring), 167–69
    reception (summer), 161–62
    transmutation (winter), 164–67
  shadow and, 46–47
  triadic model and, 127
  urge to control and, 77–79, 206
  urge to excite, 86–88, 207
  urge to merge and, 95–97, 101, 207
Relief, 154
Religion
  organized, 130–31
  readings in, 267–68
Repentance, 116
  See also Metanoia
Repression, 20, 68–69, 81, 118, 128
  experiential therapies and, 81–82
  sexuality and, 84–85
  of shadow self, 43, 118–20
Right relationships, 189–90, 195, 210–11
Rilke, Rainer Maria, 146
Ritual, 151, 228, 263
  "Healing a Lingering Attachment," 186–87
Rods of Power, 208
Rogers, Carl, 34
Romans (verse from), 114
Royal Road, 30

Sacrifice, 132–33, 165, 183
Saint Exupéry, de, Antoine, 145
Sarmouni Brotherhood, 130
Satir, Virginia, 34
Satprem, 25
Schaef, Anne Wilson, 10, 70
Science, readings in, 268
Sea Princess, The (Fortune), 178
Self, 87, 103, 104, 116, 178, 199, 204, 242, 246, 253

Self (cont.)
  addiction treatment and, 24–29
  chakras and, 73
  definition of, 16, 42
  divisions of, 27–28, 32, 135
  inner, 129–38
  quest for, 5, 10–11, 22, 30, 105, 235, 249, 254, 257–58
  psychotherapies and, 29–38
  "rule number one," 11, 37, 105
  triadic view of Self, 119–28, 133, 142
  See also Psyche
Self-actualization models, 34, 128
Self-responsibility, 57
Separatism, 76, 95, 204
Service, 204, 222–23, 231–39, 243–48, 254, 258
  four pillars of, 236–47
  "The World Server: A Guided Imagery Experience," 247–48
Seven, significance of levels, 73
Seventh Ray, 205
Sex addiction, 84, 97, 166, 173
Sexuality
  1st chakra and, 76–77
  2nd chakra and, 83–86, 203, 211
  6th chakra and, 203–4, 216–18
  repression and, 84–85
  spirituality and, 192–93
  transmutation stage and, 165–66
  "turning on" and, 192–93
  See also Kundalini awakening
Shadow (the deficient or negative ego), 16, 19, 27, 41–65, 102, 104, 246
  codependence and, 42, 55–58, 69, 70
  collective manifestation of, 48
  definition of, 19–20
  envisioning, 44
  gifts of, 53–55
  guided-imagery experience ("Meeting Your Shadow"), 59–62
  integration of, 120–23, 143–44
  manifestations of, 51–53, 86, 141
  owning, 183–84
  projections/storylines and, 45–49
  recognizing, 50–51

  repression and, 68–69, 84, 118–20
  schizophrenia and, 76
  sexuality and, 76–77
Shadow dance, 122–23
Shadow, The (radio show), 43
Shakti, 219, 220, 221
Shamanic journey, 30
Shiva, 221
Small, Jacquelyn
  accelerated transformation of, 170
  addiction therapy and, 8
  as child-abuse caseworker, 67–68, 96
  containing feelings, 179
  death/rebirth experience of, 35
  development of ideas of, 99–100, 218
  Eupsychia and, 9, 32
  "fragility pattern" of, 82
  Higher Power and, 127
  hitting bottom, 7–8, 10, 176–77
  inner work of, 238–39
  needy shadow of, 50–51, 82
  observer self of, 102
  premature birth of, 82, 120–21
  relationships
    dysfunction and, 7
    emotional seasons of, 160–69, 239
    triadic model and, 127
  shadow self and, 53–54
  son, Tom, 68–69
  spiritual experience of, 129
  synchronicity and, 240–41
  therapeutic practice of, 92–93
  therapy session/suffering, 158
  third-level "oughts" and, 202
  transpersonal groupwork and, 251–53
  transpersonal psychology and, 8, 29
  and Twelve Step program, 6
Solar plexus, 94, 158
Soul. See Higher Self
Soul group, 232, 249–50
Soul-infused personality, 19, 44, 122, 207–9, 249
Soulmates/Twin Flames, 211–12, 218–19
Soul murder, 96
Soul powers, 195, 199–209

Spirit, 33, 139. *See also* Higher Power; Psyche
Spiritual by-pass, 31, 134, 143, 212, 215–16, 218–19, 222–23
Spiritual direction/intentionality, 98–100, 156, 157, 201, 229, 258
Spiritual discrimination, 91–93, 156, 204
Spiritual experiences, 31–32, 35, 129–30
  "emergencies," 32, 140, 173, 259–60
Spiritual will, 205, 221-22
Spirituality
  intrinsic, 129–38
  readings in, 167–68
Sri Aurobindo, 25
Sri Aurobindo or Adventures of Consciousness (Satprem), 25
"Standing in the light of your own being," 11
Storylines, 45–49, 192, 201, 239
Study, 236, 241–43
Subpersonalities, 28, 86
Suffering, 154, 157–59, 194
Sufi, 216–17, 228, 250
Suicide, 173
Surrender. *See* Letting go
Sweat lodge, 263
Sword of Truth, 206, 208
Synchronicity, 140, 240–41
Synchronicity: The Bridge Between Matter and Mind (Peat), 253–54

Tantric Yoga, 217
Tao/Taoism, 30, 217
Tao Te Ching (Lao-zu), 185
Tape loop, 48
Teilhard de Chardin, Pierre, 131, 147, 255
Texas Commission on Alcoholism, 29
Theologians, 130
Third eye, 203
Thymus gland, 149–50
Thyroid gland, 200
Tibetan, The, 255, 258, 272
Transcendence, 142–45, 169, 258
Transformation, 115–45, 169–70

accelerated, 170, 171–75
readings in, 265–66
seasons of, 159–69
seven steps for dis-identification, 180–86
workshop, 171
Transformers, 11–12, 13–14, 170
Transmutation stage, 164–67
Transpersonal consciousness, 13–14, 35, 157, 250–51
Heart and, 147–59
Transpersonal psychology, 8–9, 26, 29–30, 31, 32–33, 129, 140, 164
definition of, 8, 23
groupwork, 249–54
human-consciousness researchers and, 9
Triadic view of Self, 119–28, 144, 257
diagrams of, 119, 121
Triangle (guided-imagery experience), 103–4, 119, 126, 146
Truth, 83, 110, 115, 116, 122, 125, 128, 130, 134, 136, 147, 190, 199, 201, 206, 256, 257
See also Study
Twelve Steps, The, 12, 29, 181
eleventh-step work, 238
language of, 133
work with, 124
Twelve Step programs, 5, 6, 7, 17, 25, 29, 36, 45, 82, 99, 159, 238, 247, 250
Twin Flames, 211–12, 218–19

Unknown Man (Yatri), 66
Upanishads, 143
Urge to control, 71, 77–79, 206
Urge to excite, 71, 86–88, 207
Urge to merge, 71, 95–97, 101, 207

Vaughan, Francis, 34
Victimhood, 48, 57, 163
Violet Flame, 205, 206, 222

Way of the Christ, 30
Welwood, John, 188
When Society Becomes an Addict (Schaef), 10

Whitfield, Charles L., 10, 15
Wholeness, 27–28, 34, 42
Wilber, Ken, 34, 39
Will to feel, 83
Will to know the truth, 94–95
Will to live, 76
Wolf, Fred Alan, 49
Workaholism, 97
Worship, 126–27

Yatri, 66
Yellow (and third chakra), 94

Yoga, 72
    Agni (yoga of fire), 99, 221
    Bhakti, 217
    hatha, 221
    of Self-knowledge, 215
    Tantric, 217
    See also Kundalini awakening
Young, Arthur, 73
Yuppies, 97

Zukav, Gary, 39, 242
Zuleikha, 216

BANTAM BOOKS
ON ADDICTION AND RECOVERY

ADDICTION

The most up-to-date information from the leading experts in the field.

RESTORE YOUR LIFE
A Living Plan for Sober People
Anne Geller, M.D. with M.J. Territo
From one of this country's leading medical experts on addiction, this is the most comprehensive guide available to physical, emotional, and mental health in sobriety. For recovering alcoholics and drug addicts, the book features meal plans, exercise programs, and more.
07153-X • *Hardcover* • $21.95/$26.95 in Canada

800-COCAINE
Mark S. Gold, M.D.
From the leading expert on cocaine abuse and treatment, an informative, prescriptive manual with hard facts on America's fastest growing drug problem.
34388-2 • *Large Format Paperback* • $3.95/$4.95 in Canada

UNDER THE INFLUENCE
A Guide to the Myths and Realities of Alcoholism
James R. Milam, Ph.D., and Katherine Ketcham
This groundbreaking classic emphasizes treating alcoholism as a physiological disease and offers information on how to tell if someone is an alcoholic, treatment, and recovery.
27487-2 • *Paperback* • $4.95/$5.95 in Canada

RECOVERY

From alcoholism to eating disorders, books that offer concrete tools for physical, emotional and spiritual recovery.

HOMECOMING
Reclaiming and Championing Your Inner Child
John Bradshaw
As seen in the nationally televised PBS series, this bestselling book presents the essence of the inner child workshop John Bradshaw calls "the most powerful work I have ever done," a step-by-step guide to healing the wounds of the past and discovering your true self.
05793-6 • *Hardcover* • $18.95/$23.95 in Canada

DON'T CALL IT LOVE
Recovery from Sexual Addiction
Patrick Carnes, Ph.D.
From the nation's leading expert on sexual addiction, author of *Out of the Shadows* and *Contrary to Love*, comes this extraordinary documentary look at the nature and causes of sexual addiction, plus healing advice from more than 1000 men and women in advanced recovery.
07236-6 • *Hardcover* • $19.95/$24.95 in Canada

LIVING ON THE EDGE
A Guide to Intervention for Families with Drug and Alcohol Problems
Katherine Ketcham and Ginny Lyford Gustafson
From two renowned professionals, compassionate, step-by-step advice on every facet of family intervention, from preparation to finding the right treatment options and support groups.
34606-7 • *Large Format Paperback* • $7.95/$9.95 in Canada

RECOVERING
How to Get and Stay Sober
L. Ann Mueller, M.D., and Katherine Ketcham
An essential resource for alcoholics and those who love them, a comprehensive and compassionate guide to new treatment programs that have helped many alcoholics achieve lasting sobriety.
34303-3 • *Large Format Paperback* • $9.95/$12.95 in Canada

RECLAIMING OUR LIVES
Hope for Adult Survivors of Incest
Carol Poston and Karen Lison
A comprehensive, inspiring, and supportive guide with a concrete, 14-step program for healing by an incest survivor and a therapist.
34778-0 • *Large Format Paperback* • $9.95/$12.95 in Canada

DANCING WITH DADDY
A Childhood Lost and a Life Regained
Betsy Petersen
A uniquely powerful memoir that captures an incest survivor's struggle to overcome the legacy of a horrifying childhood in order to fulfill her deepest desire: to be a good parent to her children.
07374-5 • *Hardcover* • $19.00/$24.00 in Canada

THE TWELVE STEPS REVISITED
Ronald L. Rogers, Chandler Scott McMillin, Morris A. Hill
An inspiring new interpretation of the 12 steps of Alcoholics Anonymous that clearly illustrates the path toward recovery that has worked for so many millions of people.
34733-0 • *Large Format Paperback* • $7.95/$9.95 in Canada

DON'T HELP
A Positive Guide to Working with the Alcoholic
Ronald L. Rogers and Chandler Scott McMillin
For counselors, health-care professionals, and families, a definitive and practical guide to working with the alcoholic.
34716-0 • *Large Format Paperback* • $8.95/$11.95 in Canada

ADULT CHILDREN
Essential reading for the millions who grew up in dysfunctional families.

THE ADULT CHILDREN OF ALCOHOLICS SYNDROME
Wayne Kritsberg
Real help and hope for adult children in a complete self-help program that shows how to recognize and remedy the effects of the dysfunctional family.
27279-9 • *Paperback* • $4.50/$5.50 in Canada

BECOMING YOUR OWN PARENT
The Solution for Adult Children of Alcoholic and Other Dysfunctional Families
Dennis Wholey
Television host Dennis Wholey, author of *The Courage to Change* and himself an "adult child," takes us inside a series of meetings where fourteen men and women learn to find within themselves the validation and nurturance they were denied as children. Also offers the wisdom of a dozen nationally recognized experts on recovery.
34788-8 • *Large Format Paperback* • $9.95/$12.95 in Canada

HEALING FOR ADULT CHILDREN OF ALCOHOLICS
Sara Hines Martin

A groundbreaking work that examines the spiritual and emotional healing that must take place for complete recovery from the ACOA Syndrome.
"Truly commendable"—Dr. Robert H. Schuller
28246-8 • *Paperback* • $4.50/$5.50 in Canada

FAMILY ISSUES
Groundbreaking books on conquering co-dependence and helping addicted family members.

LOVING AN ALCOHOLIC
Help and Hope for Co-dependents
Jack Mumey

The founder of the Gateway Treatment Center for alcoholics and their families presents practical advice—a way out of confusion and pain, and past roadblocks to change.
27236-5 • *Paperback* • $4.95/$5.95 in Canada

THE INDISPENSABLE WOMAN
Ellen Sue Stern

A step-by-step recovery program that will help women—and men—to relinquish control and codependence, let go of guilt, and break the destructive pattern of perfectionism and indispensability.
35231-8 • *Large Format Paperback* • $8.95/$11.95 in Canada

HOW TO GET OUT OF DEBT, STAY OUT OF DEBT & LIVE PROSPEROUSLY
Jerrold Mundis

Based on the proven techniques of Debtors Anonymous, this step-by-step guide will provide relief, support, and practical advice to the forty million Americans plagued by debt.
28396-0 • *Paperback* • $4.95/$5.95 in Canada

TOXIC PARENTS
Overcoming Their Hurtful Legacy and Reclaiming Your Life
Dr. Susan Forward with Craig Buck

The challenging compassionate, and controversial new guide to recognizing and recovering from the lasting damage caused by physical or emotional abuse in childhood, by the best-selling author of *Men Who Hate Women and the Women Who Love Them.*
28434-7 • *Paperback* • $5.95/$6.95 in Canada

HEALING RELATIONSHIPS
Books that point readers toward a healthier self and new ways of relating with others.

HOW TO BREAK YOUR ADDICTION TO A PERSON
Howard M. Halpern, Ph.D.

An insightful, step-by-step guide to breaking painful addictive relationships—and surviving separation.
26005-7 • *Paperback* • $4.95/$6.50 in Canada

OUT OF DARKNESS INTO THE LIGHT
A Journey of Inner Healing
Gerald G. Jampolsky, M.D.

The bestselling author of *Love Is Letting Go of Fear* offers a blueprint for recovery through his personal journey from severe depression, guilt, and alcohol abuse to a triumphant rediscovery of self and inner healing.
34791-8 • *Large Format Paperback* • $9.95/$12.95 in Canada

BECOMING NATURALLY THERAPEUTIC
A Return to the True Essence of Helping
Jacquelyn Small

The renowned workshop leader's inspiring guide for all who serve as listeners or counselors in the lives of others. Basing her work on landmark studies, Small helps us "straight-talk" beyond our co-dependent or controlling ways of helping others and teaches how to offer clear and loving guidance directly from the heart.
34800-0 • *Large Format Paperback* • $9.00/$12.00 in Canada

MEDITATIONALS

Daily inspiration and guidance based on the 12-step programs.

A NEW DAY
365 Meditations for Personal and Spiritual Growth
Anonymous

Offers spiritual and psychological guidance on overcoming the struggles we face each day, by the author of *A Day at a Time.*
34951-5 • *Paperback* • $6.95/$8.95 in Canada

FAMILY FEELINGS
Daily Meditations for Healthy Relationships
Martha Vanceburg and Sylvia Silverman

Valuable insights on changing destructive family patterns with one's spouse, children, elderly parents, and grandparents. By the co-author of *The Promise of a New Day* and her mother.
34705-5 • *Paperback* • $6.95/$8.95 in Canada

A TIME TO BE FREE
Daily Meditations for Enhancing Self-Esteem
Anonymous

By the bestselling author of *A New Day* and *A Day at a Time*, a new kind of daily meditational that offers insight into 52 issues as well as providing the steps that can be taken to achieve the freedom to be your best self.
35203-3 • *Paperback* • $7.95/$9.95 in Canada

FEEDING THE SOUL
Daily Meditations for Recovering from Eating Disorders
Caroline Adams Miller

Drawn from the author's own personal victory over bulimia, 366 meditations which offer spiritual and psychological support to those battling a food addiction. By the author of *My Name is Caroline.*
35279-2 • *Paperback* • $8.00/$10.00 in Canada